Rna Rachedi - Forbes
1993

PRAGUE
WINTER

PRAGUE WINTER

NIKOLAUS MARTIN

PETER HALBAN

LONDON

FIRST PUBLISHED IN GREAT BRITAIN BY
PETER HALBAN PUBLISHERS LTD
42 South Molton Street
London W1Y 1HB
1990

British Library Cataloguing in Publication Data

Martin, Nikolaus
Prague winter.
1. Czechoslovakia. Prague, 1918–   . – Biographies
I. Title
943.71203092

ISBN 1-870015-35-5

Phototypeset by Computape (Pickering) Ltd, North Yorkshire
Printed and bound in Great Britain by
Butler & Tanner Ltd, Frome and London

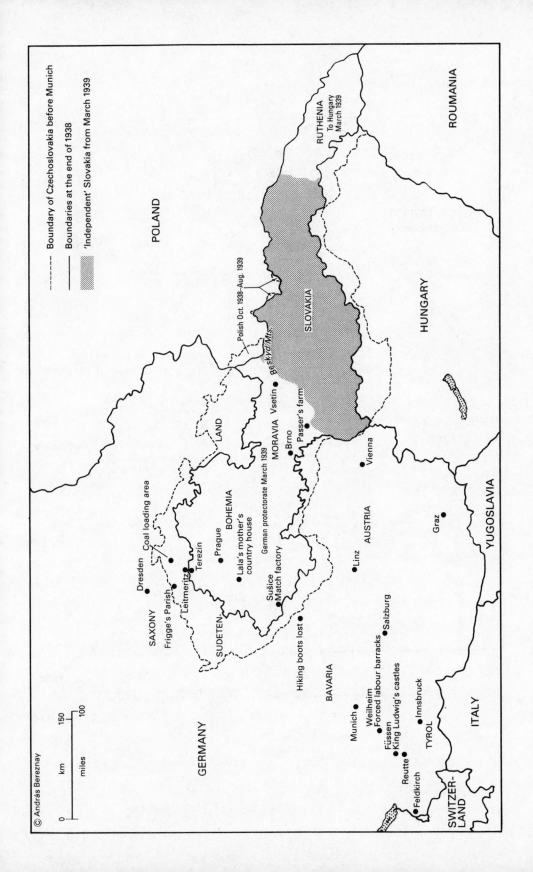

© András Bereznay

Boundary of Czechoslovakia before Munich

Boundaries at the end of 1938

'Independent' Slovakia from March 1939

POLAND

ROUMANIA

RUTHENIA
To Hungary
March 1939

SLOVAKIA

HUNGARY

Polish Oct. 1938–Aug. 1939

Beskydy Mts.

German protectorate March 1939

MORAVIA   Vsetin

Brno

Passer's farm

Coal loading area

Dresden

BOHEMIA

Prague

Lala's mother's
country house

Terezin

Leitmeritz

SAXONY

Frigge's Parish

Vienna

AUSTRIA

Graz

Linz

SUDETEN-

LAND

Susice
Match factory

Hiking boots lost

YUGOSLAVIA

BAVARIA

Weilheim
Forced labour barracks

Salzburg

Füssen
King Ludwig's castles

Munich

Reutte

Innsbruck

TYROL

Feldkirch

SWITZER-
LAND

ITALY

GERMANY

km   150
      100
miles

0

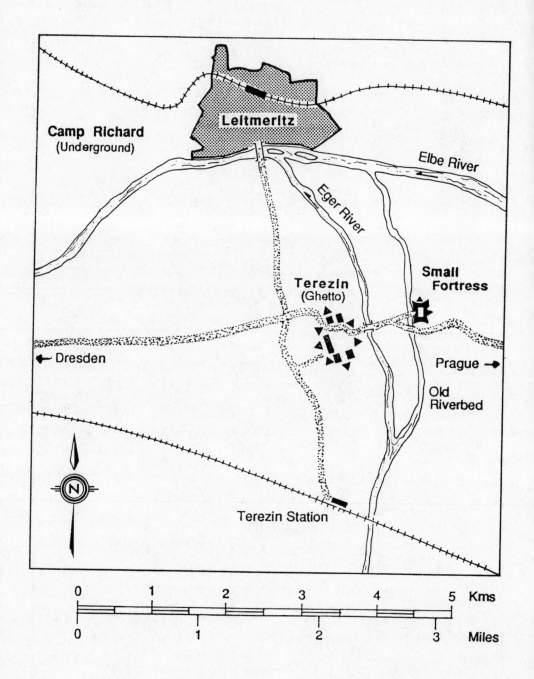

✢ Chronology ✢

12 March 1938	Anschluss.
29 September 1938	Munich Agreement—Transfer to the Third Reich of territories in Bohemia and Moravia with a majority of German-speaking people.
2 November 1938	Treaty of Vienna awards territories with majorities of Hungarians and Poles to their respective countries.
15 March 1939	Occupation of the rest of Czechoslovakia by the *Wehrmacht*. Proclamation of a Protectorate in Bohemia and Moravia and establishment of a 'Free' State of Slovakia.
1 September 1939	Germany invades Poland.
27 September 1941	Hitler names Reinhard Heydrich *Reichsprotector* of Bohemia and Moravia
27 May 1942	Attempt on Heydrich's life.
4 June 1942	Heydrich dies.
9/10 June 1942	Destruction of the village of Lidice.
18 June 1942	Death of the parachutists.
31 January 1943	Capitulation of the *Wehrmacht* in Stalingrad.
6 June 1944	D-Day.
20 July 1944	Attempt on Hitler's life.
29 August 1944	Start of the uprising in Slovakia.
Mid-October 1944	The uprising in Slovakia put down by the *Wehrmacht*.
18 October 1944	The Red Army enters Slovakia.
16 December 1944	Start of the Battle of the Bulge.
13 February 1945	Bombing of Dresden.

March 1945	Discussions in Moscow with the Czechoslovak Government in exile. Formation of a government of National Front and prohibition of right-wing parties.
5 April 1945	The Czechoslovak Government (then in eastern Slovakia) decides on nationalizations.
30 April 1945	Hitler commits suicide.
2 May 1945	Berlin capitulates.
5 May 1945	Start of the uprising in Prague.
8 May 1945	Capitulation of the *Wehrmacht* in Bohemia and Moravia.
26 May 1946	Elections in Czechoslovakia. Communist party wins 38% country-wide but over 50% in cities formerly inhabited by the Sudeten-Germans.
4 June 1947	The American Secretary of State, George C. Marshall, makes offer of US aid 'to improve the economic health of the world'. Czechoslovakia refuses the Marshall Plan.
25 February 1948	Communist Putsch.

✍ Foreword ❧

Prague Winter is my attempt to record a demented time during which I was both witness and involuntary participant. For many years I was haunted by nightmares of being recaptured by the Gestapo or of being trapped in Prague under the Communists. Perehaps the most telling introduction to those years is to report on a trial that took place nearly two decades after the events described—the trial of a mass murderer whose path crosssed mine in the last months of the war.

Nikolaus Martin
Béarn
May 1990

❧ The Trial ❧

Time September 1963
Place Graz, Styria, Austria
Defendant Stefan Rojko, aged 52—former prison guard, a stooped man of small stature with thinning hair and piercing blue eyes in a deeply furrowed face somewhat pasty from imprisonment.
Accusation 194 murder counts, 82 committed alone, 192 with other guards, 10 where he gave the order to kill.
Site of crimes The Small Fortress of Terezín near Leitmeritz, north-west Bohemia, Czechoslovakia.

Defendant's history One of 11 children, Rojko was born into a family of modest means living in a village near Deutschlandsberg in south-east Austria. His school record was poor and, by the time he was fifteen, he was employed as a farmhand. A year or so later, around 1927, he became sacristan in Deutschlandsberg, a job which he kept for eleven years.

One of the significant events in that period of Rojko's life was the aborted Nazi putsch of July 1934 when the Austrian Chancellor Dr Dollfuss was assassinated. In those critical days, Rojko, as a member of the *Sturmscharen*, a patriotic and paramilitary organization, guarded the presbytery against roving bands of Nazis. He was able to warn the authorities of a pending attack and, for this action, was decorated with the Austrian bronze medal for valour.

xi

Apart from the fact that he begot two illegitimate children, nothing of any note seems to have occurred in Rojko's life until the German annexation of Austria in March 1938. Early in 1940 he married but soon discovered that his salary as sacristan could barely support a wife and the two children for whom he had to assume financial responsibility. The Anschluss had created a lot of job opportunities and there was a war going on but, in spite of the growing shortage of manpower, Rojko wasn't particularly successful in his search. He could have opted for a career in the army but that wasn't to his liking: he admitted as much to an interrogator at his pre-trial hearing. He preferred to stay close to his wife and behind the front lines. By chance Rojko heard that the new authorities were looking for recruits for the *Schutzpolizei*, a protective police or gendarmerie. This job combined the two advantages he was looking for: no front-line duty and the possibility of a future, permanent assignment with married quarters. The *Schupo*, as the *Schutzpolizei* was commonly called, seemed the ideal solution. If his *Sturmscharen* membership and his anti-Nazi past were discovered he would probably be in trouble but he decided it was worth the risk.

Rojko's application was accepted and, after a training course in Innsbruck, he was assigned to guard duty in the prisons of St Pancras and Charles Square in Prague. By that time Czechoslovakia had been under German occupation for over a year. The prisons were overflowing and more and more guards were needed. It seems that at first Rojko's treatment of prisoners was correct but his stay in Prague was relatively short as changes were taking place in the prison system— most of the prison guards were being transferred from the Schupo to the SD (*Sicherheitsdienst*, a division of the SS) so Rojko now found himself part of the SS. In order to alleviate the overcrowding in both Prague prisons the Gestapo reopened another prison in the precinct of the Small Fortress of Terezín for prisoners whose interrogation was, in principle, finished, and who now awaited transfer to a concentration camp. Soon after this third prison was established, Stefan Rojko was sent there as a guard and administrative official. He was allotted a service flat which he could share with his wife: things were going well for him—life was better than he had dared to hope. Not only had his anti-Nazi past apparently remained undiscovered but he was being entrusted with increasingly more important jobs and was steadily advancing in rank. After assuming the responsibility of the *Hofverwaltung*, the office in charge of the formation of the different work battalions, SS *Oberscharführer* (Sergeant Major) Rojko became the third most important person in the hierarchy of the camp.

In May 1945, Rojko and his wife made their way back to Deutschlandsberg from Terezín. Soon after their return he found employment as a shipper with a local newspaper, hoping that his whereabouts and his past would go unnoticed. In this Rojko at first succeeded but one might well wonder about his peace of mind because he must have known about the war crime trials then taking place in Germany and countries formerly occupied by the Third Reich. A series of trials held in Leitmeritz in 1946 should have worried him greatly as two of his immediate superiors, SS *Hauptsturmführer* (Captain) Heinrich Jöckel and SS *Oberscharführer* Wilhelm Schmidt, along with other former guards, were sentenced to be hanged. It is difficult to fathom why Rojko elected to re-establish himself on his old home ground where many people must have known about his past and where discovery would be only a question of time. And indeed the Czechs were diligently looking for the man commonly referred to as the 'Butcher of Terezín'.

The inevitable happened in 1948 when he was arrested following a request for extradition from the Czech judiciary. Either through a bungling of the extradition procedure or due to the unwillingness of the Austrians to deliver one of their nationals to a country where certain death awaited, the demand was turned down. The grounds for refusal were that it had never been fully established that the arrested man and the killer of Terezín were one and the same person. Rojko was released in 1951 and, working again at his old job with the newspaper, led the life of an ordinary citizen for the next ten years. He may have imagined that his worries were over but new proofs of his identity were furnished—enough to warrant his re-arrest.

The Trial From August 1961 interrogating officials and the pre-trial judge had attempted to locate eye-witnesses who—some seventeen years after the end of the war and the upheavals that followed it—were dispersed in various countries. About 60 people were on hand to testify.

The names of the majority of the murdered men were not known but, as the trial proceeded, here and there a profession or at least the place from where the victim came was mentioned—a Viennese film producer, beaten by Rojko with the handle of a shovel and finished off with a thick branch; a parish priest from western Bohemia who had his head dunked in a barrel of water until he drowned; a school director from Prague and a Czech colonel, clubbed to death by Rojko in their cells in front of other prisoners; a lieutenant from a town in southern Bohemia; a Viennese engineer; a Jewish shopkeeper; a rabbi; all of whom were then identified by name.

The identity of others was impossible to establish —the Jewish prisoner beaten to death while waiting in line in front of the infirmary, or the twelve elderly inmates, hardly able to walk, whom Rojko ordered to jump a ten foot ditch, and shot as they lay inside it; the prisoner whom he pushed over the rampart, then left to lie in the moat until the workday was over, who died that night in his cell.

At one point the prosecutor asked Rojko if he knew the meaning of the word 'cruel'.

Rojko: 'The interrogating official has already explained the meaning to me.'

Judge: 'Didn't you know the meaning before?'

Rojko: 'No. I wasn't permitted to punish prisoners but sometimes I had to set one on the right path.'

Judge: 'Are you trying to tell us that you never hit anybody?'

Rojko: 'Well, possibly ... but that was to spare him more serious punishment.'

Judge: 'Wasn't there a famous Rojko punch?'

Rojko: 'At the worst I boxed a prisoner's ears. I can't remember the details any more.'

When questioned, Rojko denied having been the official executioner or even a member of the execution squad.

Judge: 'But during his trial by the Czechs Jöckel stated that you liked to be appointed to the execution squad. In fact he said that you were his best execution official.'

Prosecutor: 'You only brought the prisoners to the execution ground, is that right?'

Rojko: 'If I had refused, I'd have been a dead man myself in no time.'

Prosecutor: 'Or you would have been sent to the front. How many inmates did you normally collect at one time to bring to the execution ground?'

Rojko: 'One or more, up to five, maybe six heads.' The actual word the accused used was '*Stück*', meaning pieces.

Judge: 'How can you refer to them in such a way, these weren't pieces, they were human beings. Were you afraid of your boss?'

Rojko: 'I was an infant compared to him.' [No doubt a reference to Jöckel's size.]

Judge: 'It seems to me that you were hard and pitiless to those below you, and humble before your superiors.'

Prosecutor: 'Did you ever witness a prisoner being beaten to death? How did they die?'

xv

Rojko: 'From sickness.'
Prosecutor: 'Did you keep a record of the so-called "Daily Departures"?'
Rojko: 'No.'
Prosecutor: 'But such a book exists. Wasn't there a pickle jar with gold teeth?'
Rojko: 'No.'
The Prosecutor, addressing the judge: 'Your honour, please tell the accused that he himself admitted this to the pre-trial judge.'
Rojko: 'Yes, but not in my office, in the office of the assistant commander Schmidt. I had to deliver them there.'

At the end of the four-week trial the prosecutor's summing-up stressed that unspeakable suffering had been inflicted on defenceless people because of their political opinions or their origin. In Terezín, Rojko had murdered for the joy of killing and out of cowardice. For personal advantage he had become a faithful servant of the Nazi regime.

The defence lawyer's address presented him as just a simple person caught up in the machinery and made to serve this perverted system.

The jury returned a verdict of guilty in 34 counts out of 41. As for the rest of the some 150 cases of the original indictment, either no eye-witness had come forward, or there was no positive proof that the defendant had been the last man to have laid his hands on the murdered inmate.

Rojko was sentenced to life imprisonment.

PRAGUE
WINTER

1

My father and mother met on a train. They already knew each other as my father had courted her older sister until she married somebody else. His disappointment couldn't have lasted too long—he was with a mistress when my mother ran into him on that occasion. It was wartime, 1917, and Father was having trouble finding enough food for his dog, a Great Dane. Since Mother lived on a farm, she offered to help with supplies and that's how it all began.

I've been told that I didn't start to walk until I was three. My slow start may have been due to several illnesses, the most serious of which was one it was thought I had caught from a cow, although several doctors have since assured me that humans are not susceptible to this particular disease. When I was a baby my grandfather used to sit me on the back of one of his cows which later developed foot-and-mouth disease. My mother and Grandmother Toni took turns looking after me so I didn't end up the same way as Grandfather's cows, but their worries that I was a retarded child persisted.

One of my earliest recollections is of being on a street in my pram and seeing somebody looking down at me. At the time I must have been about three and I believe I know the exact spot where this happened: twenty years later I was marched past the same place as a concentration camp inmate, part of a work-brigade column.

I was born in north-western Bohemia, in Leitmeritz, a small, provincial garrison town on the north shore of the Elbe, about half-way between Prague and Dresden. The seat of a bishopric, it was conspicuously lacking in any industrial activity. At the time of my birth, Leitmeritz was predominantly German-speaking. However, once over the bridge to the south shore, all villages were Czech. Being born on the linguistic border of these two cultures may have made it

1

easier for me to learn languages, even though I never lived there permanently after the age of five.

Leitmeritz was built around a huge, cobblestoned market-square with one, or was it two, stone fountains and some architecturally interesting buildings. One, I think it was the City Hall, was Gothic, with arcades, another had a strange roof in the shape of a chalice; some were Renaissance but the majority were nondescript, probably built at the beginning of the nineteenth century. The house where I was born—one of the nondescript ones—was on the corner of the market-square and New Gate Street and bore the number 2 on its stone entrance. It had been rebuilt on the foundations of a much older house, since the street entrance was paved with large flagstones of an earlier date and the arch over the entrance was also very old. I was told that, according to an ancient law, a house kept the right to brew its own beer only as long as it kept its original archway entrance and ours had retained that right. The bookshop on the ground floor belonged to my father's family. The living quarters were above the shop. I was born in the living-room because the tile stove in the bedroom exploded while my mother was in labour and she had to be moved in a hurry. Of course I have no recollection of this room from my infancy but I have seen pictures of it. It was over-furnished in a kind of Biedermeier or Empire style with a harpsichord in the middle.

My father came from a line of German burghers dating back, as he believed, to the thirteenth century, more or less to the time when German settlers appeared in Bohemia. His forefathers had originally lived in a place called Martinsthal, meaning Martin's Valley, not far from Leitmeritz. He was very proud of his lineage and dabbled in genealogy, making up family trees, one of which still exists. It dates back two hundred years, that is, from the time the family settled in Leitmeritz, and it is difficult to say whether the others weren't a production of his imagination. In actual fact, I know very little about my father and that little is coloured by my mother's resentment of the fact that he never worked seriously, for example—he wanted to be a painter—and never learnt Czech, considering both beneath his dignity.

I was born six months after the dismemberment of the Austro-Hungarian Empire which followed the end of that war. The German-speaking population of Bohemia, then roughly one-third of its total, accepted the new state—Czechoslovakia—with distaste and a certain number of German irredentist societies sprang up soon after the new state was formed. One of these was the German Union, in which my father registered me before my baptism, which took place some ten months later in the local Lutheran church.

My mother was very young at the time of her marriage, about seventeen or eighteen, ten years younger than my father and, I suppose, very naïve. She had been brought up on the family farm near Leitmeritz where she was expected to help with all the chores. Apart from Czech she spoke German and had learnt French from her mother, a former teacher, and from some schooling in Switzerland. My maternal grandfather was Jewish although he never practised his faith. Instead he had pronounced Socialist views which he tried to put into practice on his farm, much to the dismay of Grandmother Toni.

Grandfather Joseph was known in the area for his generosity and once, when some repairs were needed to the roof of the local Catholic church, the parish priest sent one of the workmen to borrow a pair of horses to haul beams. Not only did Joseph lend him the horses but the driver as well. Later in the day, the distraught driver returned minus one horse and explained that it had to be destroyed when a beam fell on it. What my grandfather's comments were, I can't say, but some time later when he was again asked to furnish horsepower for the same purpose, his answer has come down through the years, 'Go tell the good Father I'll only let him have the horses if he gives them Extreme Unction first.'

Part of my Grandmother Toni's family had originally been Protestant, but at the time of the Counter-Reformation, like many others, they adopted the Jewish faith rather than emigrate or convert to Catholicism. The general attitude in Bohemia towards Jews in my grandfather's time was tolerant and, in some ways, even friendly. To illustrate this atmosphere of tolerance, Thomas Masaryk, the first President of Czechoslovakia, had become known to the general public because, during a well-publicized trial, he took up the defence of a Jew accused of a ritual murder. Racial discrimination was unknown but prejudice based on religious differences did exist to some degree. On the whole it was usually limited to expressions children used such as 'Who crucified Jesus Christ?'

There had been no mass persecution of Jews since the time of the Crusades and, in the following centuries, as the influence of the Catholic Church waned, people gradually ceased to care to what faith one belonged. This religious indifference infected the Jews as well. I cannot remember ever seeing a kosher food shop in Prague, although they probably did exist, or ever noticing any of my Jewish friends observing dietary laws. If the Jewish community continued to survive in Bohemia it was probably due to the influx from the east of those seeking better opportunities in a more tolerant atmosphere. The religious laxity on all sides resulted in social intermingling to a far greater degree than elsewhere and, inevitably, to mixed marriages. It even came as a surprise to many families when they were classified as Jewish once the Germans occupied Czechoslovakia.

My parents' marriage didn't work—their backgrounds were far too different. My mother couldn't accept the fact that her husband refused to work, that he was squandering an inheritance and living on handouts from his widowed mother who continued to manage the book and music shop. Nor did she understand his extreme German nationalism. She had been brought up in Czech, gone to Czech schools and the majority of her friends were Czech. However, the most serious stumbling block was his penchant for extra-marital affairs. My father was a remarkably good-looking man I am told, with charm to match, and had great success with the opposite sex.

My parents divorced when I was about a year old and I went to live with my grandparents who had sold their farm by that time and moved to Leitmeritz to be near their only surviving child, Mother's elder sister having died of Spanish influenza at the end of the war. They bought a house with a large garden and my first memories date from then. I remember swinging a cat by the tail in the garden; falling into a coal cellar through a trap-door on the stairway landing; smoking potato leaves until I was sick or, from the safety of the garden hedge, calling out what I thought were dirty words to passers-by. My mother went abroad for about a year and soon after her return she married again, this time choosing a Czech.

My stepfather, Loiza, had not returned from the war until the spring of 1920. He had seen service in the Uhlans, an Austrian cavalry regiment, and was taken prisoner by the Russians at the beginning of hostilities. Loiza's first years in captivity were spent in a prison camp in central Russia where he was very well treated, receiving invitations from local landowners. After the Bolshevik Revolution conditions got tough and prisoners of war were moved to Siberia. Eventually he escaped from the camp and, for a time, hid out with other escapees, all of them living off the land. After some months in the *taiga* he joined up with the Czech Legions, an army formed by the Allies to fight against the Austrians and Germans. As a reward for their help the Czechs were promised their independence.

By the time my stepfather joined the Legions they were no longer at war with Austria but were fighting alongside the White Russians against the Red Army. For a while the Czechs held control of the Trans-Siberian railway. Since Loiza spoke excellent English he served as liaison officer in Vladivostok with the American and Japanese expeditionary forces. Before the arrival of the Red Army in eastern Siberia, he left with the Japanese troops and lived for a time in Japan. His father had resided there thirty or forty years earlier, soon after Japan was first opened to foreigners.

Shortly after her remarriage, my mother moved to Prague with her husband, leaving me with her parents. Since Loiza's studies had been interrupted by the war he continued with them, passed his bar exams and hung out his shingle. The chances of his becoming a successful lawyer were good: his family was well known as his grandfather had been mayor of Prague and owned a great deal of land which in due course became suburbs.

The former mayor's project had been to create a green belt around Prague and, to this end, he donated large tracts of land to the city. However, his ambitious plan was never fully realized. Instead of being turned into parks the majority of them ended up as tram depots, barracks and even a prison—St Pancras.

I think I was nearly five when I left my grandparents and joined my new family. Now, instead of German as in Leitmeritz, I was expected to speak Czech at home. Until my move to Prague all I really knew was German, although I suppose I must have understood a fair amount of Czech, spoken between my mother and her parents, because I can't recall any problems over the change of language. Perhaps my grandparents had chosen to bring me up in German in deference to my father's family, but I suppose they must have also been aware of the advantages of bilingualism. After the births of my two sisters another change occurred when my stepfather decided I should be baptized, this time as a Catholic, so that the whole family would be of the same faith—at least I believe that was his argument at the time but my mother continued to be a Protestant as I later found out. Even now, looking back, I still don't understand the reason for my 'conversion'. Loiza went to Mass at the most for Christmas and Easter and then not every year. He was an active Freemason, I knew, and I remember our catechism teacher telling us that Catholics could

5

on no account be Freemasons. This inconsistency left me wondering, but I never spoke of it to either of my parents, nor to anybody else for that matter. It was just one of the many puzzles I grew up with.

My real father also remarried soon after his divorce. He chose a wife of Austro-Italian descent and they had a daughter whose existence I was unaware of until we met when I was around sixteen. He divorced again and died in his early forties in the house where I was born. In his last years he drank a lot, gradually ceasing to see his friends to the point where he became a recluse.

I learned some of these things from my mother when I was ten. One day I asked her why my name was different from that of the rest of the family. When she told me I can remember crying: it wasn't that I was sorry not to know my real father—I had absolutely no memory of him—rather that I felt I wasn't a full member of the family. Some time before his death, my father asked that I be allowed to visit him in Leitmeritz, but my mother refused and didn't tell me of his request at the time. I don't think she did so out of any lack of feeling, it was rather to spare me and avoid adding to my confusion.

At the age of six I went to a Czech primary school near my home. I wasn't a good pupil, more on the unruly side. My teacher used to send a schoolmate of mine to our house with little notes—telephones weren't used very much in those days—asking my mother to visit him to discuss my behaviour. When I knew this boy was coming I would wait at the top of the staircase and push him down. When the elder of my half-sisters was taken to be registered the same teacher asked Mother if he would find Marie as stupid and difficult as I had been.

At eleven I was sent to a German boarding school in southern Bohemia. By that time I was rapidly forgetting my German and my parents didn't want me to lose it altogether. I spent three uneventful years there. In a way I preferred it to being at home where discipline, at least from my mother's side, was strict and I didn't have much contact with my sisters. Any problems I had with them were never sorted out, we were simply kept apart: maybe that was one of my reasons for feeling separate from the family. At the end of my third year, when Hitler took power in Germany and relations between Czechs and Germans were becoming tense, I returned home to continue my education in Czech.

My new school in Prague was a well-known one and I was probably admitted because my stepfather had studied there in his time. This change of schools had a certain bearing on my future. It was a period during which I started to formulate my own ideas and it happened to coincide with the time when neighbouring Germany was becoming more aggressive. One could feel a growing resentment towards Germany and the German minority living in Czechoslovakia, a minority more and more attracted to Nazi ideology.

Before Hitler's ascent to power Loiza's German friends often ate with us. Of course everybody at home spoke German and my step-father's education had been, to a considerable degree, German or rather Austrian. He was a former reserve officer in the Austrian Imperial Army, half of his family lived in Vienna and spoke only German. As befitted a Freemason, his opinions were liberal and tolerant but, as time passed, we saw less and less of our German friends at table while, after each of Hitler's radio speeches, my stepfather's antagonism towards the Nazis grew. We often listened to German radio stations and could feel an increasing aggressiveness.

At school I could sense a similar attitude among friends and teachers. The approaching upheaval was felt everywhere and, influenced by this atmosphere, I became anti-German as well, even though I could guess that a conflict with Germany would be a lost cause. To counteract this feeling of hopelessness against a much more powerful neighbour, our government and the people were pinning their hopes on France with whom Czechoslovakia had a pact of mutual assistance in case of war. French cultural and commercial ties were encouraged and, probably more than just by coincidence, at this time my parents engaged a French governess for my two sisters. French gradually replaced German; we read French authors and with Mademoiselle living with us, we spoke French at table. Later I was sent to spend school holidays in Switzerland and France and it was the first time I was given an opportunity to observe a way of life other than our own.

Paris made a great impression on me. I couldn't stop admiring the wide, tree-lined avenues with their imposing buildings and the general layout of the city. By comparison, Prague now seemed to me a small provincial town. It may have been on one of my visits to Paris that I decided to live there one day.

It wasn't that Prague was a drab or boring place, quite the contrary; those who have known the city will remember it otherwise, especially the setting. Surrounded by green hills, it is intersected by a wide river, the Vltava, or Moldau, spanned by close to a dozen bridges. The oldest of these is the Charles Bridge, a huge stone structure with statues on the parapets. Gothic fortification towers terminate the bridge on either end and give access to the two old parts of the city. On the left bank is the Lesser Town, over which towers the castle complex. On the right side is the Old Town and beyond that the New Town, separated from the Old by a ring of wide streets replacing the demolished former fortifications. Actually, the name New Town is a misnomer because this part is six hundred years old.

Around the New Town and beyond the castle lies the modern city with uninteresting blocks of apartment houses but many parks. By contrast, the Old Town and the Lesser Town have kept some of their original atmosphere with winding streets, burghers' houses in Gothic, Renaissance and Baroque styles, palaces of the nobility and a multitude of churches. The New Town eventually became the business centre; it housed offices, fashionable shops, popular cafés, night-clubs and the school I attended. This was a four-storey building with a fake-stone stucco façade like all those built by the government in the previous hundred years. It was on a side street opposite a combined brewery and beer hall dating from the fifteenth century, a small, anachronistic place which had somehow survived. It was still patronized by the male population who went there for a special, dark beer unavailable elsewhere and another speciality of the house, smoked pork served with freshly grated horseradish and salt sticks.

The Czech school system was essentially a carry-over from the Austrian Empire. Secondary school lasted eight years and ended with a school leaving exam. This opened the door to university studies or to a half-way decent job in administration. The usual subjects were taught: maths, physics, chemistry, Latin and a couple of modern languages which in our school happened to be German and French. I was a rather mediocre student with the exception of these modern languages which I probably spoke better than the teachers—a fact that hardly endeared me to them. In other subjects I tried merely to pass and that was sufficient for me, I had no particular ambitions and considered school a necessary nuisance.

Since I had spent the first three years of my secondary studies in the German boarding school, I was admitted to the fourth year when I returned to Prague at fourteen. My first contact wasn't a happy one. All friendships were already established and I made no friends in my class. Furthermore, it soon became obvious that in certain subjects I was behind the rest so, in view of my lack of adequate marks in maths and drawing, I had to repeat the year. This was nothing out of the

8

ordinary, the school administration tried to discourage mediocre students from continuing because classes were over-crowded. Those weeded out either went to a technical school or were apprenticed to learn a trade. My parents, however, insisted that I be allowed another try, so I found myself in the fourth class for a second year.

This time the atmosphere among classmates seemed more friendly and I knew some of those who were repeating with me. It was from among the repeaters that I chose my friends, two boys to whom I eventually became very close. The first was the son of a lawyer well known to my parents. We were both new in this particular class but he was repeating from a parallel section and came to my attention in a rather comical way. In alphabetical order, the class-teacher read out the names of those students who had passed and then the repeaters, my name among them, adding, 'there is also Primus,' giving his family name. The first name Primus is very unusual in Czech and I wondered why the teacher had mentioned a *primus* among the repeaters—the term was usually reserved for the top student in the class. It was only a few days later that I discovered that this was his first name and didn't refer to his classification at all. Primus was rather short and stocky with wavy, chestnut hair, brown eyes and a slow, deliberate way of speaking.

A year later we were joined by another repeater from another school. His name was Franta, the son of an owner of a small factory for children's clothing. He lived about half-way in the general direction of my home, whereas Primus lived in the opposite direction. Franta was later fond of telling the story of how he first noticed me. As usual on opening day, our teacher read out the list of students who had passed, followed by those who were repeating. After finishing the names he asked, 'Whom didn't I mention?' As my name hadn't been read out, I stood up. He looked at me, frowned and shouted, 'You, you have no right to be here. It was understood you were to leave school and that's why we let you pass. Go and tell your parents, they should know what to do about it.'

I left the classroom and called home from the nearest telephone. When I got to the house my mother had already left and when she returned a couple of hours later I was told I could go back to school in the morning. Years after, Mother confessed that everything had been arranged between my uncle and the class-teacher, they had been schoolmates. From that moment on I had no serious problems and passed my final exam four years later.

My close friendship with Primus and Franta really began when the three of us were walking home from school. In Franta's and my case it would have been understandable that we walk together, but for Primus it meant a big detour. Generally, we walked along the main roads and parted at a junction where a Gothic fortification, the Powder Tower, separates the Old and New Towns. Primus and I would board different trams while Franta had a two-minute walk to reach home. Our friendship grew for another reason. Towards the end of each school year we had to catch up on what we had studied, or rather, neglected to study. By the end of May and throughout most of June we met regularly each week for cramming sessions.

2

Once my stepfather's law practice was well enough established we moved to a house on the fringe of the city centre, in a drab neighbourhood of blocks of flats. The area was squeezed between the river and a steep, tree-covered hill, with all the streets intersecting at right angles. Most of the houses were probably fifty to a hundred years old. The one Loiza bought—facing a square with a park in the middle—must have been considerably older, a fact readily established as each building had two numbers: a street number in blue and the red cadastral number allotted in sequence. The house had three floors but was somewhat dwarfed by the five- and six-storeyed, utilitarian blocks on either side. There were sculptured lintels on the yellow stucco façade and an imposing *porte cochère* flanked by a pair of conical stones that, in the past, had served to protect it from the hubs of carriage wheels. Behind the house was a small courtyard with a garage, and a flat for the caretaker. Inside, an unusual spiral stone staircase connected the floors right up to the loft, while the rooms were large with high ceilings.

Mother's parents sold their house in Leitmeritz and settled into a flat on the elevated ground floor. I lived next door to them as did Loiza's youngest brother, a medical student. The maids' quarters took up the rest of this level. The whole of the next floor was used for my father's practice. My parents and sisters and, later on, Mademoiselle, lived on the top floor which was the family living quarters as well. The whole set-up was rather reminiscent of a patriarchal society: everyone met in the middle of the day for the main meal, so that with frequent guests it wasn't unusual to be a dozen or more at table.

Primus's family home on the other side of the river had one of the most romantic settings of any private house I knew. It stood on the side-spur of the castle hill and the view from it was breathtaking. To

11

the left was the silhouette of Prague Castle along with the Gothic spires of the Cathedral of St Vitus and to the right, slightly above, the Strahov monastery and a hillside park. Within this framework, and just below, lay the city itself. In the immediate foreground were the palaces of the old nobility with their surrounding gardens and parks and the homes of wealthy burghers; beyond that the roofs of countless houses stretched to the horizon. For a large part of the year a mist—sometimes smog from all the coal heating—hung over the town, a mist pierced by the church spires and the fortification towers with the silvery ribbon of the river winding its way beneath the bridges.

Primus's house was L-shaped, modern and didn't suit its surroundings at all. In one wing were the living quarters proper, in the other a large drawing-room filled with antique furniture and subdivided by a wrought-iron grille. Beyond the living-room, in a circular arrangement to take advantage of the view, were a winter garden and dining-room.

On Primus's father's side the family was Protestant. His grandfather had founded a well-known bank while his maternal grandfather was the architect who, at the turn of the century, finished the construction of the Cathedral of St Vitus.

Franta's home was not far from the Powder Tower, about in the middle of an imaginary line drawn from Primus's house to ours. It was an apartment on the second floor of a stuccoed house built in the style fashionable before the First World War. Since it was conveniently located in the centre of town and his parents were kind and understanding, we often used his place for card games. Franta's family was Jewish. He had a much older sister whom I didn't know very well.

Franta was of above average height and slight, with black hair and dark eyes. He was always well groomed, the best-dressed boy in our class, and the only one of our group to receive regular pocket money. Primus and I often had to invent imaginary expenses—the purchase of school books, encyclopaedias and the like—to get our hands on some cash.

The three of us eventually made friends with Vladimir, or Lala as he was called, who wasn't attending our school at all. I don't really remember where or when I first met him, he may have joined our circle a year or so after Franta. He was our age, very tall and fair haired. What made him popular with us was his penchant for practical jokes and his taste for poker which the four of us used to play frequently. He had a brother, Evzen, about two years older, who sometimes joined us for cards. Their father was a government official, head of the Civil Air Transport Authority and a member of the same Masonic Lodge as my stepfather. Loiza and he were good friends and had known each other as children. Loiza used to call him Cat and I must admit there was a certain resemblance. Their mother was one of eighteen children of a well-known newspaper publisher, whose influence on public life led Emperor Franz Josef to name him to the Austrian Upper House, the equivalent of the British House of Lords.

We four saw a lot of each other. School finished at 1 o'clock for most of the term and homework wasn't too demanding, especially since we studied only the absolute minimum. When not playing cards, we used to go to night-clubs, chase girls and spend our winter holidays skiing together. If catching up on our studies became unavoidable, we worked in Primus's house or garden. We could spend hours there without ever seeing a soul. Lala didn't take part in our cram sessions since his studies were directed to the exact sciences, but he seldom missed our evening get-togethers.

Whenever we made plans for a study session I usually walked to Primus's house even though I lived several miles away. Before leaving home, I would call Franta to meet me at the Powder Tower. Nearby was a square full of street vendors selling kitchen gadgets, such as new-fangled potato peelers or celluloid shirt collars and cuffs, ties in artificial silk or children's toys. The vendors stood behind trestle tables with boxes of the goods they were selling piled underneath. They were voluble characters, calling out to passers-by to catch their attention. An associate posing as an interested buyer often stood nearby. As soon as the hawking had attracted a few onlookers, the associate would step forward and buy something in order to encourage the rest of the crowd. Once a few sales had been made and interest was slacking off, the vendor would pretend that his day was finished and begin packing up. After everybody had drifted away the spiel started all over again.

Vendors of another type—these were known as Bosniaks since they usually came from Yugoslavia—circulated among the stalls displaying their merchandise on small trays hung from their shoulders. They offered cheap mirrors, combs, razor blades, buttons, all of doubtful quality. It was best not to show any interest, because if one did so and then wandered off they would swear loudly in a comical mixture of Czech and Croatian. Here and there in this welter of people, Slovaks selling mouse-traps sat on the ground: as a matter of fact, if a Czech wanted to insult a Slovak, he called him a mouse-trap seller. The Slovak women stood out in their colourful costumes of an elaborately embroidered bodice worn over a white, puffed-sleeve blouse, the full skirt meeting knee-high black riding boots. They sold smoked sheep's cheese that sometimes had a pattern cut into the dark-brown rind. At Easter, intricately painted eggs were to be had. These were fragile and hollow—the white and yolk had been sucked out through an almost invisible hole plugged with wax.

The area of the Powder Tower was also a hunting ground for the popular-priced whores. Their asking rate was a 'bura'—a five-Crown piece—which corresponded to about four tram rides. Most of them were former maids who had come from the country and found themselves without a job. The shyer girls asked me if I didn't want a loving but the old hands approached with just a straightforward 'Would you like to fuck, lover?'

Franta was often late for our appointment. When he finally appeared we would walk together through the winding streets of the Old Town, past the Gothic City Hall towards Charles Bridge. The buildings along the way were a fascinating mixture of styles and periods. Most of the streets were paved with cobblestones rounded from years of wear. The pavements, in white and blue-black patterns of small, square marble chips, were something I had never seen elsewhere until I rediscovered them in Lisbon. The inhabitants in these parts were poor and the houses too old to offer much comfort. We passed dark, dusty shops where open barrels of smoked herring standing out on the pavement gave the district a particular odour. In other streets the prevalent smell was of roasted coffee and stale beer with a whiff of urine in dim corners. Children played football, elderly people sat in doorways observing what was going on while chatting with other old people installed across the way. In that part of town, life was unhurried and the sound of traffic rarely penetrated, but once we reached the bridge, the surroundings suddenly changed. In the open space of the river the silhouette of the castle could be seen, with tree-covered hills around it.

During those years of depression it was common to find beggars, mainly old men, but also some women with babies, sitting on the approaches to the bridge under shelter of the fortification towers. Actually, beggars on corners of busy road junctions or in front of a church were a usual sight too and there were some who didn't beg

14

outright: they could be seen hanging around snack-bars waiting for any leftovers on unfinished plates. In the trams one would notice people with highly polished but crackled shoes and frayed cuffs. Young men would ring doorbells offering to do any odd jobs around the house. The unemployment rate was high and furnished a constant subject for newspaper articles.

It was from schoolmates that I first realized just how hard times were because, when school fees came due, half the class asked to be excused payment as their parents' income was below a certain level. Then I started to really notice the poverty visible on the streets. I cannot say if, in the beginning, I considered this misery as something normal or not—it just existed, beyond my control. But political opinions were becoming radicalized in school and outside it, discussions on unemployment frequent. The rise of the Nazi regime in Germany coincided with this period of depression. The majority of those who espoused radical ideas were turning to Communism, but there were also some who, seeing the return to prosperity in Germany, wanted to copy it in our country. In the border regions of Bohemia, among the German-speaking population, where the unemployment rate was higher than in the rest of Czechoslovakia, Nazi ideology was rapidly gaining ground.

Once over the Charles Bridge we still had a good twenty minutes' walk to Primus's house, with a steep hill to climb. In this quarter the streets remained narrow but the houses were more imposing: most of the embassies were here in former palaces. We passed small wine cellars where for a few pennies one could spend a pleasant evening. The Lesser Town had rather a Mediterranean flavour, in contrast to the somewhat sombre feeling of the Old Town. At one point the slope of the street became so steep that one side of it gave way to an open space with gardens. And below the gardens the impressive panorama of the city opened up, but we could already see Primus's house a few hundred yards above.

Our study sessions often lasted late into the night. As it grew dark the lights of the city spread out below began to appear until the sight resembled an immense convex kettle lit by thousands of flickering candles. When we had finished we sometimes went to a wine shop for a night-cap along with a snack of a Yugoslav speciality—sausages or hamburgers with tomatoes and green peppers roasted together on a skewer. On occasions Primus came with us all the way to the centre of town and we separated at the Powder Tower. By that time, of course, the street vendors had disappeared but the prostitutes were still around. If business had been slow they might offer to take two or even three of us for the price of one, but none of us dared. The only lesson in sexual education my mother ever gave me must have made a deep, if not lasting, impression. It had consisted of a single sentence proffered when I made my first trip abroad. We were walking up and down the station platform and, as I was about to board the train, her parting words were, 'You know, there are bad women in this world, keep away from them: they could make you miserable for the rest of your life.'

After the war, when penicillin became available, my mother's admonition sounded somewhat hollow. Anyway, by that time I was sleeping only with 'nice' women who weren't supposed to have a venereal disease. To avoid infection before the war, we used condoms readily available from vending machines in many public toilets or restaurants and bars. Not far from our school there was a sex shop, the only one in Prague, to my knowledge. Besides the regular condoms it sold a fancy variety with feathers stuck to the tip or another type called the family condom—it was re-usable and came with a drying rack and a small box of talcum.

Once, with a girl of whose virtue I was none too sure, my condom burst and I was terrified, remembering my mother's warning. On arriving home I went straight to the bathroom and, using an eye-dropper, put alcohol into the opening of my penis. I nearly hit the ceiling with the searing pain. I avoided getting an infection all right, but for some time it hurt like hell when I urinated.

The school year was broken up by three major holidays: Christmas holidays lasted until 6 January, a week for mid-term at the beginning of February and another week at Easter. Until the age of fourteen or fifteen I spent these holidays skiing with my mother and sisters. Later, several friends who were excellent competition skiers got together and we went wherever there was a race. I didn't compete myself because I wasn't good enough, but it was more fun spending holidays with a bunch of friends than with the family.

But winters, on the whole, weren't that much fun. Prague looked grey and sad, a crisp day with sunshine was an exception and the snow soon became dirty from all the coal heating. People went around bundled up in nondescript, bulky clothing; many of the women wore kerchiefs and knee-high boots in felt, originally white but no proof against the slush and dirt of the streets.

During my last year of school I started frequenting a popular café on the river, called Manes after a well-known Czech painter. The café had once been a mill built around a stone tower; half of the building stood on an island, separated from the mainland by the millstream. It was a sprawling structure with, in addition to the café, an art gallery, a restaurant and a cosy bar. For the summer, the management anchored a sort of houseboat on the river side with a swimming pool, changing cabins and a bar. Between the boat and the buildings were terraces of different levels so that the whole complex could accommodate several hundred customers. Originally, it was probably meant as a meeting place for artists but eventually became a hangout for young people. After a while I got to know many of the *habitués*, but the greatest attraction of the place was that I was practically certain to pick up a girl there.

It was at Manes that I met most of my girlfriends, young sales-girls, office workers and the like. One was a dancer in a night-club, a fact I didn't know at the time, naïvely imagining she had very strict parents as she was seldom free in the evenings. She was a super-looking girl and I was quite smitten with her. The mystery was solved one day by Primus who had seen her performing in a club. She eventually met and married a German and had to escape from Prague before the end of the war. Some thirty years later I saw her again in Hamburg. By then my dancer had changed into a prim '*hausfrau*' and my fond memories were instantly demolished even though she was a girl I had dated longer than anyone before.

Although I lost my virginity at seventeen, I never had an affair that lasted more than two or three months and many didn't amount to more than a one-night-stand. The fact that I had no steady girlfriend didn't bother me. I had no desire to get sentimentally attached and may even have been afraid of it. Perhaps I would have made a good subject for a psychoanalyst, yet I don't think I was that different from my friends. Prague had a multitude of night-clubs, some of them posh places where I would take a girl I had met only recently and wanted to impress. The smaller clubs had a combo, the larger ones an orchestra. These clubs were expensive so I could only afford them occasionally. Night-clubs that offered shows cost even more, but there was one— where we only went without girls—with a quite innocent striptease, 'The Dream of the Maharajah'. A roly-poly man in dark make-up, wearing baggy trousers and a turban, sat on cushions while four topless females gyrated around him in a sort of veil dance. The girls were always the same and drank with the customers between acts. The place was a clip-joint with a never-varying show. After a while we stopped going there in favour of a club called 'Hell' and another, 'The Old Lady'. Both were cavernous halls below street level, frequented by prostitutes. The first time I went to Hell with Franta and Lubos, another school friend, I couldn't have been more than sixteen. We had to share a table with a man and a woman seated across the corner from me. Suddenly, I felt a hand on my knee slowly inching upwards. While she was calmly talking to her partner, I could feel her trying to unbutton my fly. Terrified that her date would notice what was going on and start a fight, and not knowing how to disengage myself from the fumbling fingers, I took a knife from the table and hit her over the knuckles with the handle. She gave me a baleful look as if to say, 'You fool, you don't know what you are missing,' and turned her back on me. Fortunately, her companion hadn't noticed anything unusual but both my friends had and were making fun of me.

'The Old Lady' was an even rougher place guarded by two bouncers who looked like boxers. It was full of not-so-young whores who competed eagerly for the favour of each newcomer to get a commission on any drinks ordered. This couldn't have added up to much as most people drank beer or slivovitz, a cheap plum brandy. A trick some of these women used to perform was to have the customer place a five-Crown coin on the edge of the table which they would then proceed to pick up with their cunt, another way of supplementing their income.

After a visit to these joints our next stop was often 'The Crown', a snack-bar on a corner at the junction of the two busiest streets. Besides the house speciality of tripe soup, one could buy a sandwich or cold salad by inserting a one-Crown coin into a slot in the display case. But the best by far was still the tripe soup with marjoram, served with a slice of dark rye bread—even now I recall it with fondness for it had a magical power to sober one up. Once I ran into Franta there at an early morning hour when he had just come from a party and was so drunk he could hardly stand. That time the potion didn't have its usual effect so I had to drag and carry him home, a distance of several blocks.

Lubos was the one who originally introduced us to these dives. He was a heavy-set fellow, older looking than his age, who had joined our class in the same year as Franta. At the time he made himself known in an original way—by circulating trash like *Paris Sex* and *La Vie*

Parisienne. Later on he lived alone in his parents' flat when his father was Ambassador to Turkey; nominally he was under the supervision of his grandparents, but they were living in the country. Lubos knew all the bordellos in Prague and the prostitutes addressed him as Doctor, probably because he was generous with money. However, the allowance he was getting wasn't enough for his sort of life-style. To supplement it he played in night-clubs as he was an excellent pianist but his studies began to suffer from late nights and lack of sleep. Once, after an outing, he invited me to his flat for a night-cap. We hailed a taxi and on arrival discovered that neither of us had any money left, so he calmly took off his shoes and handed them to the driver. Lubos's constant need for money finally got him into trouble with the police. He either advertised or answered marriage proposals in classified ads and, after a few meetings brought his supposed future wife to the apartment to show her where they would live. This was the opportunity to ask for some money as a contribution towards paying for the furniture. The women he conned must have been quite gullible: the flat had some exquisite pieces worth far more than what he pretended to have paid for them. Before long, Lubos was denounced for breach of promise and extortion and the affair was only hushed up when his father reimbursed the victims. The family threw him out and he had to live with a relative, but that didn't last long either.

In our final year of school, when Lubos ceased coming to school altogether, the class-teacher found out where he was living and, in a last ditch attempt to make him see reason, sent our best student—a true *primus*—to speak to him. According to what we were told afterwards, Lubos was living on the third floor of a run-down apartment house in the suburbs. A woman in her late thirties answered the bell but banged the door in the student's face when she found out the purpose of the visit. On the way down the stairs a voice through a half-open door asked the *primus* if he wasn't ashamed of himself, so young and already visiting a whore. After that we completely lost track of Lubos and never heard of him again except for once, at the beginning of the war, when somebody told me he had become a collaborator.

3

In our last school year, Lala and his brother approached me and a few other friends with the idea of fixing up a cellar in their parents' house and making it into a place for parties. It was roomy, two or three levels below the ground and soundproof, ideal for our purpose. The floor directly overhead was a Masonic lodge, but not the one our fathers belonged to. We lost no time accepting the proposition: we were always short of cash and a place like that would be more economical than the bars and night-clubs we were frequenting. Everyone lent a hand fixing it up with old furniture collected from attics and carted to the cellar. I remember that one of the so-called rooms was known as the Portuguese corner because of the red and green flag used to hide the holes in an old sofa. Lala had snitched it from his father, the honorary consul of Portugal. Once arranged, we christened the place 'Cojar' which we mistakenly took for the Spanish 'to copulate'.

Later, when house owners had to provide air-raid shelters for their tenants and walls between cellars were pierced to make escape routes, it was discovered that our hideout had another advantage. The wall separating Cojar from the wine cellar of the Masonic lodge was partially torn down and we made expeditions there to help ourselves to their impressive supply of liquor. Upstairs we found small, white kid aprons with pink and blue bindings which we then put to use in our own initiation rites.

Cojar soon proved its worth in other ways as well. If a party lasted into the early hours of the morning, or if we were facing an examination and weren't prepared for it, we left home as usual in the morning but instead of going to school went to the cellar to sleep or to arrange for a game of cards. Depending on the situation, we stayed there the whole morning or showed up later at school where our

20

absence went unnoticed. Our schoolmates had instructions not to report us absent at the morning roll-call: if discovered they simply said that so-and-so had been sent by another teacher on some errand outside. One day when I came home for lunch after a whole morning in Cojar my mother asked me about school. My ready answer was that everything was fine, I'd had a Latin exam that I felt I'd passed satisfactorily. The phone rang while we were all at table and the maid came in to say that Mother was wanted by my class teacher. All I could hear from where I sat was her insistent 'but he says he was at school'. Nothing was mentioned on the subject during the rest of lunch but afterwards she took me aside for a memorable dressing down.

The fact that I was living on a different floor from my parents gave me more freedom than my friends had. I could leave the house at any hour without their knowing about it. Once I came home just as the caretaker was opening the *porte cochère*. He greeted me with a smirk. 'So, I see you are now taking early morning walks; keep it up, it's good for your health.' Another time I mislaid my key to the gate and, since I had a pressing appointment and knew I wouldn't be back until morning, I jumped out of my window, some eight feet from the ground. A passing taxi driver saw me and gave the alarm, thinking I was a burglar.

Loiza's half-brother, Jan, had the room next to mine. Then in his mid-thirties, he was a sort of eternal student still a long way from finishing his medical studies. Jan had a mortal fear of presenting himself for exams and postponed them whenever possible. Because he was chronically short of money he didn't go out much; most of his time was spent in his room, studying and smoking up the place with cheap cigarettes. It was cluttered with medical books—I even recall a human skull—and everything was covered with dust as he didn't want the maids to come in to clean. There was a special reason for this. At the beginning of each month Jan received some money from his relatives plus a small income from an inheritance. He changed everything into coins and threw them under his bed and cupboard to be fished out progressively as the month wore on.

He was popular with my friends: if they had reason to suspect a venereal disease they came to him for diagnosis. In spite of our age difference, he and I were on good terms, enjoying long chats until he used me as an excuse to Loiza as to why he hadn't presented himself for an exam. Jan finally got his degree when he was close to fifty and

I've heard that he made an excellent psychiatrist.

On the whole, I could say that life was unstinting to me until I reached my nineteenth year. I had no worries except those concerning approaching exams. Of course, there was that nagging, subconscious apprehension at the back of my mind that this pleasant, irresponsible life would soon have to come to an end. What kind of end, I had no idea—perhaps because my school years would soon be over and I would have to apply myself more seriously to studies at the university, or it may have been a presentiment that some unforeseen event would drastically change everything around me.

I felt that we were living in a pervading atmosphere of uncertainty and fear of the future. In this sentiment I may have been influenced by the mounting nervousness around me because of what was going on in Germany. The annexation of Austria was the signal that these forebodings were justified. Shortly before this event, cousins of Loiza's had been visiting us from Vienna. Hearing on the radio that the Austrian Government was organizing a plebiscite on whether or not to join Germany, they cut short their visit to be there for the vote, but their hasty return proved unnecessary. Under pressure from Hitler, the plebiscite was called off and German troops entered Austria.

In a flash, the desperate strategic situation of Czechoslovakia became obvious. The whole western part of the country was surrounded by Germany, like those drawings showing the head of a small fish in the mouth of a much larger one. The news reaching Prague was depressing and, at the same time, hard to believe. Suicides, arrests, mistreatment of Nazi opponents, flights into exile, all these were now daily subjects of conversation. I discovered that there is something strange, however, about human reactions: a lot of people try to discount or ignore facts difficult to stomach. Although the tragic situation which now faced us should have been evident to everybody, the majority of those with whom I talked tried to belittle it. The argument went that the Czechs had a well-equipped army, modern fortifications and the will to fight back, all of which the Austrians had lacked. They chose to overlook the fact that half this army was made up of Slovaks, ethnic Germans, Hungarians and Ukrainians, peoples with little incentive to fight for a country they hardly considered their own; that the fortifications were located in German-speaking borderlands and, at any rate, the *Wehrmacht* was ten times larger. All these facts were dismissed and hopes pinned on the defence treaties

Czechoslovakia had with France and the Soviet Union, futile as they turned out to be. Neither of these countries had a common border with Czechoslovakia and the Soviet Union didn't even border with Germany. I have always wondered about this general tendency to play down disagreeable realities. The majority of my friends and acquaintances didn't really believe that what happened in Austria might repeat itself at home. We were soon commiserating with the Austrian refugees who started flooding into the country, just as we had with the preceding wave from Germany. Their stories were listened to with disgust but without drawing any conclusions, just as if these things were happening on another planet.

Nearly everyone was clinging to the hope that some unforeseen miracle would reverse the pattern of events. Only when things did take a turn for the worse did some people consider leaving the country but by then it was too late. Other nations began closing their borders to would-be immigrants from Central Europe. Oddly enough, this simplified everybody's life; the would-be exiles didn't have to liquidate their assets under pressure nor those without means face an uncertain future in a strange country. I still vividly remember a conversation with Franta on this subject. 'I'd rather sleep in my own bed with worries than under a bridge in a strange town,' he told me. Little did we know then that sleeping under a bridge would have been a picnic compared to what was awaiting him.

With Austria occupied, the German pressure on Czechoslovakia increased. Politicians representing the Sudeten Germans were pushing their claims, more and newer demands were being voiced. It soon became evident that only a complete separation of the German-speaking regions of Bohemia and Moravia and their annexation to the Reich would satisfy them. Hitler's radio speeches increased in virulence. Graffiti, slogans like 'One Nation, One Reich, One Führer' began to appear in German-speaking towns. Serious incidents between Sudeten Germans and Czechs became a daily occurrence. Many Germans and Czechs, who until then had been friends, stopped speaking to each other, mixed families split up. A showdown was fast approaching.

When I was in my early teens, the whole family regularly spent summer holidays in a good fishing area in the mountains close to Bavaria. Loiza was an ardent fly fisherman and often let me tag along.

He always rented the same house from the owner of a glass factory who had a daughter my age—we had quite a crush on each other. Later, I stopped spending holidays with the family but I still went there occasionally for a long weekend. On my last visit I met this girl on the street. She was wearing a dirndl, the Bavarian national costume—a white blouse, cotton skirt and laced bodice in a bright print plus a decorative apron. The dirndl, like the *lederhosen* for boys—leather shorts worn with white knee-length stockings—represented the outward sign of German nationalism. When I saw her coming towards me I raised my arm in greeting, but before I could say a word she turned abruptly and crossed the street. There was no doubt that she had seen me and it was equally obvious that she didn't want to talk to me. This happened in 1938, at Whitsun. A few days later the Czech Government decreed a partial mobilization after reports that the *Wehrmacht* was concentrating troops on the border. I met some fellows in uniform whom I knew by sight, but nothing happened and it proved to be a false alarm.

In late June I went to England via Paris. While passing through Stuttgart in the train, I saw half a dozen military planes circling over the city at low altitude and, while I didn't know much about planes, I couldn't help but notice how advanced in design they looked. It was my second trip to England and by then I could speak English quite well. There was no apparent war psychosis there, not like home. The papers were certainly full of reports from Berlin and Prague, but I felt that the British didn't concern themselves unduly with this news. One day I listened to a speaker on Hyde Park Corner talking about Fascism and the danger of war. The speech seemed hollow to me, with a lot of inaccuracies as if he had learned it by heart without actually knowing much about his subject. I could sense that the onlookers were not too taken with it. When I later mentioned this to my landlady she told me he was most probably a Communist because relatively few Englishmen, apart from the Communists, had any outspoken opinions on the subject. Later, I wondered about his being one, not once during his speech had he given any indication of his convictions.

My own political opinions were neither to the left, nor to the right. Of course, I was aware of the purges taking place at roughly that time in the Soviet Union but that was far away, in a country I really didn't know much about. Anyhow, it was all overshadowed by much closer events happening in Germany. There were Communists in my class, but none of them were particularly close friends of mine. When

24

Czechoslovakia's mutual assistance treaty with the Soviet Union was discussed in class, I accepted our history teacher's opinion that the Russians were gradually abandoning Marxist theories and turning into nationalists. On several occasions some of my schoolmates suggested that I participate in anti-German street demonstrations the Communist party was organizing, but I refused. Had somebody asked me the reason for my refusal I probably would have been embarrassed to say exactly why. If pressed I might have said that since my father was an ethnic German I had no business demonstrating against them: besides, I felt that the notions of German and Nazi were being lumped together too indiscriminately. Probably another reason was that none of my close friends, with but one exception, had shown any Communist leanings; it was a subject we somehow never even discussed. The exception sat next to me in class, a boy with a solid middle-class background. Jiri's academic record was similar to mine. As a matter of fact, at the beginning of our final year each of us was failing in half the subjects, fortunately not the same ones. As the school year progressed we put this mutual deficiency to good use. I helped him with German and French and he helped me with Czech literature.

Until our last year, Jiri had carried on a rather vocal propaganda for a semi-Fascist party whose slogan was 'Nothing but the Nation' and wore a lapel badge with an 'N', the party's symbol. When he had a radical change of opinion and became a Communist, though surprised by his sudden about face from one extreme to the other, I thought it merely a passing whim. But I was wrong. He stuck firmly to his new beliefs and, although I lost track of him, I eventually learned that he made a career for himself when the Communists came to power. He became rector of the Academy of Arts and, during the period of the Prague Spring in 1968, before the intervention of the Soviet troops, he steadfastly maintained his orthodox and pro-Soviet orientation. Unfortunately for him, his faithfulness was of no help when his son escaped to Switzerland a few years later. The defection created a scandal impossible to cover up and my former schoolmate was forced to appear on television and abjectly confess to 'narcissism', a term I had never come across before in the Communist vocabulary of self-criticism.

When I returned from England at the beginning of September 1938, I found the country preparing for the inevitable conflict. People in army uniforms were everywhere, with columns of soldiers marching through the streets, and tanks and motorized guns in evidence. The park in front of our house was criss-crossed with trenches as a shelter against aircraft attacks. Far more ominous were Hitler's speeches transmitted by radio, interrupted with shouts from his audience of 'Heil' and 'We Want War'. There was no doubt that a confrontation was imminent.

While this tension was building up, the British Government initiated talks with Hitler in an effort to prevent an armed conflict. At first these talks were inconclusive but, by the end of September, Hitler, together with the heads of government of Italy, France and Great Britain, concluded an agreement in Munich that forced Czechoslovakia to cede to Germany all regions with a majority of ethnic Germans. Everything happened with such speed that there were very few protests and the country, on the whole, was relieved to have escaped a war it would have had to fight on its own. The president, Eduard Benes, fled the country, as did Jan Masaryk, the son of Tomas. Of course, patriotic pride was deeply hurt and the breaking of the mutual assistance treaty by France was resented. But, except for those who had to leave the regions now occupied by Germany, life went on more or less as before. Certain political organizations, along with the Freemasons, were banned and a new government was installed—one more amenable to Germany. By the same stroke territories with a majority of Hungarians and Poles had to be ceded to their respective countries.

Geographically, the new state looked even more absurd than the old one. Following the language borders, the political frontier went meandering over the countryside without heed to any logical or economic necessity. Railway lines and roads crossed and re-crossed borders with deep salients here and there. At one particular spot the new German territory was only twenty miles from Prague. My birthplace, Leitmeritz, became German.

The prevalent feeling among the Czechs was that they would watch the approaching war as uninvolved bystanders—after all, hadn't Hitler proclaimed time and again that he didn't want a single Czech in the German Reich? Only a few seemed to realize that this was a temporary respite which couldn't possibly last but, in view of the desperate economic situation facing the new state, where factories were cut off from supplies and workers from factories, with refugees from the lost territories crowding the truncated country, many began to admit that the dismemberment of the old Austrian Empire had been a tragic mistake—a dismemberment in which the Czechs had played

26

the leading role twenty years previously. It was now evident that the Austrian Empire had been the only viable entity allowing for the existence of the multitude of small nations settled between Germany and Russia. The present destruction of multinational Czechoslovakia was the direct outcome of the earlier destruction of the multinational Austrian Empire. Inevitably, these small nations had to come under the sway of either Germany or Russia, whichever country was stronger at a given moment.

The hopes of the Czechs that the new state would now be left in peace never materialized. On 15 March 1939, less than six months after the occupation of the German-speaking borderlands, the rest of Czecho-Slovakia—the name was then hyphenated—was invaded and occupied by the *Wehrmacht*. A few days earlier, alarming news had started to circulate. It was reported that there had been riots between Czechs and Slovaks as well as between Czechs and the handful of Germans left in Bohemia. The Slovaks, the eastern partners of the truncated country, half encouraged, half forced by Germany, seceded and declared independence. At this point, Emil Hacha, the new Czech president, a former supreme court judge with little political experience, was ordered to Berlin where, under intimidation and blackmail, he asked Nazi Germany for protection for Bohemia and Moravia.

⧫ 4 ⧫

While the new crisis was building up I was on a skiing holiday in Slovakia. Although I heard of the troubles they didn't sound serious and, anyway, the holidays were coming to an end. I returned to Prague on 14 March. The next morning, on my way to school I saw a handful of uniformed Germans getting out of an ordinary car in front of one of the leading hotels and entering the lobby. From their black uniforms, red and white swastika armbands and the skull and crossbones emblem on their caps, I immediately recognized them as SS officers. At a distance, a small cluster of bystanders was silently watching, some of them crying. The morning was overcast with occasional snow flurries as I continued on my way. When I arrived in the classroom all I could see was despair written on all faces. There was no question of lessons and we were sent home. While making my way back through half-empty streets, tanks and trucks full of soldiers suddenly appeared from around the corner watched by groups of silent people. No shouts were heard anywhere, everyone was in a state of shock.

At home the mood was sombre, to say the least. According to German law my mother was Jewish and I, if considered an ethnic German, was at that time still liable for conscription into the *Wehrmacht*. Later, conscripts having a Jewish parent had to serve in the organization Todt, building bridges, roads and fortifications. Laws concerning Jews, the Nuremberg Race Laws, had been decreed in 1935, two years after Hitler came to power. Until then, the interpretation as to who was considered Jewish had been hazy. These laws stipulated that anybody with more than two Jewish grand-parents was a Jew, regardless of whether he or his parents belonged to the Jewish faith or any other.

In my case, the decision on my being Czech or German would

28

depend solely on an interpretation by the authorities. For the 1930 census—and that was the general guideline—my parents had declared that Czech was my mother tongue yet, in that year, I was attending a German boarding school and my father, an ethnic German, was still living.

At this point in family discussions, my proposal was that we all try to leave the country. The question was, however, where to go? Although we were reasonably well off we had no money outside the country and monetary restrictions didn't allow funds to be transferred abroad. In any case, in the new situation, the family couldn't expect to maintain the same living standard. Loiza's most important clients were the big industrial trusts like the Skoda Works. How could he hope to keep these accounts and a Jewish wife as well? Discussions and speculations were endless.

The most noticeable change occurred the first night after the German troops entered Prague. It was decided that traffic would now circulate on the right-hand side instead of on the left. Insurmountable difficulties might be imagined, but the change-over was effected smoothly in spite of the fact that all public transport was by tram so rail-switches had to be reversed overnight. Bilingual street signs appeared soon afterwards and tram conductors were instructed to call out the names of stops in German and Czech. This led to comical situations when the name of the stop was untranslatable or identical in both languages. For instance, the conductor had to call 'museum, museum' or 'viaduct, viaduct', both pronounced with a strong Czech inflection, the assumption being that the first 'museum' was in German. The city began to fill with uniformed personnel, not only army grey and the black SS uniforms, but also the brown uniforms of the SA, and those of the Todt Labour Organization, railway employees and others we couldn't at first identify. Until then Prague had been a cosmopolitan city, but foreigners were gradually leaving and embassies closing down. After the take-over the country was proclaimed The Protectorate of Bohemia and Moravia with Konstantin von Neurath as *Reichsprotector* and a State Secretary as head of the executive. Emil Hacha was left in office as well as his government; however, their functions were limited to executing the orders of K. H. Frank, the German State Secretary.

Schools were reopened and teaching resumed without, for the time being, any change in the curriculum. At the end of May I passed my final exams, giving me the right to enter University. Nevertheless, I was firmly resolved to clear out. By that time, German propaganda had begun directing verbal attacks against Poland: there was no doubt that it was to be the next target. Rumours circulated that Czechs were escaping across the border to Poland and forming an army in exile. Without mentioning my intentions to anybody, I decided to join it.

On occasions there had been vague talk in the family of my studying law and eventually joining my stepfather's practice, but I had never been interested in a career in law and given the political situation there wouldn't have been any sense in doing so. Instead, I proposed that I study chemistry, to which my parents agreed. To get some practical experience it was arranged that I spend the summer at a brewery in eastern Bohemia. Two days after my arrival there, without letting anybody know, I boarded a train heading towards the Beskyd mountains of north-eastern Moravia.

I wasn't familiar with the terrain through which the new Polish border ran but I knew the general region vaguely—a favourite holiday spot for people living in the heavily industrialized centres to the north of it. After travelling overnight I got off at a station some fifteen miles from the spot where I planned to cross into Poland. The area was thickly wooded and sparsely populated. Here and there were clearings planted with rye and oats, with simple farm buildings and a cow grazing nearby. I climbed a steep footpath and eventually caught up with a group of hikers heading in the same direction. We started talking and I found out they were Czech school teachers on a walking holiday. They intended to spend the night at the same resthouse where I had planned to stay before the crossing. I had chosen this resthouse from a map because it was built astride the Moravian–Slovakian border, about five miles from the Polish frontier, close to where the three countries met. My intention was to first cross into Slovakia because I thought the Moravian–Polish border might be more closely guarded than on the Slovak–Polish side. Judging from the map, the route I planned to take led over uneven and steep terrain without settlements or paths. In my opinion, there was little likelihood that this corner of Slovakian territory would be closely guarded.

Among the group of teachers was a single woman in her late thirties who seemed very friendly so I decided to walk with her thus making myself part of their outing—less conspicuous than hiking alone. We were approaching the Slovakian border and, as if to put me at ease, the woman told me there would be no problem if we kept to the path:

she knew because the group had come this way from the opposite direction a few days earlier. We did meet a few border guards, but they just looked at us as we passed. Naturally, I was dressed like a hiker in shorts and heavy boots and carried a knapsack. From her questions I had the feeling she suspected my true intentions but was tactful and didn't press me too closely. By the time we reached the resthouse I knew a lot about her and thought she would have been quite willing to pursue our acquaintance. Though I wouldn't have minded either, I decided to let it go as there was an important day ahead of me.

Next morning I studied my map again to memorize the lay of the land, then got rid of it so I could claim to have lost my way if I was stopped by a patrol. Perhaps my fascination with maps dates from that time. I always have a feeling of satisfaction when I recognize a landscape from a map I have previously examined. It was still early morning when I left the hostel and the day promised to be hot. I retraced my steps for about a mile along the path that had brought us to the resthouse the previous evening and veered off down a wooded slope into Slovakia. With the sun on my back I headed in a north-easterly direction. Crossing small streams and ridges I hoped to have remembered correctly from the map, I finally reached a saddle which marked the border. On my walk I hadn't met a single living thing except a large viper sunning itself on a tree-stump. In the distance I could hear lumberjacks at work but not in the direction I was heading. It was noon when I stepped on to Polish soil: it had all been easier than expected. After a while I came to a path leading down into a valley. As I followed it, the small clearings became more numerous and larger as well until I saw a cluster of houses ahead of me. Since I thought the worst was behind me and that from now on I had nothing to fear, I passed right beside them out in the open.

Just then a voice from behind called out to me. I turned to see a Polish guard standing in a doorway. He motioned me inside where he and another man in uniform began asking questions. Who was I? Where was I heading? Did I have any identification papers? I showed them my old Czech passport. They spoke Polish but I could understand them fairly well since Czech and Polish are related though the pronunciation is different. Communication was helped by the fact that they spoke slowly and asked simple questions. What was I doing in Poland? I explained that I wanted to join the Czechs who were forming an army. The interrogation was informal and the guards

31

seemed relaxed. After some twenty minutes of this I was told I could leave the room but to stick around—one of them would take me to the village in the valley later in the afternoon.

Outside, a woman came up to me saying she had overheard me—she was Czech herself and married to a Pole. We chatted for a while and I found out there were already quite a few Czech refugees in the country, but she didn't know where, maybe in Cracow. I sat there in the sun with children playing around and later the woman brought we something to eat.

At around six, two new guards arrived at the house and one of my interrogators came out with a bicycle and told me to follow him. He pushed his bike while I walked alongside him on a dusty road winding beside a small stream. After an hour or so we arrived at the village. On a knoll a short distance away stood a house surrounded by a fenced-in garden. As we went through the gate I noticed the red and white Polish flag above the entrance and underneath it the words Police Station. The guard handed me over to a heavy-set man in mufti: there was nobody else around so I supposed he represented the whole police force of the village and probably lived in the house as well. He led me into his office on the ground floor, a big room with a sturdy oak table in the middle and a wooden chair behind it. Pushed back against the white-washed wall was a bench where he motioned me to sit while he installed himself behind the table. Two lithographs of high-ranking Polish officers hung on the wall; a saucer served as an ash tray, but there were many butts on the floor as well as a white enamel spittoon.

The questions he put to me were essentially the same as the ones the guards had asked me earlier but this time my answers were being written down so it took a while. Judging from the frequent pauses before committing my replies to paper, the policeman seemed to be having trouble with either syntax or spelling. His attitude throughout was friendly. At one moment he asked me casually if I had any money with me. What I had was very little and it was in Protectorate Crowns. I could see he didn't like that so I told him money wouldn't be a problem because I was confident that friends abroad would send me some as soon as I had a chance to contact them. His last question was whether or not I had served in the army, to which I replied that I was too young to have been called up. For a while he continued to write and it was getting late.

Finally, he stood up and, asking me to follow him, led me upstairs and showed me into a small room with an army cot. He told me I

32

would be given something to eat, then left without locking the door. I was pleased to note that the window had no bars. Later a woman, probably his wife, brought me a plate of stew with potatoes. She told me I could leave the room if I wanted but should not go too far. I sat down on the cot and, while I ate, wondered what would happen next for the policeman had left me completely in the dark about his intentions and everything was strange. After all, this was to be my first night in a police station.

In spite of my unaccustomed surroundings, I slept well. My previous day's walk over rough country, and the excitement that followed, had tired me out. I was still half asleep in the morning when the door opened and the policeman came in. He had heard from his superiors and was sorry to have to report their decision to send me back. If I didn't cause any trouble I would be escorted to the border to make my way across Slovakian territory as best I could. Should I try to escape or return, his orders were to turn me over to the German border guards—the surest way I knew of ending up in a concentration camp. This news was a great disappointment. If the Poles wouldn't let me stay I saw no other solution but to comply. Nevertheless, I was more firmly resolved than ever to try again but at a different spot further east in Slovakia, this time with money and, if necessary, pretending I had done my military service. My first experience had taught me that getting over the border was only one of the hurdles.

Later in the morning the same man as before came to collect me and, at the houses where I had been stopped, passed me on to two other border guards. The three of us made our way back to the saddle with me leading. Finally we stopped and they told me to be careful, to avoid certain places which they described in detail. They wished me luck, we shook hands and I continued on over the now-familiar terrain and crossed into Moravia without a hitch. So, there I was, safely back from my adventure and nobody the wiser. The following day I walked back to the station and took a train to Prague. As a reason for my unexpected return I told my parents that I hadn't liked the brewery but would still register for chemistry at the end of the summer holidays.

Some time before, my paternal grandmother in Leitmeritz had died and left me a half-share of her house, the house where I was born: my sister from my father's second marriage inherited the other half. My intention was to sell my share to finance a second escape.

The first step was that I had to be declared of age, which could be done from eighteen on by a legal procedure. I was twenty at the time and pretended to my parents that since the situation of the family had changed I wanted to finance my studies from the sale of the house. Loiza had the necessary papers drawn up and ready in a few days.

My second step was a bit more difficult. For this I went to Leitmeritz to see my sister Utta's legal guardian and stepfather, Dr Burian, a longtime friend of both my parents. Dr Burian advised me not to sell as he felt the property should remain in the family. At the same time he made it clear that my sister couldn't afford to buy me out, but when he saw that I was determined to go ahead, he suggested I contact my uncle, my father's younger brother who lived not far from Leitmeritz.

I had not met Ernst before but had heard he was a Nazi. He was a member of the party and had spent some time in jail on political charges under the Czech regime. When I telephoned him he was affable and agreed to see me. Before the meeting I felt ill-at-ease but everything was all right: my uncle wore the Nazi badge in his lapel and that was the only thing that bothered me. He avoided touching on politics, mainly asking me about myself and my mother. Unfortunately, when I offered to sell him my half of the house he wasn't interested, but he did tell me, however, that the bookshop owner who was renting the space in the building might be interested, which he was. Within a few weeks my share was sold and I now had the money to finance another attempt to get out.

The last step was to contact one of the few foreigners still left in Prague, a Swiss composer, who earned his living by giving music and French lessons. I had met him through Primus some time earlier, I think he taught his sister. Maybe he didn't want to return to Switzerland because of legal problems there, since he never bothered to hide his preference for boys. In Prague, he continued to indulge his penchant, picking up conscripts whose army pay was just enough to afford one tram fare per day. This activity kept him chronically short of money, a situation he remedied by selling Swiss Francs on the black market. I deposited the larger part of my inheritance in a Prague bank: with what was left I got some Francs from him in cash and the rest of the money was to be waiting for me in a bank in Switzerland.

During the summer, while I prepared my second escape, war hysteria mounted. The Czechs now favoured an armed conflict as the only solution for getting rid of the occupying Germans. The majority believed that with England, France and Poland fighting together, Nazi Germany would be defeated quickly. Weren't the Germans already suffering from shortages? At any rate, I went on with my preparations as fast as I could, but not fast enough.

In the early hours of 1 September, Germany invaded Poland. On 3 September Britain and France declared war on Germany. Obviously the borders would be more closely guarded than ever, so my plans had to be shelved. Besides, from listening to foreign broadcasts, it was evident that the *Wehrmacht* was advancing faster than expected. Even the start of hostilities on the French border a couple of days later didn't slow down their advance in Poland and it was soon clear that Polish resistance was collapsing altogether. About two weeks later, the occupation of the eastern part of that country by the Soviet Union left a lot of people bitter and disillusioned many Czech Communists.

In late September I started attending lectures at the Prague Technical College. Right from the start the anti-German mood among the students was noticeable: leaflets were circulated inviting everyone to demonstrate against the occupation on 28 October—the Independence day of the old republic. A student was shot during these disturbances and more troubles broke out at his funeral. The German reaction was both swift and ruthless. In one night all student dormitories were raided, a few students summarily shot and most shipped to a concentration camp. Those who lived at home or were boarding in private houses were left alone, but Czech universities were closed for the duration of the war.

Students still free scrambled to find a job. There was the danger that those who were unemployed would be sent to Germany to work in factories. Through Loiza, who was on the board of directors, I was taken on right away at the head office of a cable factory. The job wasn't very demanding and, without much effort, I soon knew it all by heart. I had to compile statistics of different types of products the company was manufacturing and keep track of the quantity of metal in any given one, since a private buyer was expected to furnish scrap metal equal in weight to the metal content of his order. In this way the authorities made sure that all copper and aluminium released to the cable factory from government stockpiles was kept exclusively for army orders.

With the fall of Poland, opportunities for escape were considerably reduced. I would have to think of a different route if the war went on, but I wasn't too sure it would, France and England might well sign a peace treaty. Now, all escape routes except one led through Germany, which posed a problem. Czechs were not permitted inside the Reich unless they volunteered to work in factories or had some specific business there. Even if one tried to enter Germany illegally, the distance to a neutral country was great and conditions unknown near Switzerland, or Belgium and Holland, which at that time were still neutral: moreover, it was common knowledge that German trains were constantly checked. The only practical possibility still open was to cross illegally into Slovakia where a sizeable portion of the population remained friendly, and from there through an underground organization into Hungary, the Balkans and the Middle East. It was a route set up by the Czech exiles in Paris mainly for the use of former officers.

5

It proved difficult as well as time consuming to find the right contact to this underground organization but, by the beginning of February 1940, I had finally succeeded in getting an introduction to a mysterious person to whom I gave my telephone number. Within a short while he called with instructions on time and place to rendezvous near the main railway station. All I was to take along was a knapsack with a minimum of personal belongings. When we met, his instructions were that I should immediately board a train leaving for Brno, the largest town in Moravia, transfer to another local train and get off at a small village station. I was to wait inside until picked up by somebody who would greet me with a password. He also told me not to worry if two other men waited there with me.

The trip, including the transfer, took a whole day. The second train was nearly empty, but two other passengers got off when I did. One was a middle-aged man, the other looked about a couple of years older than me.

The three of us paced around the cold and dingy waiting-room observing each other but not daring to start a conversation. The only employee, busy in the ticket office, paid no attention to us. To kill time, I studied the time-tables posted on the wall. About an hour after our arrival a young girl came into the waiting-room and quietly spoke to each of us in turn.

After an exchange of passwords she asked me to follow her, the other two were already waiting outside. The village was a mile or so away and we set off towards it at a brisk pace. No lights were to be seen anywhere: it was a cold, dark evening with frozen snow that crunched under our feet. More snow began to fall as we crossed the village and came to a large house on the outskirts which our guide told us to enter. She led us upstairs into a big, unheated room with several beds and said we were to rest but not to show any light, since the windows had no blackout blinds. The younger one, with whom I spoke in general terms, was a mechanic, but nothing was said about why we were there—the less we knew about each other, the better. The older man looked like an officer and kept apart most of the time. Hours passed and nothing happened. Finally I stretched out on one of the beds and fell asleep.

When I woke up it was getting light and I could hear people talking on the floor below us. Around nine the door opened and the girl came in bringing us breakfast. She said that we should leave the empty plates outside the door but should not venture out ourselves. After eating we went back to the waiting game. The room seemed even colder and through the window I could see that it was still snowing. I had a paper from Brno and occupied my time by reading and re-reading it. It was getting dark again when the girl came with supper. She told us to get ready as we would have to go back, the snow had made the track across the border impassable. We were to be contacted again when the situation improved. So ended my second attempt, but I never had another call from the mysterious man. Decidedly, this business of escaping wasn't going to be easy.

When I arrived home, my mother didn't even ask where I had spent the last two nights, although by that time we were all living on one floor and she was certainly aware of my absence. Marie, the elder of my sisters, had died of leukaemia just before Christmas and Granny Toni had died a little later. In their grief, my parents locked themselves away from the rest of the world. The family had shrunk considerably in the space of a few months. Mademoiselle left for Paris just before the outbreak of the war and Jan had moved elsewhere.

We were living far more modestly now, but due to my mother's efforts food was still plentiful. We had staples like rice, something which had disappeared from the stores in the autumn. Loiza absolutely hated it, it reminded him of his time in Siberia. There were rows of olive oil cans stacked in the cellar along with bags of split peas sent to us by relatives in the country.

Food had been rationed from the beginning of the war and for many, black-marketeering became a flourishing occupation in spite of its hazards, with draconian punishments meted out to sellers and buyers alike. Many families with cash to hand had their own suppliers who risked their lives to smuggle food in from the country. Farmers weren't permitted to slaughter their own livestock and farm controls were efficient. Checks were frequent on trains, at railway stations and on roads leading into Prague. Even so, food came in regularly, but the prices were increasing constantly: they were multiples of the controlled ones.

Our black-market supplier was, on the whole, a decent sort and her prices remained reasonable for a long time. Thanks to her there were usually whole sides of smoked bacon hanging in the larder. She was enormously fat which no doubt helped her in smuggling, as the bacon slabs were hung under her ample skirts. On arrival, she would lift them in the kitchen to hand over the bacon and, in spite of her offensive body odour, we were glad to deal with her.

As the months passed rations became smaller with marked deterioration in the quality of the little food available. Housewives developed a knack for inventing new recipes and omitting ingredients in short supply. Ration coupons were needed for flour, fats, milk, meat, eggs, coffee, tea and bread. Textiles and shoes were rationed, as were cigarettes, which became a currency of sorts. At one time there was a rumour that matches would be rationed so there was a run on them. Everybody ended up with plenty of boxes at home but they never did disappear from the stores.

Black-marketeering was not the only risky activity—there were many other offences punishable by death. Black-framed notices started to appear regularly in the newspapers announcing that some poor soul and his entire family had been executed for listening to the Czech broadcasts from London. Each radio set had to have a small, official notice on the tuning knob—'Remember that listening to foreign broadcasts is punishable by death'—it wasn't just an idle threat. Falsification of identity papers, hiding people, or even hiding belongings liable to confiscation, carried the death sentence: those arrested for anti-state activity frequently had their property taken away as well. This policy of wholesale terror was used to crush all opposition to the Nazi regime. Confiscation must have helped, at least to a certain degree, in financing the German war effort.

Among the people I knew well, one of the first victims of this policy was the father of my friend, Primus. Before the occupation Primus's father had been legal advisor to one of the wealthiest families in Bohemia—Jews who had extensive interests in mines and industry and also owned a bank. In the six months between the annexation of the Sudetenland and the take-over of the rest of Bohemia they had the foresight to liquidate their holdings, although at a considerable loss, and emigrate to the States. The loss was so great that at the time we joked about it, saying they had exchanged a large fortune in Czechoslovakia for a small one in America.

Among the many items of value for which they were unable to obtain an export permit was a painting by Rembrandt. Whether it was sold to Primus's father or only deposited with him for safe-keeping is not clear. I do seem to remember that the Rembrandt was openly displayed in their home. The likelihood of a person being arrested and sent to a concentration camp was often in direct relation to his wealth and this policy applied to Primus's father as well. He was arrested either for hiding Jewish property or simply because he was wealthy. Whatever the reason, the Gestapo confiscated not only the Rembrandt but the family's house in Prague, their estate in northern Bohemia and other holdings. One of the few assets to escape confiscation was a small factory which, under German licence, was manufacturing tools for lathes and happened to be in Primus's name.

The family had to move, and his mother was later reduced to starting a laundry with a former maid in order to make a living. A few months after the father's arrest the family was notified that he had died in the infamous quarry of the Mauthausen camp. In the early days of the war the next of kin were often informed of the death of a camp inmate and the ashes arrived in a shoe box. Later, this practice was discontinued and relatives were left in the dark as to the fate of the arrested person.

Meanwhile, fighting went on. The continuous victories, first over Denmark and Norway, then over the Low Countries, were depressing and demoralizing and it was even worse when France capitulated. While other occupied nations may have lost more lives and property, the Czechs had to endure German occupation longer than any other and hopes that the war would soon come to an end were fading. Now, every month, week and day brought further restrictions, oppressions and reprisals, more arrests and executions. The art of terror was constantly being perfected as the war progressed. Executions of prominent personalities, such as General Alois Elias, the Prime Minister of the Czech puppet government, or a well-known artist, a scientist or maybe a former politician of the old regime were well publicized on the radio and in the papers. Small, blood-red posters with the emblem of the eagle and swastika were stuck up on street corners and in public buildings announcing in black script in both German and Czech, 'So-and-so was executed for anti-state activities'. The charges were sometimes changed to *Volksschädling*, referring to an individual who was harming the economic interests of the nation, in other words, a black-marketeer. It often happened that a person arrested at night was shot the following day and, along with the rest of the population, the family found out about it from a news broadcast. The authorities didn't even bother to pretend that the execution had been carried out after a trial, as they had allowed no time for one—the sentence was an administrative decision made by the Gestapo.

Restrictive measures against Jews were also increasing. Nobody molested the Jews—as had been the case in Vienna—when the Germans entered Prague. The first measures came only after several months. Jewish businesses had a '*Treuhand*'—a trustee with executive powers—imposed on them. This trustee would be German, usually a member of the Nazi party who knew something about book-keeping and management. If these businesses proved prosperous they were eventually confiscated; otherwise, they were liquidated.

Next, the identity cards of Jews were stamped with a 'J' with each ration coupon marked with a 'J' as well: that meant they had no right to certain foods, especially meat. Many Jewish families had to vacate their homes and were assigned a flat which they were forced to share with several others. Jews weren't permitted to leave the city, use trams, enter parks, walk on certain streets or even own pets. Finally, before the Jews began to be assembled in ghettos, they were ordered to wear a yellow star with the word *Jude*—printed in black lettering faintly resembling the Hebrew script. This applied not only to adults but to children as well and, to add insult to injury, these stars had to be paid for with textile coupons.

Many of these petty restrictions were calculated to humiliate and undermine morale rather than cause real suffering but, as everybody knows, far worse was to come. Many people wonder today how it was that the Jewish population, on the whole, accepted this treatment without the slightest murmur of protest. To understand their seeming complaisance, it must be remembered that all these measures were taken one by one, that each represented only a slight tightening of the screw, which didn't in itself warrant a desperate counteraction. Sadly enough, each new restriction was believed to be the last and the Jews thought that nothing worse could happen to them. Much of this harsh treatment went unnoticed by the majority of the population—even if they had noticed nobody would have lifted a finger, they themselves were terrified.

Practising Jews were readily identifiable from records kept by the Jewish congregations and left intact when the Germans entered Bohemia. Why they were not destroyed is inexplicable since the Czech Jews were well aware of the treatment meted out to the Jews in Germany and Austria. Perhaps the records were left intact because of the speed with which the Germans took over, or else the registrars were simply afraid of possible sanctions against themselves and their families.

There were many non-practising Jews, probably as many as practising ones, or converts and descendants of converts who, according to the Nuremberg Race Laws, were considered Jewish. Of course, they had a somewhat better chance of escaping recognition but, in the majority of cases, that was impossible. Every important step in life meant showing birth certificates going back three generations—entering school, getting a job, opening a bank account and so on. Furthermore, in a multitude of everyday dealings, Gentiles had to declare and sign under oath that they were 'Aryans'.

Strange as it might seem, all these repressions and persecutions and the plain terror felt everywhere hadn't modified my way of life to any great extent. Just because I was living in difficult times, when there was no way of knowing what might happen tomorrow, I wanted to take advantage of every opportunity to enjoy myself and in this I wasn't alone. Most of my generation, even those who had suffered a tragedy in their family, continued to live it up as much as possible. I had enough spending money from my job in the cable factory as I was keeping most of what I earned for myself. There was also the money from my inheritance so, for the first time in my life, I knew financial independence.

Night-clubs were still operating, but this pastime had become less popular due to frequent police controls. My crowd spent more time in private homes playing cards—especially poker—for ever higher stakes: in one evening it wasn't unusual to win or lose as much as some people earned in a month. We also had private showings of old American movies. Jazz was very popular with us and somehow there was always a supply of recent records by Louis Armstrong, Duke Ellington, Glenn Miller or Benny Goodman circulating among the group. I don't know how they got into our hands but we knew the latest hits almost as soon as the jazz fans in the States, which was surprising as this type of music was considered decadent and 'racially impure' by the Nazis. Our private bar was no longer in existence so, since most of us lived at home with our parents, we had to find a place where we could meet and take a girl. Empty flats were nearly impossible to find, but I was lucky enough to hear of a two-room apartment in an old, narrow house and I took it without hesitation. The rent was modest because it had no bathroom and the toilet was on a common landing. This wasn't a real problem, there was only one other flat in the building besides the janitor's and we rarely saw the other tenant who lived on the floor above. The flat did have one serious inconvenience, however. It was located on a square facing the Czernin Palace, the seat of the *Reichsprotector*. There were a lot of Germans coming and going and the place was closely guarded. Once Jews had to observe a curfew, it became increasingly risky for Franta to attend our parties and after Primus's father was arrested, I decided to give up the flat. Primus and Franta had shared expenses and shouldering the cost by myself wasn't worth it.

When we no longer had the flat I soon discovered that it was adversely affecting my love life: I now had to limit my interests exclusively to women with a place of their own. Around this time I began to notice the frequent visits to our home of the fiancée of Eric, an Austrian cousin of Loiza's. She was Viennese and had moved to Prague a couple of years earlier, soon after Austria was overrun by the Germans. The reason for her change of residence was that she was a Jew and, if this had been known, Eric would have been in trouble. A Gentile having sexual relations with a Jew committed a crime known as *Rassenschande*—shame to the race—a crime punishable by arrest and deportation to a concentration camp. Feli was posing as a Gentile and her chances of being found out were less in Prague where nobody knew her background. However, her papers might not have stood up to close scrutiny. As I later had reason to know, Eric was an avaricious person so he may have felt that installing her in one of his flats in Prague would be cheaper in the long run than hiding her in Vienna.

Feli was probably receiving her subsistence money through my stepfather, money which had to be given to her under the table—at least that was my explanation for her periodic visits. She was a good-looking blonde in her mid-thirties, always tastefully dressed and well groomed, with an impressive frontage that of course caught my attention. One day, after her visit to Loiza's office, Feli stopped at our home for a courtesy call. These visits were always short as my mother couldn't stand her and Feli probably felt her antagonism. That day I was on the point of going out but delayed long enough for both of us to leave at the same time. As we were walking away from the house, she invited me to her flat and I enthusiastically accepted. From then on I became a regular visitor and it wasn't long before we started an affair. Until that time my amatory art had been rather rudimentary and I somehow like to think of her as my first real teacher. Feli was about fifteen years older than I was and very demanding. She already had another local boyfriend, a gynaecologist, who knew about our affair but tolerated it with good humour: as a matter of fact, the three of us got on well together.

It was now the summer of 1941 and the German armed forces were reaping one success after another on the war fronts. Yugoslavia and Greece were occupied and the campaign against the Soviet Union was in full swing. The Germans were exultant. Every day, loudspeakers installed on street corners would blare out the staggering losses the Russians were suffering. Posters with pictures of Soviet–Mongolian prisoners were displayed, with the caption 'Are These Your Brothers?', insinuating the Slavic kinship the Czechs felt for the Russians. As allies of the Reich, Romania, Hungary and Slovakia were sending troops to the eastern front, so escape through these countries had become impossible. Depressing news was reaching us from everywhere. It seemed that Great Britain, in addition to sustaining heavy naval losses, was in difficulties in North Africa. Even the inveterate optimists who, a year earlier, were declaring that the retreat from Dunkirk was only a British ruse, began having doubts about the outcome of the war.

With their successes, the Germans stepped up the pressure against the civilian population, especially against the Jews. Franta, like some of his age group, was conscripted into what we thought at the time was just a labour battalion and sent to a small town in north-western Bohemia called Terezín in Czech and Theresienstadt in German. It was a fortified site built by the Emperor Joseph II in the late eighteenth century as a defensive position against the Prussians. Erected on former swampland, it was not far from the confluence of the Elbe and the Eger. Terezín, like most fortresses conceived in that period, was surrounded by moats, ditches and walls with a few gates, and lay astride the principal road from Dresden to Prague. In the days of the

Austrian Empire and, later, of the new state Czechoslovakia, it housed a fairly large garrison along with a civilian population of about five thousand, mainly tradespeople catering to the military. To the north, across the Elbe and some three miles distant, was Leitmeritz.

To the south-east, on the opposite bank of the Eger, about half a mile from the town of Terezín, was the Small Fortress, an outpost of the fortified site, used under the monarchy as a political prison. Princip, whose assassination of the Austrian Crown Prince, Archduke Ferdinand d'Este, triggered World War One, was imprisoned and died there. During the Czech republic some Nazis were held in this jail, possibly my Uncle Ernst among them. It was once again put to use about a year after Germany occupied Czechoslovakia.

After the arrival in Terezín of the Jewish work battalion into which Franta had been conscripted, the town was gradually emptied of its civilian population and made ready to receive Jewish families from Bohemia and some parts of Germany for internment. The reconversion process was gradual, the work spread out over several months. At first, the labour battalion was housed in empty military barracks and, as long as there were still some Czech families living there, it was possible, with some risk, for an ordinary civilian to enter Terezín. As time went on it became more difficult and later impossible. The town, planned like a citadel, was easy to guard, as was control of the points of entry. The only weak spot was the main road.

The labour battalion was run by a detachment of *Sicherheitsdienst*, the SD, a division of the SS in overall charge of guarding and administrating concentration camps and certain prisons. In Terezín the SD were helped by conscripts from the Czech police. This had certain advantages for the internees because in most cases the Czech police tried to look the other way if there was some illegal traffic going on. Their leniency couldn't be taken for granted, however, as they themselves, under pain of death, were responsible for the strict separation of Jews from the outside world and some policemen did indeed apply all regulations to the letter.

Franta's parents were still living in their same flat in Prague and I kept in touch with them. After his departure rumours began to circulate that the food given to the work battalion was extremely poor. On one of my visits they asked me if I would be willing to smuggle in a food parcel. To get one together must have meant great self-denial on their part: food was short everywhere but more so for

Jewish families who were getting smaller rations than the rest of the population. We agreed that the parcel had to be a small one, something I could fit into a briefcase. Even so, it would represent a great deal of money, money difficult to come by when their bank account was frozen.

On the train I wondered how to contact Franta. In case I was stopped and questioned I had a ready story that the food parcel was a present for my sister in Leitmeritz. Leaving the briefcase at the small station serving Terezín, I set out on the half-hour walk to the town to check the layout: this was at a time when a certain number of Czech families were still living there. While wandering through the few streets I finally came across the familiar face of a friend of Franta's who led me by signs to a courtyard behind a butcher's shop. When I told him I had a parcel for Franta at the station we arranged that I would return in an hour's time.

Franta was waiting for me when I got back. We quickly exchanged news—he couldn't write or receive letters—set up a meeting for the following month and separated. I repeated the trip on our agreed date and Lala replaced me for the next delivery. Unfortunately, on my third trip I discovered that the butcher had been moved out and practically no civilians were to be seen in Terezín. I felt too conspicuous so made my way to the Dresden–Prague road which by then was fenced off with seven-foot-high planking. The only thing I could think of was to walk up and down as though waiting for a bus as there was still a service connecting the villages in the vicinity. After a while I noticed faces watching me from the window of a building behind the fence. From the signs they were making I understood that as soon as it got dark I should leave the parcel at a certain spot against the fence and that, with relief, was what I did.

On my return to Prague I told Franta's parents what had happened and also that I thought the whole undertaking too risky to be repeated. Shortly afterwards I heard that somebody did get caught. Franta's parents were themselves deported to Terezín not long after. Eventually word came through that Franta was working in the ghetto kitchen and had a relatively better life: he rose to become a foreman of a shift cooking for five thousand people—a position he had certainly never envisioned. After leaving school he had worked with his father in the clothing factory then operating under the control of a German trustee. This new job not only allowed him to eat what he needed but to distribute some additional food to his relatives and friends—the majority of internees were subsisting on starvation-level rations.

In the autumn of 1944 Franta was deported to Auschwitz and, without his protection, his parents soon followed him there never to return. His sister and her husband disappeared in the same way.

6

A few months after the beginning of my affair with Feli, she received a visit from the Gestapo, who suspected that she was Jewish. Her papers stated that her real father was an Austrian cavalry officer, a Gentile, but I learned about that only much later. It seems that Eric had paid a certain sum to this officer in return for his declaration under oath that he had had a longstanding relationship with Feli's mother and that she was his daughter. These 'Aryanizations' usually carried little weight with the Gestapo. In most cases all parties concerned ended up in a concentration camp.

When these problems started, Feli's interest in sex cooled considerably and, as a consequence, so did mine in her. She had been Eric's fiancée for many years without his ever making up his mind to marry her. They used to spend much of their time on his property in Upper Austria where he had a small castle on a lake in the Salzkammergut, a region between Salzburg and Linz. I have heard it was an attractive place and they entertained a lot. Feli told me an amusing story about one weekend there. One of their visitors took her fancy, but there was never a chance to pursue her interest in him as Eric was always around—until she hit on the idea of sending Eric out on the lake. He was a keen swimmer so Feli encouraged him to swim out to a raft in the middle. While he was at a safe distance from shore, Feli and his friend had all the time necessary to satisfy their urge in the boathouse.

My affair with Feli came to an abrupt end the day she introduced me to a striking blonde. The moment I saw this woman I felt an instant desire for her: this had never happened to me before, it usually took me some time to warm up. I was able to accompany her home that evening and found out she had been widowed fairly recently—her husband had been shot as a black-marketeer. Helena had a small flat and earned her living as a designer and occasional actress. Within

48

a few days we were on friendly terms and I began to see more and more of her. She probably felt lonely and may have been looking more for companionship than what I had in mind. Whatever Helena expected from me, I was soon into a new relationship that was to last longer than any before. To whomever cared to listen, Feli declared that I had been taken over still 'bed-warmed'. Helena's job left her with quite a bit of free time and being with her was stimulating and fun. She was a little older than me—I never found out her exact age—was well read and spoke fluent German and French. Helena's place was some thirty minutes from my office so I often went there straight from work.

One day when I got to the flat she said she had some urgent work to finish: I wasn't to disturb her, just settle down and read. I did as she asked, trying to be patient, but scanning through magazines didn't hold my interest for long. After a while I got up to see what she was working on. At the drawing-table Helena made no move to hide the man's photograph she seemed to be re-touching, nor the ID card I noticed among the drawings and artist's paraphernalia spread around. It wasn't too difficult to guess what was going on, so right away I asked if she didn't think she already had enough trouble. Helena explained that a good friend of hers was on the run, a comrade from before the war, when they had been members of a Communist youth group.

Of course I was well aware of Helena's leftist leanings, we discussed politics quite often. Sometimes, half in jest, she called me a rotten bourgeois, but I never took these barbs seriously: after all, she herself was of bourgeois origin. Her father was a school teacher if I remember correctly. While she continued her work—and I could see that she was experienced—Helena admitted she occasionally did some service for an underground set-up. What she was most often asked to do was to falsify documents or, as she put it, arrange them a little. The group she was in contact with was part of a Communist organization re-activated after the attack on the Soviet Union. From what I understood, it was a sort of back-up cell to replace those people rounded up when the Nazis realized that the Communists were again taking up anti-state activities.

I have to admit that until then I'd had no inkling of her involvement, it came as a complete surprise. After leaving Helena that evening I had time to go quietly over the whole thing in my mind—my discovery and the conversation that followed. I couldn't get rid of the feeling that my finding out wasn't accidental. Helena had been expecting me and had made no attempt to hide what she was working on. She obviously thought I was trustworthy and may have had the idea of enlisting me for some of the work. However, in our discussion she hadn't come out openly with any proposition. She may have realized from my remarks that I would have nothing to do with a structured organization, especially one whose aims were not the same as mine. I could have asked, but didn't, why it was that the Communists had lain low until the moment the Soviet Union was attacked.

The discovery of Helena's involvement didn't really affect me one way or the other: after all, if she was determined to stick out her neck that was her business. I didn't share her leftist opinions but at least we had one thing in common, our loathing for the Nazis. Helena knew I would be willing to help her out of friendship and affection should the need arise, but that was as far as I was prepared to go.

Then came the day when she asked me if I could accompany her and another woman to a small town near the Slovakian border. The trip there took nearly ten hours. We got off the train not far from the village where the heavy snowfall had aborted my second escape attempt. She must have known the town well because, without asking anybody for directions, she led us straight to a farmhouse a little away from the town. The farmer was expecting us: he was to guide the woman over the border. We spent a short while talking to him and saw his wife briefly, then said goodbye to our companion and walked back into town to look for a guesthouse. There was no train until the next morning.

In those days, small railway lines were still using coal. On the return trip I was sitting by an open window and a speck of cinder got into my eye which became irritated and very painful. Helena asked me to spend the night at her place so she could bathe my eye. It was a memorable night—never before had she heaped such affection on me. I noticed on later occasions that whenever I did some service for her group she became aroused and let me make love to her in a way she wouldn't usually consent to.

A couple of times I went back to that farmhouse alone, either to bring something or to deliver a message. These trips threatened to become too frequent for my liking: it took two days to go there and back and I was having trouble justifying my absence from the office. In the end I sent Lala to the farm with a message without first mentioning to Helena that I couldn't go myself. She soon found out about it and as a result we had a terrific row.

After this quarrel my interest began to wane. I was getting fed up with her endless political discourses between intercourses. She also suffered from an overdose of narcissism and would suddenly hop out of bed at the worst possible moment to admire herself from all angles in front of a large mirror. Her technique in love-making was definitely inferior to Feli's: besides, I resented her using sex as a reward for any services rendered to her cause. Gradually I saw less and less of her and went back to my old habits of evenings of cards with my crowd and picking up girls at Manes. Nevertheless, a strong friendship continued between us that was to have a direct bearing on my future.

Spring had come again and for the holidays that were due to me I planned to visit my sister in Leitmeritz. On my last visit, in 1939, when I went there to sell the house, it was relatively easy to get a travel permit and the actual sale hadn't required my presence. This time I was surprised when, after some weeks, my request was refused and, as a result, I decided to stay in Prague. The weather was exceptionally warm for that time of the year and I spent the mornings on the roof terrace of my habitual café on the river, sunbathing and girl-watching. Manes was one of the last places where there was still some life.

Towards the end of my time off there was a particularly hot day for late May, when I installed myself on the roof terrace earlier than usual. The place was half empty: just a handful of German soldiers and one or two people who looked vaguely familiar but nobody I really knew. I reclined on a deckchair with a glass of beer, leafed through a newspaper and, out of boredom, finally fell asleep. It was past noon when the waiter woke me to present the bill. There was still time to reach home before lunch was served so I started walking slowly in that direction. Half-way there I met a friend who stopped me to ask in agitation, 'Have you heard what happened? Heydrich was shot this morning.' He had no details and we separated. Continuing on my way I wondered if it was true and what the consequences would be. We often heard rumours that there was no way of checking at the time and only later proved to be false.

Reinhard Heydrich was the *Reichsprotector* of Bohemia and Moravia, the omnipotent regent who represented Hitler in our country. It was Heydrich who, a few months earlier, had ordered the execution of Alois Elias, the Prime Minister of the Czech puppet government, because he didn't find him sufficiently pliable to his wishes.

51

Years later I read that the British Secret Service had framed the man by sending him a phoney cable or letter from South America with a passage which could have been interpreted as a coded message.

At the outset of the war Heydrich was not well known to the general public. His name began to appear in the papers when he tried to annihilate the Norwegian underground, hence his sobriquet, 'Butcher of Norway'. Heydrich was a good-looking man in his late thirties, tall, blond and blue-eyed: to the Germans he was the personification of the Aryan race and his rise through the Nazi ranks had been spectacular. There were whispers, however, that one of his grandmothers was Jewish, that her gravestone had been made to disappear from the cemetery—in Leipzig, I believe it was. Naturally, this was not general knowledge, but it leaves one wondering if the fact wasn't known to Hitler and Himmler, who could have blackmailed him into carrying out the most secret and unsavoury tasks, for instance the organization of the Final Solution, the annihilation of the Jews.

Heydrich's political plans for the Czechs became obvious soon after his arrival in Prague. He set out to eliminate the middle and upper classes while at the same time wooing the workers with a sort of stick and carrot policy. Even though this policy wasn't making any noticeable headway, the Czech government in exile in London was worried. It was true that underground activities in Bohemia and Moravia were negligible and couldn't be compared to those in Poland and Yugoslavia. It wasn't that the Czechs felt any more love for the Germans. The reason for the apparent lethargy was twofold. The Czechs, on the whole, are a down-to-earth and practical nation, not given to heroic feats. Their character is best personified by the anti-hero in *The Good Soldier Svejk*. Svejk is a clever sort of fellow who fights the authorities by playing the fool. He messes up everything, not by open rebellion and defiance, but by executing all orders to the letter, while at the same time committing such imbecilities that the original purpose of the order is defeated. This ploy might have worked under the easy-going Austrians but certainly not with the Germans.

The second cause is simpler, it had to do with Bohemia's geographical location. The Czechs were surrounded on three sides by German-speaking peoples. For sheer numbers there were more Germans, both army and civilian, in the Protectorate than in any other occupied territory. The country was small and densely populated, with only a few places where an illegal and hostile activity could have escaped attention for any length of time.

In an attempt to put some punch into the underground, the Czechs in London parachuted a handful of men into western Bohemia with guns, grenades and a shortwave radio. It seems the action was ill-prepared and the volunteers neither well-chosen nor properly trained. They made contact with the local population, moved to Prague and started tracking Heydrich's movements. His elimination was their primary objective. Heydrich's opinion of the Czechs as being a rather passive nation, one not given to extremes was, on the whole, correct. He must have thought they would never dare to make an attempt on his life. Every day, he defiantly travelled without escort in an open Mercedes, never varying the route from his home—a confiscated castle some fifteen miles outside the city—to his official seat in Prague. On this day in May 1942, two men were standing by a sharp curve where his car had to slow down. As the car passed, the first man pulled out a submachine-gun from under his jacket, took aim but it failed to fire. Heydrich or his driver may have noticed the gunman and slowed to a stop. At that, the second man lobbed a hand grenade into the open car where it exploded behind Heydrich's seat. The explosion was deadened by the upholstery but some grenade fragments hit him in the back. He got out of the car, pulled out his revolver and fired at the second man who tried to take cover behind a lamppost. Heydrich collapsed a few instants later just as a baker's horse-drawn cart was passing by. His chauffeur commandeered it, stretched him out inside and took him to one of the larger city hospitals a hundred yards down the road. The hospital was immediately cleared and Heydrich installed close to the operating theatre.

During the afternoon, street-corner loudspeakers began blaring out the news of the attempt on the *Reichsprotector*'s life. The wording of the announcement left no doubt that revenge on a huge scale was in the offing. That same evening special trains carrying police from all over Germany converged on Prague. A curfew was proclaimed, streets were cordoned off and a roof-to-cellar search of literally thousands of houses was begun. Many people who were in hiding but had nothing to do with the attack were arrested. However, the task was so gigantic that scores of others, so-called submarines, escaped, either in secret hideouts or because they could show well-forged papers. Thousands of people, those in hiding and those who hid them, were executed in the days immediately following, and this was only the beginning.

As a first retaliatory measure, the already insufficient food rations were further reduced. New waves of arrests began at once on a greater scale than ever before. A new crime was invented for which a single sentence was decreed, and that without trial. This crime was defined as 'approving the attempt on Heydrich's life'. Everybody realized it was merely a pretext to get rid of all public personalities of the old Czech regime as well as the intelligentsia and the wealthy. Arrests were simplified by the curfew since all inhabitants had to be in their own homes from eight in the evening until six in the morning. Squads of Gestapo men descended on the residences of people previously selected and sometimes took them away still in their pyjamas. Many of those expecting arrest took to sleeping in their clothes. In the majority of cases the families of those taken never saw them again— twenty-four hours later they would hear their names read out on the news broadcasts as being among those executed for having approved the *attentat*—the murderous attempt on Heydrich's life.

Lala's family had an old and battle-scarred smooth-haired fox terrier whose favourite pastime was to roam the streets. It had an uncanny sense of orientation and we often used to meet it in the most unlikely places far from home. The dog knew me and would come to greet me before continuing on its errands. There wasn't much that was attractive about the animal—its coat was unkempt and dirty most of the time—but it was a great favourite of Lala's father who considered it his mascot. Before the occupation he had taught the dog to bark when asked in company, 'How does Hitler speak?' Every morning it was let out and didn't return until the evening meal. It was very regular of habit and seldom stayed out the whole night. A few days after the attack on Heydrich the dog disappeared and didn't return that night or the next. The family was worried and Lala later told me that his father began to have a strange premonition. On the third night after the dog's disappearance two Gestapo men arrived at their home, made a cursory search of the apartment and took Lala's father away with them.

I learned about the arrest first thing next morning and talked about it with Loiza who believed he had been arrested either because he was a high-ranking Freemason or for having organized the flight into exile of Eduard Benes, the former president. Lala's father, in his capacity as head of the Civil Air Transport Authority, had arranged for the flight, as the removal of Benes had been one of the conditions for the normalization of Czech–German relations after the giving up of the

Sudeten region. President Benes had been Hitler's *bête noire*. At one time there was seldom a speech in which he didn't refer to him in a derogatory way.

There was a sort of tragic irony in all this. When the German army entered Prague, Lala's father happened to be in Paris negotiating with Air France. The French immediately offered him political asylum which he declined because of his family and probably also because he was sure the Germans would have nothing to hold against him.

We all rushed to look at the morning paper as soon as it arrived and found his name almost immediately in the middle of the dreaded, black-framed column. Lala's family also learned about his execution from the same source. Nobody had had the courage to listen to the newscast the previous evening when it was made public the first time. Later in the day Lala phoned to ask me to meet him on a street close to his home. When I got there he wanted to know if I would help him to carry some of the valuable paintings to his brother's flat—he was practically certain their home wasn't being watched as the Gestapo would be too busy arresting other people. There was nobody at the flat, his mother had left the same morning to be with her sisters in the country. We took the pictures down, but their outlines were clearly visible on the wallpaper and it wasn't washable. Wondering what could be done about it, Lala remembered that some time before he had won several paintings at poker. These were family portraits of a Jewish friend who was awaiting deportation. Nobody cared what happened to the paintings, they couldn't be taken along so were lost to them anyway. Lala and I started matching the outlines on the walls with the pictures and I suppose we finally found the appropriate places. When we had finished and looked around, a collection of patriarchs confronted us, some of them with pronounced Semitic features. We debated whether we could get away with it, but there was no other handy solution and we just had to hope the Gestapo wouldn't look too closely when they came to collect them. We wrapped up the original paintings and carted them to Evzen's place on the other side of the city. As it turned out, the police never did return and we could have left everything as it was, but there was no way of knowing that at the time.

Much later I heard two other possible explanations for the execution of Lala's father. In one, from Lala, it appears his father had arranged to hide some spare parts for planes which would have amounted to sabotage. The other is mentioned in Otto John's book

Twice through the Lines. According to John, Lala's father had been in contact with a group of German opponents of the Nazi regime. After the start of the war this group planned to get rid of Hitler and it is possible the Gestapo may have had some inkling of these plans. Several of the conspirators were arrested some ten months after Lala's father was shot. Among them were Dietrich Bonhoeffer and Hans von Dohnanyi. Others, General Beck, Admiral Canaris and Colonel Oster were left at liberty until their arrest after the unsuccessful attempt on Hitler's life in July 1944. What is left to speculation is whether the Gestapo was aware of the contacts Lala's father had or if his execution was just a coincidence.

Unable to find the culprits of the attempt on Heydrich's life, the mood of the Nazis was becoming uglier. The columns of names framed in black grew longer every day. Two villages in different parts of the country were surrounded by the SS. The inhabitants were allowed to enter but nobody could leave. In the evening, all males over sixteen were assembled in front of the church and machine-gunned down. Mothers and children were separated and the mothers carted away into concentration camps. Some of the children were given to German families and others were never heard of again.

One day posters appeared on the streets offering an unheard of financial reward to anyone coming forward with information on the whereabouts of the perpetrators of the attempt on Heydrich's life. There was a promise of amnesty should the informer be himself involved and prepared to inform on his accomplices: the amnesty would apply to the informer's family as well. A rumour was started, no doubt encouraged by the authorities, that everybody whose ID number ended in a certain figure would be shot—in view of what was happening around, the population was willing to believe it. Out on the street, sheer terror could be felt as if it hung in the air.

Still, there were no leads to the parachutists in hiding. All that the Gestapo could show for their work was an abandoned leather briefcase, its photograph shown in newspapers and on thousands of posters. The police went from house to house, showing the picture and making everyone sign a paper declaring that he couldn't identify it. No stone was left unturned, no lead, however flimsy, ignored. Thousands of people were brought into the Gestapo headquarters for interrogation. Some were let go, others simply disappeared.

7

I was among those brought in. The Gestapo came to our house one morning, asked where I was and wanted to see my room which they proceeded to turn upside down. My mother had to tell them where I was working in the Old Town.

Normally, all visitors to the office were received in a room apart as the factory worked on armament contracts classified as secret. Therefore, I was quite surprised to see two unknown men come into our office right on the heels of the usher and stop at my desk. When the plain-clothes men showed me their police identification telling me to follow them I was taken completely off guard. I could feel the stares of my colleagues.

Out in the corridor they wanted to check my ID papers and, once they were sure I was the person they had been sent to collect, put handcuffs on me. As we left the building I wondered if this would be my last trip down the familiar staircase. A car and driver were waiting. I was put in the back with one of the men beside me and driven to the Gestapo headquarters, a former bank building, where I was signed in at the entrance desk and taken up in a lift. I noticed we were going to the fourth floor and then realized that my mind was registering trivialities when it should be occupied with more urgent thoughts. Nobody had said a word on the short car ride so I had no idea why I was being brought in—was it for something in connection with Helena?

We walked down a long corridor with doors on both sides. Men were standing beside some of them, their faces turned to the wall, a few looking as though they had been roughed up. There were two desks in the room we entered and four men were standing around as if waiting for me. The Gestapo man who came with me spoke to one of them, but I couldn't catch what he said. The man spoken to came over, sat on the desk in front of me and put his feet on the chair. He was in civilian clothes, rather young-looking with a square face and sparse, brown hair.

'What were you doing on 27 May?' he shot at me. I must have looked surprised because it took me several seconds for it to register that that was the date of the attack on Heydrich and a moment or two more to remember just what I had been doing that day.

'In the morning I was at Café Manes, the one on the river. I went home for lunch and stayed there all afternoon.'

'Who were you with at the café?'

'With nobody, I was alone.'

'You have a job, why weren't you at work?' I said I had been on holiday for the last half of May. The reason for my arrest was becoming clearer and suddenly I realized I didn't have an alibi for that morning. There had been nobody on the terrace who knew me, unless the waiter could remember.

'If you were on holiday, why did you stay in Prague?' I explained about the *laissez-passer* that was refused for my original plan to visit my sister in Leitmeritz. He seemed satisfied.

'What do you think of the attempt on the *Reichsprotector*'s life?' he threw in casually. 'Have you any idea who could have done it?' Remembering the penalty meted out to those who supposedly approved the attack, I replied with feigned indignation, 'I really can't imagine who could have done such a cowardly act. It must have been the work of some crazy fanatic, somebody completely un-balanced.'

His question had been put in an offhand way but I knew my reply had to sound sincere: this was probably the most important moment of the whole interrogation.

The questions were in German and it seemed that speaking it fluently was to my advantage. The whole exchange was more like a polite conversation, but I couldn't forget some of the men I'd seen in the corridor who showed traces of a beating. Finally, I was told to step outside and stand with my face to the wall. So many thoughts were flashing through my mind as I stood there waiting for what might happen next. Numb with fright and worry, I didn't know if I had been standing there for a few minutes or for hours when my interrogator called out to me to return to his office. Now there were two women there, one about forty, rather small with dark hair and the other a blonde, plump, young girl. They were staring intently at my face and I had to turn first to one side and then the other. They both noticed a scar low on my left cheek.

'How did you come by the scar?' the interrogator asked.

'I was bitten by my grandparent's dog when I was seven.'

'Yes, the scar looks old and healed over,' he said and the two women were dismissed.

A briefcase was brought to me for inspection: it was the battered old leather one shown on the posters. He wanted to know if I had ever seen it before. To satisfy him I took a good look and told him I hadn't. With that my interrogator went over to exchange a few words with a man sitting at the second desk, then came back and told me to follow him. While we were going down in the lift and passing through the reception hall I could no longer think of anything, I was utterly drained. At the entrance desk the guard gave me a form to sign declaring I would not divulge anything I had seen or heard while in the building, at least I think that was what it stated. I signed it and was told I could go. What an immense relief, I was free. Still in a daze, I was out in the sun with people hurrying past me. Instinctively my steps were carrying me home. I don't remember if I walked or took the tram, but I know the janitor of the house next door looked at me curiously as I passed. Using my own key I went in and met my mother in the hall, crying. She knew, I thought.

'They came here first, I had to tell them where to find you,' she said.

'Why didn't you phone to warn me?'

'I was afraid you might run away and they would come back to arrest us all,' my mother replied. It was only later that it came to me why I had been called in—my travel permit to Leitmeritz, of course. The police were following up every possible lead. There must have been thousands who were hauled in simply because of something out of the ordinary they had done that day.

The terror continued. At first there were rumours that Heydrich was dying. Then the rumours became more precise, that he had blood poisoning and probably a ruptured spleen. When the hand-grenade splinters went through the back of the car seat they carried with them bits of the horsehair upholstery and these had infected his wounds. Heydrich died about ten days after being taken to the hospital. Black flags were ordered to be hoisted throughout the city, public buildings were draped in black. With the agents still at large nobody knew what might happen next—the whole country was gripped by fear. Kurt Daluege, another police general, was named *Reichsprotector*.

Suddenly, one morning, posters with photographs and names appeared in public places, on the streets and in newspapers. Everyone was ordered to inform the police immediately where and when these men had last been seen. A few days later, in the early hours of the morning, a Greek Orthodox church near the city centre was surrounded by an SS detachment and all streets leading to it cordoned off. In spite of machine-guns, hand-grenades and tear-gas bombs, nobody from the SS could get close to the church. As a last resort firemen were called in and, under covering fire, managed to insert a hose into an opening to the crypt near street level. The men inside chose suicide rather than drowning. They were the group of parachutists sent by London to eliminate Heydrich. All the church elders and their families were shot in reprisal, while some 250 relatives of the parachutists were arrested and either executed or sent to camps.

It was only after the end of the war that the complete story became known. One of the agents hadn't hidden with the rest but had gone instead to his parents' home in southern Bohemia. There, exposed to the constant fear and anguish of his family, he was persuaded to go to the police to denounce himself and the other members of the group. His denunciation left a bloody trail which eventually led to the crypt. The Nazis, true to their promise, let him go free and left his family unharmed, but he didn't survive for long. Soon after the German defeat the Czechs brought him to trial and he was executed for high treason.

It would be impossible to enumerate all the victims of this wave of terror and there is no doubt that the overwhelming majority of them were innocent. When it was over, except for those who had spent the war years in exile, there were practically no political or intellectual leaders left. I sometimes wonder if those exiles felt at least a twinge of guilt for having sent a handful of young, ill-prepared and inexperienced volunteers to a certain death, causing a bloodbath the like of which the Czech nation hadn't experienced for centuries.

My firm belief is that the ease with which the Communists installed their regime after the war was to a great extent due to the political vacuum left by the Heydrich affair. Moreover, the elimination of the *Reichsprotector* had no political or economic impact whatsoever on Germany's war effort: it amounted only to a symbolic gesture. Instead of disposing of Heydrich, it might have been more effective if those men sent by London had concentrated on destroying archives in city halls and parishes and the records of labour offices and agricultural centres. Had the local population followed their example it would have created an administrative chaos far more damaging, and probably cheaper in human lives.

If the wave of terror receded, it didn't cease altogether. No explanations were given as to why so many people had been killed and villages razed. After the perpetrators had been found, and when it became evident that there was absolutely no connection between the handful of parachutists and the tens of thousands of innocent victims, neither Kurt Daluege, nor his State Secretary K. H. Frank, ever expressed any regret for the mass killings.

For the Czechs, the Heydrich affair represented a psychological break in the German fortunes of war. Throughout the summer the *Wehrmacht* was still advancing, the loudspeakers continued to blare out the successes of the *Luftwaffe* and the submarine packs, but the victories didn't seem as resounding or frequent any more. The offensive against Stalingrad and the Caucasus was an attack limited to the south. Obviously, the German armies now lacked the strength to attack simultaneously on a broad front from the Baltic to the Black Sea as they had previously done. The defeat before Moscow in the winter of 1941 must have cost dearly in men and equipment. Such was the reasoning of the Czechs at that time.

Although we couldn't know it then, the late summer of 1942 was indeed the turning point of the war. The British succeeded in stopping the advance of the *Afrika Korps* at El Alamein. Even if the battles were still inconclusive, hopes were rising. The times of the blitzkrieg, the lightning strikes and the subsequent destruction of the forces opposing the *Wehrmacht* were definitely over. Four months later the German armies would be on the defensive everywhere—the 8th Army would take the initiative in Libya, the Americans land in North Africa and the Russians start an offensive to relieve Stalingrad.

At the same time as we were getting encouraging news from the war theatres, the situation in our family was, unfortunately, quite the reverse. My mother received her not unexpected notice to be ready for deportation to the Terezín ghetto on 12 September. Grandfather Joseph, who had continued living with us after Granny Toni's death, had been deported earlier. Mother was considered Jewish because of three of her grandparents and she was no longer protected by her marriage to my stepfather—soon after the German occupation Mother had insisted on a divorce to safeguard Loiza's law practice.

When they divorced for appearance's sake only, nobody ever imagined that Jews would one day be deported.

When I first found out about Helena's activities I had considered offering to furnish my mother with a false birth certificate, but by that time it was too late, she was registered and nothing could be done about it. I well remember the days preceding her deportation. She had to prepare a suitcase—each deportee had the right to only one of a stipulated weight—and think of what to pack for a period of which nobody could estimate the length. Deportees were not permitted to take money or jewellery with them or any other valuables which could be used for barter: anyway, within the closed circuit of the ghetto such items lost their value. When she got there Franta was working in the kitchens and helped her as much as he could.

Not long after my mother's deportation but unconnected with it, I left the job I had held for three years. My work was so boring and repetitive that I had trouble concentrating on my calculations so inevitably mistakes crept in. When my immediate superior threatened to have me transferred to an even more boring job our discussion became heated and that was it, I quit. It may not have been a smart move, but at that very moment I didn't stop to consider either an alternative or the consequences.

That autumn, with the changing situation on the war fronts, the German High Command needed to replace their losses. When German factory workers were called up for the *Wehrmacht* the vacant jobs had to be filled by labour from occupied countries—in the early days it had been more on a voluntary basis. In the Protectorate, all males of a specified age not already involved in work essential to the war effort were liable to be drafted. Now, in order to trap all men who might be of interest to German industry, the issuing of new food coupons was tied in with a visit to the Labour Office. Each potential draftee had to submit to a medical check-up along with an interview, the results were compared with an existing file and the demands of the Reich were, to a certain degree, satisfied. For this stepped-up war effort a new word was coined: *Totaleinsatz*—more or less the equivalent of throw-everything-into-the-breach.

The question of my being classed as a *Volksdeutscher*, that is, an ethnic German having citizenship other than that of the German Reich, was no longer under consideration so, as a Czech, and jobless, I faced the likelihood of being drafted for forced labour. All posts in the armament industries in Prague were already filled by those as anxious to avoid the draft as I was. My situation suddenly threatened to become serious. Through a skiing friend who had a minor clerical job in the Prague office I found out that the whole process was being speeded up and I could expect my call-up towards the end of the year or early in 1943. If I wanted to avoid or, at best, delay my order to report I had to act quickly. I had had an umbilical hernia from birth. It never gave me any trouble and only made me a bit self-conscious when I undressed in front of somebody, and that I was doing fairly often—love-making was one of the few pleasures to be had without coupons. Now was the moment to have it seen to. More as a rearguard action than anything else—I knew I wouldn't be able to avoid conscription forever—I checked into hospital shortly before Christmas. It so happened that my summons arrived much later than expected. By then the scar from the operation was practically healed, but as it still looked rather fresh I was given a new date a few weeks away. Even if the chances of being deferred a second time were more or less nil, I managed an invitation for the night before my next medical. I had never slept with this girl before and was hoping the novelty would have the desired effect on my constitution. When I arrived at her flat on the fateful evening, armed with a bottle, I discovered she was already in bed—not because she wanted to cut short all the preliminaries but because she had a high fever and was feeling rotten. So, instead of playing the indefatigable lover I had to content myself with being her nurse. While wiping off her perspiration-soaked body I was well aware of her attractions. At the same time I realized that there was no hope of combining the useful with the pleasurable without confessing the pressing reason for my visit. Somehow I never managed to go back to see her and can only presume she wondered about my sudden interest and subsequent lack of follow-up. I have sometimes wondered myself.

The next morning I went straight to the Labour Office and passed my medical with flying colours. After I had dressed again I was directed to an office on another floor where I found two or three dozen men impatiently pacing in front of a closed door—they had been waiting for at least an hour they told me. I sat down on a bench a few feet away, quite content to respect their precedence. Once in a while the door would open and a squat German would appear to call out a name. After some time I heard mine called and entered a large room with a desk in the middle, forgetting to close the door behind me. Most of the desk was piled high with files and the official was sitting behind it in a swivel chair under a large picture of Hitler, studying my file. There was no chair for visitors so I stood in front of the desk. As he was leisurely leafing through the file I could see it contained the certificate needed for the re-issuing of my food ration coupons. Just then the telephone rang and the official mechanically reached for the receiver. The moment he realized it was a personal call, he swung his chair completely around and went on talking, gazing absent-mindedly out of the corner window. While his back was turned the men waiting in the hallway began slowly filing into the room to the point of hemming me in and filling up the space between the desk and the door. The conversation went on and on—he obviously wasn't a model of German efficiency. At last he turned back, hung up and lifted his head, surprised to see the crowd in the room.

'Damn, who gave all of you permission to come in here?' With that, he jumped up, spread out his arms and started to push the intruders out. '*Raus, raus*, everybody out,' he shouted. Those behind began backing up and slowly leaving, the men around me retreated too, but more hesitantly. His attention was no longer on me and all I heard was 'out, out', that would include me as well and there was my file on the desk. I grabbed it, quickly shoved it under my coat and let myself be pushed out into the hall with the last of the crowd.

Clutching the hot file I left the building and from a nearby telephone called my useful friend to tell him I absolutely had to see him at his lunchtime break. When we met I showed him the file.

'How did you get hold of it?' he asked in astonishment. I told him the story and wanted to know if there were any copies.

'No, just your name on a filing card in the archives. But the card shows only your age and address.'

'Could you destroy it?' He thought it might be too risky and probably unnecessary as well because it was seldom referred to. I kept on pressing him, but he let me know he had already taken a risk as it was, and he was right, a year later he was arrested for passing on some confidential information and spent the rest of the war in jail. When I got home I went straight to the basement, took out the ration certificate and burned the rest of the file in the furnace for the central heating.

When I presented the certificate at the City Hall for a new coupon issue I was somewhat uneasy, but there was no hitch. For the time being the problem of ration coupons was solved. I felt that as the weeks passed there would be less and less chance of the Labour Office finding out about the missing file so I convinced myself I had nothing to worry about on that score either. Therefore, instead of working somewhere in Germany for victory, I spent most of my free time—and most of my time was, fortunately, free—playing cards in Prague often late into the night.

8

However, soon after the episode with my labour file I was introduced to a German officer. Eric's nephew, who was serving in the Signal Corps in Berlin, passed through Prague on his way to Vienna fairly often and used to visit us. Although he was popular with the family we didn't like him coming during the daytime because our neighbours would notice a German in uniform. We finally told him, so from then on he used to let me know and I would meet him in a café between trains. One day he was there with a friend of his, a lieutenant. After my cousin left us, his friend told me he would be interested in getting hold of some diamonds—he had heard they were cheaper in Bohemia—and he immediately proposed that I act as his buyer. Some Germans were beginning to have second thoughts about the outcome of the war and were thinking of ways to provide for themselves in case of a possible draw or defeat. It came out in our conversation that the lieutenant's family owned a brewery in East Prussia. He believed that should Germany have to settle on a compromise with the Allies, East Prussia might be ceded to Poland, they would lose everything and diamonds should be a good hedge if the currency became as worthless as it did after the First World War. I told him I had no experience or knowledge of diamonds, but he kept insisting, saying he knew no-body in Prague and on his short visits couldn't very well go round in uniform purchasing jewellery. He was prepared to pay a good price for whatever I could find. Beer was one of the few unrationed commodities so money was flowing into his family's business as never before. Other possibilities for investing ready cash were limited therefore diamonds, even at somewhat inflated prices, were a sensible buy.

His proposition suited me extremely well. My inheritance, except for what I had changed into Swiss Francs, was almost gone, lost at

66

cards or spent in black-market restaurants. Within a week of our meeting I received a notice from a bank that an amount of 100,000 Crowns, the equivalent of 10,000 *Reichsmark*, had been transferred in my favour—could I let them know what to do with it as I had no account there. This was a substantial sum, even for wartime—my cousin must have given me a good reference—and I was to keep a commission of ten per cent on all deals. I would have nothing to worry about, at least money-wise, for the rest of the war. I soon established my contacts with jewellers and private individuals. Every two weeks or so I sent a small parcel to a given address and in return received the amount I had spent, plus my commission.

The diamond business left me with plenty of free time, and Helena, knowing this, asked on occasions if I could do some errands for her if she was too busy. We remained good friends and the most important thing in our relationship was the knowledge that we could depend on one another. It was understood that anything I did was out of friendship for her and had nothing to do with her group. Of course, it was sometimes difficult to draw the line between the two. Perhaps due to my inexperience in political matters, it didn't occur to me that I was collaborating, indirectly maybe, with people believing in an ideal which in practice treated the individual with the same disdain as the one I was opposed to. I was blinded by events around me which made me lose all sense of objectivity and fall victim to an oversimplification: if the Nazis represented utter villainy, all opposing them must be righteous. This argument was skilfully exploited by Helena. She waved aside any shortcomings in the Communist system as details that would straighten themselves out sooner or later. She had the right answer for everything and any questions confronting her were either black or white, no intermediate tones existed. Helena simplified all issues, as if to prevent me from forming my own opinions. With time, I resented being fed pre-digested and pre-packaged solutions to everything but continued to see her fairly often.

Nevertheless, I was aware that as long as I was in contact with Helena, I was exposed to the danger of being arrested and felt the need to be ready to go into hiding or to escape on short notice. It was now over three years since my last attempt to get out and the situation had become even more complex. The underground I once had vague access to was probably dismantled by now and to establish new contacts was nearly impossible, as I had learned from experience. The only way out I knew of at present was through Helena's group and the escape route they offered was to Slovakia which didn't interest me as I considered it nothing more than a stop-gap. What I was striving for was to get out of reach of the Gestapo once and for all. Getting away to England would have been the ideal solution but that was out of the question. There were partisan groups operating in Yugoslavia and Poland but how was I to get there to join them? My target would have to be a neutral country and Switzerland was the obvious choice. Anyhow, there weren't that many neutral countries left.

Once I had decided on Switzerland, the next step was to get hold of a Swiss passport. Naturally, I would have to steal one and there were very few Swiss citizens left in Prague in those days. There was still the composer who had sold me the Francs, but he was much older. A better bet was a distant cousin, Richard. His mother, a relative of Loiza's, had married a Swiss but made sure that her son learned Czech—he actually spoke it better than German. I figured it would be easy to get into his flat during an absence I could foresee with reasonable certainty. It had to be my cousin Richard, in spite of the fact that he was boarding with a student studying at the German university—a former soldier who had been discharged from the army because of a serious head wound suffered during the assault on Moscow. Once I had timed the absence of both, I would break in to get hold of the passport. I supposed that normally he didn't keep it on him—for identification purposes he had an ID card for foreigners— and a Swiss passport was too precious to cart around. To start with, I had to get hold of his keys and copy them, then choose the time and finally decide where to leave the passport. It would have to be with someone I could blindly trust and where I could leave it until the possibility of a police search at our house had passed. Once I was reasonably certain that there was no longer any danger, I would give it to Helena for a change of picture and description. Richard and I were close in age but he was shorter and had darker hair.

The most complicated part of this scheme was to find out what had to be done before crossing the Swiss border. I imagined that in wartime one would need an exit visa and this I planned to find out from the composer. Even if it proved too risky to apply for one, at least I could get as close as possible to the frontier without drawing too much attention to myself, then make the crossing on foot. However, these were conjectures for the future. At present all I wanted was to be ready. Later, I would have to play it by ear.

The first step of my plan was simple, the only tricky part was the timing and to find out where Richard kept the passport. He and I were not on particularly close terms—I considered him a bit of a bore. So, on what pretext could I invite him to our home? I remembered that he had shown interest in our maid, a pleasant wholesome-looking girl. I called on him to ask why we hadn't seen anything of him lately and mentioned that our maid was also wondering where he was. I invited him for supper, an invitation he eagerly accepted. The maid prepared a good meal and I sacrificed an old bottle of wine for the purpose. After the meal, since he was in a relaxed mood, I continued plying him with hard liquor. At last he was so drunk that I was able to persuade him to have a rest before returning home. The maid helped me to get him on to the bed where we left him to sleep it off. When I was sure that he was lost to the world, I took his key-ring out of his pocket to make wax impressions of his house keys.

Next day I went to Helena to ask her to have copies made by one of her contacts. A week later I got a set of keys from her but didn't proceed with my next step right away. Some weeks later, quite by coincidence, I found out that Richard's fellow-lodger had left for a visit home. This was unexpectedly good news so I decided that now would be the perfect opportunity to get into the flat. One morning I waited and watched until Richard left for the brewery school he attended, then followed him to the tram stop. After he boarded the tram I gave him another few minutes just to make sure he wasn't going to return for any reason. I even rang the bell when I went back to the flat—of course there was no answer.

The third key fitted. I was nervous but fairly confident Richard wouldn't denounce me even if he caught me in the act. Finding the passport didn't take long. It was where I had suspected it to be, in the drawer of his desk. I stopped at the door to make sure the coast was clear before leaving. When I heard voices on the stairway I stuck the key into the lock so it couldn't be opened from the other side, and waited. The conversation seemed to go on and on. The whole thing was getting a bit nerve-racking but I felt reassured I couldn't be surprised and would have time to return the passport to its original place. I stepped away from the door and went into the other bedroom. A letter was lying open on the desk and, while waiting, I began reading it absent-mindedly. It was from the Wartheland, a region of Poland incorporated into the Reich. A line drew my attention and even to this day I am unable to explain why, '. . . we load them into trucks, drive around the country for a while and when we get back everybody is dead . . .' The letter was referring to Jews but somehow I panicked and couldn't continue reading, just put it down and went back to the door. There was no sound outside now. I stepped out, turned the key and left with the passage I had read buzzing through my head. Richard's passport was burning a hole in my pocket, I had to get rid of it right away. I went straight to Primus and asked him to keep it for me for a while. He had led a quiet life since the death of his father, doing nothing to bring himself to the attention of the authorities and, furthermore, was to be trusted. I told him to hide it anywhere he thought it would be safe and he accepted without hesitation, or so it seemed to me.

Next I visited Helena and told her what I had read in the letter. She immediately asked me if I could bring it to her, but I refused, I was too scared to go back. She wanted to know if at least I couldn't give her more details. All I knew was where the letter was from, not who had sent it nor the date. The only further information I could give her was the name of Richard's fellow-lodger. We discussed all this at length and came to the conclusion that it was probably an isolated incident. Still, what bothered us and left us wondering was why they hadn't been shot or hanged, the usual methods of execution.

I knew that some Jewish families, instead of being shipped to Terezín, had been deported eastwards, most probably to Poland. There had been rumours that either the Germans had come to some kind of agreement with the Vichy Government to establish a Jewish colony in Madagascar or that Jews were to receive tracts of land in Poland or western Ukraine where they could support themselves by farming. According to these rumours, the original owners of the land were resisting expropriation, forming partisan bands to fight back against Jews and Germans alike. None of this made much sense but for a long time it was all that filtered through. However, a month or two after my break-in, the information about gassing was confirmed by another source, so it became evident that it hadn't been just an isolated incident.

My mother's friend Hilda was Viennese. She had been living in Prague for about twenty-five years and was the widow of a high-ranking official in the Ministry of Public Works. She lived in a modern apartment house in a good residential district, opposite a large park. The flat was roomy and, as there was an acute shortage of housing, she had to accept a German lodger. This man probably didn't realize that Hilda was a Czech national and thought her Austrian on account of her very pronounced Viennese accent which she never lost. Hilda was on fairly friendly terms with her lodger and on one occasion he told her, in confidence, the same story I had read in the letter and she passed it on to me.

While I was waiting to see if there were going to be any repercussions about the passport, I had a call from Lala. He asked me to meet him after work, it was important, he didn't want to discuss it over the phone. We met later that day and he came straight to the point.

'Did you give Primus a Swiss passport to keep for you?'

'Yes, I did. What happened?' I asked with apprehension.

'Well, he hasn't got it any more. Why the hell didn't you leave it with me?'

'What happened?' I insisted.

'He sent it to the Swiss Consulate. You're a complete idiot, how could you have entrusted Primus with something like that? Haven't you noticed how he's been behaving lately?' I explained to Lala that I'd thought Primus was the ideal person to keep it. He steadfastly refused to get involved in anything illegal and the chances of his being arrested were more remote than those of anybody else I knew well and could trust.

As for his odd behaviour, well there I had to admit that I knew about the strange way he was running his factory. His accountant had already mentioned to me in despair that Primus was changing the accounting system practically from month to month and there was another unusual thing—a questionnaire drawn up by Primus had been found in his desk drawer. It was a long list of names—relatives, friends and even his father's former chauffeur—that had to do with some business problems he was facing. Primus had come up with an original solution. Alongside the names he ruled off a YES and a NO column, then made a check mark against each name in one column or the other. His decision was made with respect to the opinion of the majority. The odd thing was that as far as we knew he never really bothered to ask the advice of any of those listed and simply surmised what their answer might be. Somehow, it never occurred to me that this strange behaviour could have an adverse effect on the passport episode.

According to Lala it seemed that Primus hadn't been able to sleep for worrying about where to hide the passport. Finally, when the strain became unbearable, he took it out on a rainy night and threw it into a mud puddle to obliterate any possible finger prints. Then he put it into an envelope addressed to the Swiss Consulate in Prague. When Lala told me the whole story I was flabbergasted, I just couldn't believe it.

'If he was so scared, why did he accept it in the first place, why didn't he simply give it back to me?'

Apparently Primus had thought about it and dismissed the idea because, if the theft were ever found out, I might implicate him. I still wasn't a hundred per cent sure that this wasn't another of Lala's practical jokes, so I went to face Primus.

'Yes, it's true,' Primus admitted, 'I sent it back a week ago.' He explained he just couldn't have it around. He was truly sorry, but as he told me, he thought it was all for my own good. 'Do you realize what you were risking?' he went on, 'besides, I couldn't have you on my conscience. You might have got into trouble because of my help.

There was nothing to be done about it and I was terribly upset. All my careful plans had come to naught, there was no question of repeating the operation and I had no idea for an alternate plan.

Apart from this set-back and considering the general circumstances, my life wasn't too bad. In the mornings I sought out people who had jewellery for sale. Mine was certainly a leisurely occupation when compared to the jobs of all those who had to get up early every morning, six days a week, to stand in front of lathes and drills in armament factories and return home late in the evenings, exhausted, from unaccustomed work.

I was mainly after big stones over one and a half carats. The prices I was prepared to pay were rather generous, in line with what the brewer had in mind. In principle, he was interested in flawless stones, but it wasn't always easy to find them. Other diamonds had the so-called old-fashioned cut, which brought down their value. The colour of the stone was an important factor too. I learned these things from a jeweller whom I had known for a number of years who gave me good advice when I started out. Ten per cent represented a nice profit, considering that I didn't have to finance the purchase, and the risk of getting caught for black-marketeering was minimal—there was no explicit regulation prohibiting dealing in diamonds.

During these transactions I discovered that most people had no idea of the real value of what they had for sale and often asked ridiculous prices. It was up to me to bring them down to what I considered a realistic price and, if the stone was interesting, it often involved several haggling sessions before I purchased it. I made it a rule never to give my name or phone number. This was not only a precaution but it also kept the seller in the dark as to whether I would turn up again. About half the characters I came across looked like thieves or fences, or black-marketeers who were paid for their goods in jewellery when they would have preferred cash. I had no qualms about doing business with them. The others were people in financial difficulties, sometimes those with relatives in jail. Then it wasn't pleasant doing business, I hated it. They were often so helpless that I was sorry for them.

Occasionally, I had a twinge of conscience but avoided dwelling on it for too long or too often. Granted that buying what was maybe the last piece of jewellery from impoverished families for a currency that could buy little in stores and even less on the black market was ethically questionable, I still wasn't contributing in any way to the war effort of the Reich. Choices were limited and everybody somehow got caught up in the contradictions of the times. There we were, everybody hating the regime while at the same time supporting the war machine in one way or another. Any overt act of defiance was promptly followed by retribution that helped nobody and achieved nothing—whole families suffered from resistance on the part of one individual. The line between doing the strictly necessary to protect one's life and collaboration was indeed a thin one. Many who couldn't distinguish this line or who, in their jobs, couldn't avoid collaborating, paid very dearly, either to the Germans during the war or afterwards to the Czechs.

9

With Franta away and Primus acting strangely, I now spent most of my time with Lala. After his parents' apartment had been confiscated he found—through connections—a bachelor flat on an elevated ground floor in a modern part of Prague. It consisted of a rather large living-room, a small entrance and a bathroom which doubled as a primitive kitchen but cooking was never much of a consideration. At lunch-time he ate in the canteen of the film studios where he was employed as an architect–decorator—work considered essential as German propaganda films were being turned out there—and over the weekend he usually went to the house in the country where his mother now lived with her two sisters.

I spent many weekends with him there. It was a comfortable house with a vegetable garden and orchard some thirty miles from Prague: when the weather permitted we bicycled there. Food in their village had remained adequate but I suspect the three sisters ruined themselves buying extras for us on the black market. One of the specialities of the house was homemade bread which in itself was worth the trip. Sometimes several of Lala's friends came with us and we were all able to fit into rooms in the attic. His mother used to come to the city once a week to bring him food. She had her own key because, by the time he came home from work, she had to be on her way back to the country.

Lala had a few sets of keys in circulation which he lent to friends for the pursuit of their love affairs. Hotel rooms were hard to come by and anyway most girls refused to go to them because it meant showing their ID cards. Normally, the best time to use his apartment undisturbed was at weekends when he was in the country, but fairly often it was put to good use while he was at work. Lala was very liberal about lending his flat and if he ran out of spare keys and someone's urgent need arose he would tell him where to go for one.

I've heard of some who, in desperation, criss-crossed the city by tram and on foot on this errand.

One day the inevitable happened. Lala's mother arrived in town and called him at the studio as usual to say she would be going to his flat. Completely forgetting he had lent the apartment to a friend he told her to go ahead. When she arrived and found it impossible to get her key into the lock she went to the janitor for help. He knew perfectly well what was going on but how was he to explain it tactfully to this well-born woman? He tried to tell her there was no cause for alarm, that the flat was often occupied during her son's absence. This Lala's mother refused to believe—if there was someone in there it had to be an intruder. She kept banging on the door, causing such a commotion that finally, to settle the question, the janitor put a ladder up to the open window and suggested she go and find out for herself. From half-way up, she could see two naked bodies on the couch against the opposite wall. For the straight-laced woman she was known to be, this was something of a shock.

'What on earth are you doing there?' she asked from her perch on the ladder. 'This happens to be my son's apartment.'

One of the bodies jumped up, covering himself with his hands. 'Can't you see madam, we're repairing the electricity,' realizing too late whom he was addressing. The electrician happened to be one of the crowd who sometimes joined our weekends at her home in the country.

Using Lala's flat for amorous adventures was normally all right in the afternoons but the girls I dated were rarely free except at weekends. Using it in the evenings was more problematic because it was rather far from home, not to mention the fact that Lala hoped to get some sleep. Trams stopped running around one a.m. and taxis had ceased to exist at least two years earlier. If I didn't leave before midnight, the chances were that I had to hike all over town, first to take the girl home and then to get home myself. This could mean a long walk. I once left Lala's flat at two in the morning, arrived home at five, and worse still, I don't even recall if it was worthwhile. Another evening I made it in plenty of time for the tram but, due to drink and exhaustion, fell asleep, passed my stop, and was woken up by the conductor at the terminal. The tram turned round for its final run and the next thing I knew I was at the other terminal across town. There were never many people on the streets late at night and the blackout was strictly enforced. The busy night life of earlier days had gradually disappeared as people were tired from working long hours. Occasionally, before using Lala's flat, I would invite the girl for a meal and drinks in a restaurant where I was known and could eat without ration coupons, but these outings were expensive since the owners had to get their supplies on the black market.

It was following such an evening session, one well lubricated with plenty of alcohol that, after separating from my partner, I was walking home along one of the main roads when I felt an urgent need to empty my bladder. As I continued towards home the urgency increased with every step and I desperately started looking for an appropriate place to relieve myself. There was an occasional pedestrian so I decided to turn into a side street hoping for a suitable corner. After taking a dozen steps I found a particularly dark spot and quickly unbuttoned my fly. The first gush gave me a fantastic feeling of relief but, at the same time, that familiar sound of piss hitting the pavement was missing as if the stream had dispersed into the air. This puzzle was solved within a fraction of a second. An irritated male voice, not more than a foot away, boomed into my ear, 'Couldn't you go somewhere else?' The impact of surprise hit me like a bullet. At the same moment, in the darkness of the blackout, my eyes could make out the outline of a couple in a doorway. The absence of all sound was due to the fact that I was urinating on his overcoat. I can't remember what I answered in my astonishment but I do remember that I just couldn't stop the flow and only stepped back to continue. While I was finishing, I could hear the woman complaining to her companion, 'The swine, he pissed all over my stockings.'

This carefree interval came to an abrupt end the day Helena called to tell me that somebody she knew who had escaped to Slovakia several months before had been arrested. He had used the same underground contacts as the woman we had both accompanied about a year earlier. For the time being there was no need to get alarmed as she knew this person only slightly. According to Helena there were still many people between this man and herself, but the news was upsetting enough for us to talk about it the whole evening. It was only too well known that once someone was arrested the Gestapo had ways of following the chain, picking up link after link.

Soon we received word that a second person hiding out in Slovakia had been caught. Evidently, the Gestapo had made the first one talk. It was imperative that we find out if the farmer who led them over the border was still free and, if so, warn him. He had no phone and sending a letter was out of the question. Helena discussed the situation with her friends and it was decided that she should make the journey. When she mentioned it to me I dissuaded her. She was the type people would remember and, on top of it, she knew too many who were directly involved. I proposed that I go instead, but with the understanding that she keep it secret from her group. Except for her, nobody knew my name, at least that was what she had always assured me: neither the farmer, his wife, nor the woman we had brought there. Helena saw my point and agreed that I replace her.

Leaving the station in the small town where the farmer lived, I stopped for a beer, then wandered around the few streets, retracing my steps from time to time. It seemed nobody was following me. Then I walked out into the open fields in a slightly different direction from the one to his house. After strolling in the open for a while I veered off and went on until I could observe the entrance of the farm. Nobody was to be seen and I could wait without drawing attention to myself. I had no preconceived plan and was wondering how to make contact. I was afraid of walking into a trap if I went straight up to the farm.

It might have been two or three hours later when I saw a woman open the gate and set out towards the town. I thought it would be best if I could talk to her there: I left my observation post and walked quickly back, passing the farm without stopping. I was pretty certain the woman I had seen leaving was the farmer's wife. She continued on a way ahead of me until I lost sight of her between the houses at a bend. When I reached the bend she was nowhere to be seen. If it was really his wife I was tailing she would be coming back the same way.

Near the farm, in the direction of the town, was a baker's shop. I went in and asked the woman behind the counter if she knew where so-and-so lived, mentioning an unusual name. She, of course, answered that she didn't know anybody by this name. Continuing my inquiry would give me an excuse to be on the street when the farmer's wife returned and I could then speak to her without arousing suspicion. I went from house to house asking for the person with the unusual name until I saw her coming back. I stopped her and asked the same question. No, she didn't know anybody of that name and I could see, with relief, that she didn't recognize me. Then I asked if her husband might perhaps know him.

'My husband isn't at home,' she said, not looking directly at me.
'When will he be home?'

'I don't know, he won't be home tonight.' And I thought I noticed her mouth quiver, as if she were trying not to cry.

'Will he be home tomorrow?' I persisted.

'No, I don't think so,' she managed to answer. 'He was arrested a week ago.'

'Oh, I'm sorry,' I mumbled and walked away. That was all I needed to know. To keep up the pretence I stopped at another few houses to ask my usual question, then left for the market-place. To make sure I wasn't being followed I went from there to the next village to board a train for home.

The return trip was a long one with plenty of time to reflect on the bad news. Would Helena talk if she were arrested? Not under normal circumstances, I was sure of that, but they could make her. Everything depended on her and I decided that after making my report I would cease all contact with her and hoped she would understand.

Helena took the news calmly—she must have prepared herself for it. No, she didn't think she was in danger, at least not immediately, a few more contacts would have to go first.

'You've got to stop seeing those people,' I urged her. 'Maybe they're already being watched.'

'No, you don't understand, I can't stop. There's too much involved and there's probably nobody to take over from me at the moment.' She did promise to take more precautions and to keep me informed should the arrests come closer. In parting she tried to reassure me, 'You have nothing to worry about, nobody knows you and even the farmer's wife didn't recognize you. You can be sure I won't give you away.'

I took leave of Helena with a mixture of relief and regret, but at the same time, I must admit, I felt like a coward.

Before long more bad news reached me. The Labour Office had again begun checking the files for new call-ups: this time it wouldn't be for work in factories but in labour brigades. Since my original file no longer existed I didn't know when I would be called or if at all, but my name was still in the archives. My friend from the Labour Office was in jail by that time, so I had no way of making sure. I had heard of a few people who for different reasons had escaped attention: some had even been called up, informed that they should await further news, then nothing more happened. With time, the rumours about brigades became more persistent.

At last, in late April, a summons arrived for me to present myself for the usual medical check and I went on the stipulated date. Luckily, no reference was made to the disappearance of my previous file—at least that was good news. The official who interviewed me didn't dwell on the fact that I had no visible occupation—had there been any complications I would have told him that from the time of my first medical, shortly after my hernia operation, I had never received further notification. As I left his office, he told me I would hear from them shortly.

If I were conscripted into a labour brigade Helena obviously wouldn't be able to warn me in time should anything go wrong at her end. Just before my summons she had let me know that a couple more people had been arrested, one of them the woman we'd taken to the farmer. The situation meant that I couldn't take the risk of not being in Prague to follow events from close at hand. Either I had to stay in the city in hiding or try to escape to Switzerland—the passport would have come in handy now, but that was all water under the bridge. As for hiding out in Prague, I didn't know where or with whom. In my opinion, Switzerland was the better bet. Richard was back in Zurich so if I had difficulties with the Swiss authorities he would probably intervene on my behalf. The important thing would be not to get caught immediately after crossing the frontier. I had heard the Swiss border guards often turned back escapees without bothering about formalities. My chances of fighting extradition would be better if I were caught as far from the border as possible.

Once again I studied all available maps. There shouldn't be any problem while in Bohemia. The crossing into the Sudetenland could be trickier, but I didn't think this border was heavily guarded. The main drawback there was that it was patrolled by guards who could change back and forth from Germany proper to the Protectorate as the need arose. I decided I would have to cross at a point where I was familiar with the countryside and my choice fell on a spot close to a small town where my stepfather and I used to go trout fishing. Once inside Germany, additional uncertainties would be facing me: first, would my ID card be good enough? I believed it would because two or three years earlier my age group had received cards identical to those issued to Germans, but with the difference that Czech IDs had a red stamp at the bottom stating that the bearer was a national of the Protectorate. Fortunately, the red stamp was missing from mine, either because I was born in a town that was now part of Germany or because my status—that is, was I German or Czech?—was still undecided at that time. I had noticed this omission without calling attention to it and now it would come in handy. My main disadvantage was that I was of an age when all Germans, unless they were obvious invalids, were in uniform. The best way out of this dilemma was to pose as a student. To avoid close scrutiny I would have to keep away from all likely check points and sleep either in the open or in private homes since all guests were required to show identification when registering at hotels.

There was another important, unsettled question. Was the border open between the Sudetenland and Bavaria, and what about between Bavaria and the old Austrian territory? None of the people now working in Germany who returned for holidays had mentioned that these old borders were checked, but all insisted there were frequent controls on trains. Under these circumstances the safest way would be to go by bicycle which would add to my cover story. Only the essentials could be carried. German currency would be no problem as marks were circulating freely in Bohemia at the rate of one *Reichsmark* to ten Protectorate Crowns, but Crowns were not accepted in the Reich.

A further problem had to be solved: German ration cards were different from the ones issued to us. I either somehow had to get hold of those coupons or bring enough food to last my trip, but food with a high calorific value was practically unobtainable. I just had to get hold of the currently valid German coupons to buy my supplies on the way, but again a catch: coupons were valid for a month only—colour changed with each new issue—and I had no way of knowing just when I would be leaving. This seemed the most difficult hurdle until I recalled that visitors from Germany used travel ration coupons with a longer validity in restaurants and shops. I contacted a waiter I knew well and asked him to keep these coupons for me, promising him a tip as well. In exchange I would give him the Protectorate ones I could buy on the black market. The restaurant was well frequented by Germans so he had no trouble getting me a good supply.

Now I had to decide on my itinerary and especially the spot at which to cross into Switzerland. The most obvious ones, near Basle or Schaffhausen, were ruled out as I expected both areas to be more heavily guarded than the Austrian sector. The drawback with the Austrian frontier was that most of it followed high Alpine ridges and I was no mountain climber. My choice finally fell on a compromise spot near Liechtenstein where I would have to cross the Rhine. There I expected to find the river to be not too wide. If I had to swim over instead of wading it wouldn't matter if the current was swift: on the contrary, much better for cover than a placidly flowing stream. Naturally, either way I planned to cross under cover of darkness.

❧ 10 ❧

Why I procrastinated when the arrests of members of Helena's group were increasing, I cannot say. There were, I suppose, a number of reasons. Immediately after the medical check-up would not have been an ideal time for sleeping in the open and, besides, I planned to pose as a student on holiday from the German University in Prague and could, therefore, do so only in July or August. Also I was having a good time then and wasn't in a particular hurry to plunge into a dangerous situation. So I waited and decided to let Lala in on my plan, expecting him to agree with it, but this certainly wasn't the case—he strongly advised me against it. In his opinion crossing the Swiss border would be too risky and the way there too long. Lala thought I should go underground instead and become a submarine.

There were three kinds of so-called submarines: those with genuine papers who felt it prudent to disappear because they were expecting arrest or deportation; others whose false papers could stand only a cursory glance, and, of course, there were some with no papers at all. For the latter, life was much more difficult because they could rarely leave their hiding places. Hiding out in the country was easier than in town because of the availability of food, but a stranger was more likely to be noticed. Whether one left the hideaway or not, the possibility of an accidental discovery always loomed.

Submarines had to have a great deal of patience. They could usually emerge only at night and their allotted space was often rather confining. From the point of view of company and morale, it was easier, on the whole, for two to hide than one. Obviously, somebody had to provide the space and food as well. The punishment for concealing a submarine was death and, more often than not, the entire family involved was executed. For this reason it was extremely

82

difficult to find people willing to take the risk. There were many, however, who hid out successfully for the entire war and I know of a couple who stayed in Prague in the flat of their own janitor and were never discovered.

Lala proposed that he keep me at his place but I rejected his offer for several reasons. As it was an elevated ground-floor flat anybody from the house opposite could see in. The janitor living on the other side of the stairway would surely hear somebody moving about when the place was supposedly empty. Everybody knew of my close friendship with Lala so the police could easily trace me to him if they started a serious search. Above all, I felt I couldn't do this to his family, not after what had happened to his father. Lala spent some time trying to convince me, minimizing the risk with the explanation that, should I be discovered, he could claim he had no idea I was a submarine. As for food, it wouldn't be a major problem, his mother was providing him with enough for two. But I still didn't see how I could accept—I knew myself well enough to be positive I was incapable of staying holed up for an indefinite length of time. I would be unable to stand the strain and my nerves would eventually give way.

The convocation from the Labour Office was taking its time. A month passed, a month during which Helena contacted me again. An associate of hers in Prague had been taken in the night before. We agreed she would phone me without fail every second day at a set time. If there were no call or message it would mean she was in trouble. I didn't worry about her calls being traced, she had no phone and always used public booths.

The tension I was under was slowly having its effect on my nerves. I began to consider the alternative of making a break right away instead of going through this interminable waiting. While weighing the merits of an immediate move my notice arrived at last. I was to present myself at the central railway station in ten days' time, equipped with enough clothing for three weeks. Well, that was it and in a way I felt relieved that the decision had been taken out of my hands. At home I hadn't mentioned anything about my intentions, believing it would be better for Loiza and my sister, Lida, if they were kept in the dark—there wouldn't be any conflicting testimony if they were ever interrogated. When Helena made her next pre-arranged call I asked her not to contact me any more after the date set for my departure, giving as a reason that I was leaving for the country and would send her a message on my return. The only person fully in the

83

picture was, of course, Lala.

I now proceeded to get rid of all papers and photographs, anything that could even remotely connect me to anybody else. My bike was waiting for me at Lala's aunts' house to the south-west of Prague, a direction which happened to suit me. I tried to think of everything I might need for the journey—it had to be as little and as light as possible. Naturally, the selection of clothing was important: something to keep out the rain and the cold, but everything had to fit into a knapsack as I would have to carry it all, plus the bike, in places where I couldn't ride. As emergency food rations, I included two jars of rendered pork fat plus a box of sugar. Heavy hiking boots, a pullover and an anorak were bulky but indispensable. I felt that in shorts, a shirt with rolled up sleeves and tennis shoes I would be inconspicuous enough and look the part of a student on a biking holiday. With all my identification papers, German ration coupons and marks plus a blanket I was ready to set off.

On the morning of my convocation I left home but, instead of showing up at the main station, I took a tram to a small station on the outskirts of the city and from there made the short trip to where Lala's mother was living. She and her sisters weren't particularly surprised to see me arriving unannounced. I told them I had come to collect my bike, hadn't Lala let them know? No, they didn't know anything about it, he had probably forgotten to mention it. I was invited to stay for lunch. This would be my last decent meal, I thought to myself, and as it turned out, I was more or less right.

When I went to collect my bike from the shed, I saw it had a flat tyre and looked for a repair kit, but couldn't find one. The village where the sisters lived was small and only the blacksmith in the neighbouring one, a couple of miles away, would be able to fix it. Since the smithy was in the opposite direction to the way I planned to go, I left with only the wheel. It was late afternoon by the time I got back and I was again invited for supper and to stay overnight. Even if the flat tyre hadn't been a good beginning, there was no special hurry. At least this way I could be sure of a good night's sleep.

When I took my leave the next morning, I was mentally prepared for the long trek ahead of me. During breakfast we had listened to the news—it was 21 July 1944—the previous day there had been a bomb attempt on Hitler's life. That was really bad news for my plans: what a shame, I thought, if only the attempt had succeeded the situation would be quite different for everyone. Now all roads would be far more closely watched—but there was no way of changing anything, I had passed the point of no return. The broadcast said that most of the conspirators had been rounded up and some had committed suicide. They had been planning to sue for peace. According to the announcer the war would go on to ultimate victory. All traitors would be exterminated without mercy and, in spite of the setbacks, new wonder weapons would soon change the course of the war. In contrast to this depressing news it was a glorious morning with not a cloud to be seen. I was pedalling along leisurely, and enjoying the countryside as if I hadn't a worry in the world. Whenever I approached a town I took care to circumvent it—my papers were in perfect order but if I ran into a roadblock I didn't want to be asked why I wasn't at work. After several hours of pedalling I stopped in some woods to attack the sandwiches the ladies had packed for my return trip. There was little traffic. Private cars had been banned a long time before; petrol was reserved for the exclusive use of the army and official cars. I met a few horse-drawn wagons that day, a bus with a charcoal-fuelled engine, some cyclists and, late in the afternoon, two Germans in army uniform who zoomed past me on motor-bikes. It was getting dark and I had to find a place to spend the night.

The region was familiar as we used to motor this way when Loiza went fishing. Ahead was a railway crossing where my cousin's husband and Loiza once nearly had an accident. They were driving fast and didn't notice that the barrier was down until it was too late to brake. Luckily they managed to swerve into the field at the last moment. After this unnerving experience, when someone asked Loiza what his last thoughts as the passenger had been, my stepfather remarked, 'Well, it was a close call all right. As the carriages flashed by I was wondering if we'd be travelling first or second class.'

Not far away was the village where one of our former maids lived. We had stoped there once or twice to pick her up. I thought it would be a good place to stay overnight, so left the road and went around the village. After the day's heat, storm clouds were gathering on the horizon—if I didn't want to get drenched I needed to find shelter. Some distance beyond the village, close to a footpath, was an old stone hut, probably a sheep-cote. The floor of the hut was covered with straw but it was too dark inside to check how clean it was. Regardless, I gathered up the straw to make a bed, wrapped myself in my blanket and promptly fell asleep.

I had slept soundly. It had rained heavily during the night and there were puddles on the path in front of the hut but the shelter was waterproof, everything inside was dry. With the storm over it looked like another hot day ahead. I collected up my belongings and crept out into the open. The border was close to Susice, a town I knew well, and beyond it were mountains covered with dense forests supplying lumber for a match factory close to the centre of town. I felt there was no rush to get there and it might even be better to reach it around two in the afternoon when shifts were changing. There would be a lot of people in the streets at that hour and I could mingle with the workers. I slowly made my way towards the town taking small paths whenever possible. From the maps I had studied I had a good idea where the new border ran.

At exactly two o'clock I rode into town and went straight to the market-square. In the middle was a map of the town and, as I had hoped, the outline of the 1938 border, close to the southern outskirts. The city park above the river was now almost an enclave and I went there to survey my crossing point and kill time. It was full of mothers with children taking advantage of the still-sunny afternoon. I sat on a bench and started talking to a woman watching a child.

'Yes, the river separates the town from what is now Germany,' she said in answer to my opening question. 'It's a nuisance having the border so close. In the old days we had a choice for Sunday walks and now everything is cut off, even the good mushroom places.'

We continued chatting for a while as I felt less conspicuous in her company and anyhow I had to wait for darkness to wade across the river and get into the woods on the other bank. Storm clouds began to gather again and I noticed people preparing to leave. The woman I was talking to got up so I left too but, instead of heading towards the town, wheeled my bike in the opposite direction to where the terrain changed into proper woods with a lot of undergrowth. From a hidden spot in the bushes I could observe the goings on on the other side of the river: there was nothing unusual—the place looked deserted. The river was a typical trout stream, shallow but swift, spilling over boulders. More thunder clouds were gathering and fast coming towards me. Soon there was a steady downpour and I was soaked to the skin. It was too late to take out my anorak, I hadn't thought of it in time.

This would be the right moment to cross, I decided. The guards, if any, would probably have taken shelter and I was wet anyway. Scanning the surroundings once more, I scrambled down the steep embankment, the knapsack on my back and the bike held above my head. Within a few steps the water reached my hips and I had to brace myself against the current. That I mustn't lose my balance, fall and soak the knapsack was all that was on my mind as I struggled across. I was too busy watching where I stepped to look around to see if I was being observed. The other bank of the river was flat and, as I made my way through the water, the stream became shallower, so with each step the going got easier. The whole undertaking couldn't have lasted more than a few minutes and immediately after reaching dry land I melted into the woods, then stopped to listen. All I could hear was the sound of the rushing stream and the rain.

From former trips I knew that the road ran parallel to the river for at least half a mile before coming to the next village, a long, strung-out place inhabited mainly by lumberjacks. Without getting too close to the river I continued through the woods, safely staying away from the road as I had no idea of the exact location of the border post. It was important to bypass the first village in German territory just to be sure I was well beyond the checkpoint and out of immediate danger of being challenged. That meant a walk of at least an hour alternately pushing and carrying the bike. My wet shirt and shorts were clinging to me but I didn't pay them much attention. I had to leave the border area as fast as I could.

In pre-war days, the mountainous region I was moving into—the Bohemian Forest—had been the frontier between Bohemia and Bavaria, the watershed being the border. It was a sparsely-populated, poor and heavily-wooded area, many of whose farmers couldn't live off the land and had to supplement their income either as lumberjacks or by working in small glass factories as blowers or cutters. I re-crossed the river over a small bridge. There was no need to be concerned now—I was well inside German territory. It was getting dark and I was cold, really chilled. I would simply have to risk it and ask to stay with a farmer. Nobody would be surprised by my wet clothes, the recent downpour explained them. The farmhouse I chose was a bit away from the village and I waited until it was completely dark and quiet. Covering the bike with some branches I left it in the bushes and came out into the open. A dog barked as I approached the house. Through a slit in the blackout curtains I could see a light so I knocked on the door and waited.

'Good evening. How far is it to the next village please?'—that I knew was several miles away. 'I lost my way and got caught in the rain.' The farmer looked me up and down and invited me in.

'About three hours of good walking.' He began explaining how to get there. His wife came to the door and interrupted him. 'Is that all you are wearing?' she asked.

'Yes. I didn't expect the thunderstorm, my spare clothes in the knapsack are wet too.'

'Why don't you stay for a while and dry some of your things?' she offered. The kitchen was warm and I asked permission to change my shirt, the one from the knapsack was drier. The table was set for two.

'I'm sure you could manage a bowl of soup with us,' she said and without waiting for an answer began to lay another place. During the meal we discussed the war. My host thought things weren't going well but fortunately their son was with the mountain troops in Norway— much better than on the Eastern Front.

'What are you doing, are you on leave?' I was expecting this, everybody of my age was in uniform, so I told him my prepared story—I was a student on holiday from the German University in Prague.

'You're lucky not to be in the army,' was his envious comment.

'Next year, as soon as my studies are finished I'll have to join up.'

'The war won't last that long.' From his expression I could see that what he really meant was that Germany would have lost by then.

'Oh, one never knows. With the wonder weapons things will turn round fast,' I thought it prudent to say. Then he wanted to know where I was from, so I told him I was born in Leitmeritz—no need to hide the fact, it was right on my ID card.

'So you're a Sudeten German as well. You know,' he continued, 'the Czechs weren't so bad after all, at least there wasn't a war on. Our son could have been here helping us. I'm getting on and with just my wife it's hard running the farm. If only I could get a war prisoner, but they don't want to send any here. They say the farms are too small. Besides, I think they're afraid the prisoners would escape into the forest. There are a few around now and once in a while they catch one.' By 'they' he meant the authorities who, it seemed, were none too popular with him.

'How do they get caught?' I wanted to know.

'Oh, usually when they come out and start stealing food. I would leave them alone as long as they don't cause any trouble.'

Our conversation was taking a tricky, even dangerous slant, so I was immediately on my guard. I wondered if he was baiting me and answered, 'You can't leave them alone. If there were too many at large they might start forming bands and attack you. They could be dangerous.'

'I don't believe that,' he said shaking his head, 'I've heard they are badly treated and not given enough food, especially the Russians.'

'We treat them the same way they're treating our people and there are too many Russians anyway. A few less of them wouldn't do any harm,' I countered, echoing the official propaganda. He wasn't mincing his words but I still didn't trust him.

'You see,' he went on, 'I fought the Russians in the last war, I know them a bit, they're not that different from us. It's true, they have a rotten government but the people can't have changed all that much, they must be the same as when I knew them. We haven't changed either, even if our governments have. I was born Austrian, then came the Czechs and now we are German, but I'm still the same person. You're young, people in town give you ideas you accept and believe in without questioning them. One day you may discover that not everything you learn today will still be valid tomorrow.' His talk was beginning to border on high treason. His wife must have been thinking the same and intervened at this point.

'Don't listen to him,' she said, 'he doesn't understand that life will improve when the war is over and our son comes back. He misses him a lot and is bitter. Your shirt is dry now but it's late, why don't you stay with us? You can leave in the morning, we always get up early. We'll give you our son's bed,' she added turning to her husband for confirmation. I was glad to end our discussion on this tone. They offered me a tumbler of schnaps and we went to bed.

Even if the conversation had been engineered in order to provoke me into making anti-Nazi statements, nobody would go to the police at this hour. Anyway, I hadn't said anything objectionable, it was rather the farmer who would be in trouble had he spoken in those terms in front of a Nazi. I guessed he hadn't had much formal education but was probably well read and his ideas were well formulated—a shame there weren't more Germans like him. I often wondered what happened to him after the war. Most likely he was expelled by the Czechs and his farm confiscated when they re-occupied the village.

I got up at the same time as my hosts. We had a filling breakfast of very good dark rye bread, even butter—unusual for the times—with homemade jam. I thanked them and left a bit of money under the plate. They were kind and genuine people and I was certainly lucky to have ended up with them. It was still raining but only slightly and my anorak protected at least my back. I walked to where I had hidden my bike. My estimate was another three hours to the Bavarian border. Most of the going was uphill and I frequently had to get off and push. The previous night's conversation was still on my mind. Suppose the farmer really believed what he was expounding, how many others thought along the same lines?

While I was thinking about all this I pedalled or pushed ahead on secondary roads, many of which I remembered clearly. In spite of the constant drizzle I felt fine, the wildness of the scenery was so beautiful. In keeping with my student-on-holiday pose I hadn't dared to ask the farmer if the former border still had a checkpoint—better to avoid the road and go over the mountains.

Here and there as I climbed, the green of the hillsides was marred by grey concrete block houses—the vaunted fortifications the Czechs had put so much faith in and never used. There were still two small villages to circumvent before the old border. At last I reached a high plateau of marshland interspersed with tall fir trees and nearly stumbled over a granite marker about the size and shape of a milestone. The 'CS' had been roughly effaced, the 'D' on the reverse side left intact. To my right and left, spaced some hundred yards apart, were identical markers—the old border line. Beyond the stones the plateau ended abruptly in a steep descent. It was also the last of the territory I was familiar with.

11

My little path disappeared and I had to carry the bike balanced on my shoulder. The going was difficult on the wet, slippery ground, my boots were soaking and progress was extremely slow. Finally, late in the afternoon I came to a cobblestoned road and there was still nobody around. Since the morning I hadn't caught sight of a single person—just as well. The road followed a small stream on its far side and behind it the woods sloped upwards. It seemed better to get on to the road—if anybody happened to see me carrying the bike on the other side of the brook it would look strange when there was a perfectly good road alongside.

Soon the valley opened up with, in the middle of it, a small village which I pedalled right through and then through another. Nobody paid any attention to me. The going was easy now, mostly downhill on a good surface. In a town I knew from hearsay I stopped at a baker's, bought a loaf of bread, paid and handed over the ration coupons while at the same time watching for a reaction—there was none. The shopkeeper simply put the coupons into a drawer and served the person standing next to me. So far so good. As soon as I was out of the town I stopped and attacked the bread. I was ravenously hungry, my last meal had been breakfast at the farm. Also, I was getting tired. Crossing the mountains had been harder than expected and I wasn't as far ahead as I had hoped to be. In spite of my anorak my clothes were wet, it had been raining steadily, but my confidence was growing the further I rode into Germany.

At a bend I overtook a country girl with a little boy. Here the way was steeper so I got off and, since the girl was walking beside me, we started a conversation. She had a broad Bavarian accent in contrast to mine which is rather hard and characteristic of the German spoken in north-western Bohemia. She remarked on how wet I was.

91

'No wonder,' I answered, 'it's been raining the whole day.'

'You'll get a chill that way.'

I told her I was planning to stop soon for the night, did she know of an inn nearby? No, there wasn't one for a long stretch, until well down into the Danube valley, but there was a small one in the town I had just passed through.

'No, I don't want to go back, I'm rather tired and a bit cold. Would you know where I could stay overnight, somewhere closer?' I ventured.

'You could probably sleep at our place, but I'd have to ask first.' The girl wanted to know where I was from and where I was going. She may have found my accent unusual, it was clear that the name Leitmeritz meant nothing to her. I gave her the same story I had used the night before. To ward off her personal queries I started questioning her. She was a hired help from another village, working for the mistress of the farm we were going to—the little boy was the woman's grandson. On top of the hill we took a farm track to the left and soon reached the house. The girl excused herself and went inside with the child. When she came out she told me it would be all right if I didn't mind sleeping on a cot in the attic. The elderly woman scarcely spoke to me and I followed the girl upstairs. After leaving me there I imagined I wouldn't see any more of her so I undressed, spread out my wet clothing and put my boots close to the chimney coming up through the loft. With that I settled myself on the cot and was soon asleep.

I woke up with a start. The girl was standing over me holding a light in one hand and in the other a plate of cottage cheese with a couple of slices of bread. She offered me the plate and sat down to talk. Somehow I had the feeling she had come for more than just conversation and I wasn't really surprised—men of my age didn't exist in the country any more. We chatted for a while and she probably felt that I wasn't particularly interested in her. After finishing I handed back the empty plate with thanks.

In the morning I left without breakfast and, as I later discovered, without my hiking boots as well. Where the lane joined the highway a *Feldgendarm*, a country policeman, stood as though waiting for me.

'Your papers, please.' I handed over my ID card, he looked at it, asked me a question or two and gave it back. 'Enjoy your holiday,' he said pleasantly, touching his cap. Coasting downhill I wasn't sure if this was just a coincidence or if the girl had advised the police—maybe her interest and our conversation had been a pretext to get more information out of me. The village seemed too small to have a police station so she could have phoned the last town I had pedalled through. Anyway, I had passed the test and this lifted my spirits considerably. Moreover, the weather had cleared during the night.

The mountain peaks around me were lower now with the woods receding. The road ran downhill and villages were more numerous. I passed horse-drawn carts, people on bicycles and on foot. Suddenly, around a bend, a plain opened in front of me and stretched as far as I could see. Soon there was a large bridge ahead and the Danube. I was apprehensive that there might be a control point on it but there was nothing. On the other side I stopped in front of a bakery, got a loaf of bread and next door, at a butcher's shop, a smoked sausage—so far I hadn't had to touch my iron rations from home.

My progress was good all that day. If I continued at this pace I should pass through Munich by the following one. No longer bothering to leave the main road I pedalled on. Except that there were no young men to be seen, one wouldn't have thought the country had been at war for five years, everything looked so peaceful. The day was warm so I made up my mind to sleep in the open that night.

Towards evening the landscape began to change imperceptibly. There was a wooded ridge on my left and slightly rolling country ahead. The ridge looked inviting—this would be the place to sleep, no need to tempt fate again and expose myself to a denunciation. At the first opportunity, and well before sunset, I veered off on an isolated path, crossed a small bridge and installed myself in a thicket. I ate the rest of my bread along with most of the sausage and lay down.

The night was warm, I slept well, woke up when the sun was high and returned to join the road. Quite a few people were about, mainly women and elderly farmers, but there was nobody in uniform. At one point I was overtaken by a convoy of cars and trucks with the inscription 'Dr Joseph Goebbels Propaganda Train'. For that there was still enough petrol. I supposed they were heading for Munich to prop up civilian moral.

I reached Munich in the afternoon. The city was vaguely familiar to me from a previous stay there with Primus when he lost his passport on a skiing trip in the Bavarian Alps. The nearest Czech Consulate was in Munich. Once inside the city I tried to identify places which on first sight looked familiar, but the place had changed considerably. Some parts had been bombed and at one spot I saw concentration camp inmates in blue and white striped uniforms clearing away rubble. I crossed the city without stopping, looking out for signs to the Alps. After Munich the country became hilly and my progress slowed.

Towards evening I neared Weilheim, a medium-sized town and, just as I was entering it, I overheard three young men talking Czech with an unmistakable Prague intonation. When I stopped them they told me they were labour conscripts working in a local factory. Then I asked where I could stay overnight and they told me there was plenty of room in their barracks. There were some fifty people in the part reserved for men and on the other side was a smaller section for women. Most of the workers were Czech but there were also Poles and some Belgians.

A Polish girl took me under her wing by spontaneously offering me a hot brew resembling coffee. She was quite friendly and we spent a pleasant evening chatting, without her asking me what I was doing among them. She seemed sorry to learn that I would be leaving the next morning. The atmosphere in the barracks was animated, some were playing cards or chess, others just talking and cracking jokes. The thought crossed my mind that I might have been one of them if I hadn't stolen my file in the Labour Office.

In the morning the girl woke me saying she had to go to work and on impulse I gave her half of the sugar I was carrying. She insisted on writing down her address in Cracow and made me promise that I would visit her once the war was over. Of course, for her safety, I had to get rid of the paper.

Beyond the town were the foothills of the Alps. The road climbed more than it went downhill and my progress was at a snail's pace, but the good weather was holding. By the afternoon it was so hot that I looked longingly at the lakes I was passing. A swim would have been the ultimate luxury, but I didn't know if that was permitted, nobody seemed to be bathing. Besides, before evening I wanted to reach Füssen, a town close to the Austrian border where I could treat myself to an overnight stay at an inn with a hot bath. By now I was far from home, the further away the safer I felt. There would be plenty of guesthouses—I had heard it was a popular resort area. The fairytale castles built in the nineteenth century by the crazy King Ludwig of Bavaria were close by. Maybe I was getting reckless, but it seemed better to take chances now rather than near the Swiss border. The difficult part of the trip lay ahead and I should be as fit and rested as possible.

Once in Füssen, I stopped to relax in the garden of an inn with typical Bavarian paintings decorating the exterior stuccoed walls. I ordered a beer and watched the small number of guests sitting in the shade of the trees. Soon afterwards a young woman came to sit down at the table next to mine, not a striking-looking girl but a sort of wholesome, attractive one. When our eyes met I could discern a faint, encouraging smile. The absence of men of an interesting age seemed to have had its effect on the female population. No wonder the authorities prohibited foreign workers from having anything to do with German women. There might have been a lot of unexplained births with the husbands at the front.

No harm picking her up I thought, she might furnish useful information. I smiled back, started a conversation and that was enough for her to move to my table where she talked incessantly—I had opened a floodgate. My well-rehearsed student story was repeated and she told me she was on holiday from the Ruhr where her home had been bombed. I was a bit disappointed to hear this as I had hoped she lived in the town—it would have been perfect if she had had a place of her own. She was staying in a boarding-house nearby and thought there would be a room free for me.

We left the inn together, heading in the direction of where Hannelore was staying. As I walked alongside her pushing my bike, she continued to talk animatedly, explaining she would introduce me as a friend of long standing to preserve her good name with the owners of the boarding-house—this suited me too. The proprietor was a jovial Bavarian who didn't seem to me the type to overly concern himself with reputations. Yes, he had a free room because there hadn't been that many tourists lately. With a wink he gave me my key and directed me to my room. I was surprised he didn't ask for my ID card and I made no move to show it. My companion's room was next to mine and she suggested we have our evening meal together. I told her I badly needed a bath, would put my things in order and join her in an hour or so.

When I knocked and went into Hannelore's room a surprise awaited me. Instead of our going to a restaurant with a menu offering only tasteless wartime dishes as I had expected, here was a table set with cheese, sausages, bread and pickles, a real peacetime supper. I reproached her for the quantity of food coupons such a spread represented, but she waved aside my objections, saying it was a long time since she had had anybody to talk to and it was worth it.

Her holiday had been spent alone and she was happy that I was there.

Just before sitting down, Hannelore produced a bottle of white wine which I had to open. She told me she had brought it all the way from home but, until this evening, there hadn't been an opportunity to drink it. We started our meal with a toast. She kept on talking and asking questions, fortunately seldom waiting long enough for a reply. At the same time she almost finished the bottle alone as I had only two glasses, too conscious of the fact that I could slip up on my story. I don't think she noticed my reserve. Still, there were occasional questions that made me uneasy.

Hannelore was either from Dortmund or Duisburg, I can't remember which. During an air-raid she had taken shelter in the cellar of her home, the building had collapsed and blocked the exits. She and some other tenants had had to wait forty-eight hours before the rescue team had dug them out. Her employer gave her a two-week holiday to get over the experience which is why she had come to Bavaria ten days before.

She was dreading going back to being exposed again to the bombings, accusing the Allies of being barbaric and inhumane. I listened patiently without comment, nor could I tell her of my joy at seeing British and American planes overhead while bicycling through Bavaria. Her reference to the air-raids was the closest we got to speaking of politics.

'Fortunately, everything here is peaceful so let's enjoy it,' I told her and sat down on the bed, motioning her to sit beside me. The fact that Hannelore wasn't exactly my type, a bit too hefty, didn't bother me unduly, since our affair would be a one- or, at the most, a two-nightstand. I felt I needed a respite before attacking the Alps and spending the whole day with her would provide an ideal cover, especially as the proprietor hadn't registered me. That way the police wouldn't know about my presence in the town.

What bothered me about Hannelore, however, was her incessant talking. Even when we made love she didn't stop and the disconcerting part was that it was about subjects having no connection with love-making. At first I thought it was because my efforts left her cold, but that wasn't the reason either, quite the contrary. After each session she described her feelings, sensations and emotions in detail and with vivacity, which was quite a new experience for me. I don't remember when we finally fell asleep. I must have been doubly exhausted from all the bicycling and now from love-making. Fortunately, the two activities bring different muscles into play.

We got up late. After lunch Hannelore and I went for a walk in the direction of the castle but never got there. For years I regretted this, as I was curious to see the place and I had read a lot about it. At least she was less talkative and the evening with her was short—I guess she thought I was recuperating. That night I slept in my room and, to avoid explanations, checked out early. I told the proprietor of the boarding-house that I would be back in a couple of days to collect my bike. Parting with the bike would leave Hannelore under the impression that I was coming back and perhaps stop her from having second thoughts about the background I had made up. The other consideration was that in the Alps the bike might prove to be more of a hindrance than help. To get out of town fast I boarded a local bus that stopped at a bridge a quarter of an hour later. There I got off, crossed the river and was in Austria.

Now the third and last lap of my escape had begun, the most difficult one. I walked through a wide valley and saw the little town of Reutte ahead. A couple of elderly *Feldgendarmes* riding bicycles passed by. They greeted me with the old-fashioned '*Grüss Gott*'—not the usual *Heil Hitler*, and went on without stopping. This different salutation, although in itself insignificant, seemed a much less enthusiastic attitude to Nazism which I considered a good sign.

When I reached the town it reminded me right away of my birthplace, in spite of the different architecture and the Tyrolean dialect I heard spoken around me. The old street signs were obviously of the same origin as those in Leitmeritz—they could have been made by the same company, identical in size and Gothic script: the trade names for shops were the same as in Bohemia. I had to remember always to be on my guard, however: many Austrians were Nazis, maybe even more ardently so than the Bavarians.

I bought some provisions and continued on my way up the valley of the Lech river. It was going to be another hot day—my knapsack felt heavier with each step. Perhaps it had been a mistake to have left my bicycle behind for although the road was climbing it was not so steep that I should have had to push it. An hour or so after leaving the town, a cart overtook me and the driver reined in his horse.

'Are you going far?' I gave him my destination.

'That's still quite a hike, climb up,' he said. 'I'm going the same way.' I was happy to jump up beside him. The man talked about the weather and the villages we were passing through but asked no personal questions. The two *Feldgendarmes* I had seen earlier came pedalling back towards us, again a '*Grüss Gott*' and they went on. It was close to midday when the driver stopped.

'This is where I stop but you still have a couple of hours of walking, *Grüss Gott*,' he said in parting and I answered with the same. On the dusty, uphill, unpaved road I could feel every little pebble through the soles of my tennis shoes. Now I sorely missed my hiking-boots, the ones I so stupidly left by the chimney: without clothing coupons, there was no hope of replacing them.

Just before the village I had mentioned to the driver as my destination, I turned up the slope. The valley was much narrower now. Hiking on paths should be more comfortable than on the road and I would avoid a reception committee if the farmer had alerted the police. He didn't seem the type but, whatever the situation, I had to be extremely careful. It was important that I never divulge to anybody the exact itinerary I intended to follow. Banner headlines in newspapers I had seen in kiosks along my route left no doubt that a mammoth headhunt was on for the conspirators involved in the attempt on Hitler's life. From a paper bought in Munich I had read that the general public was invited to join in the search and report on any suspect. All those known to have taken part were much older than myself which might, in a way, explain why nobody had paid me any special attention. All in all it seemed better to avoid unnecessary contact and continue my way on small roads for as long as possible.

Woods gave way to meadows as I climbed higher. Here and there cattle grazed but nobody was to be seen anywhere. By now my feet were really bothering me, so I stopped several times to cool them in streams. At last I just had to quit, I'd had enough. There were small huts strewn over the slopes which didn't seem large enough for storing hay and I imagined they were where the farmers milked their cows. It could be risky to sleep in one of them, what if the owner suddenly paid a visit? Instead, while there was still some light, I selected a haystack. The day was warm but nights could be cold at this altitude. The grass felt good on my feet when I took off my tennis shoes. Most of the bread and sausage I had bought in the morning made up my supper. The haystack looked inviting, so I prepared my bed, crawled in and promptly fell asleep. During the night I woke up several times with the cold and because of my feet, which were bothering me a great deal.

In the morning, I felt as if I had hardly slept at all. My feet were aching and, even worse, the sky was overcast. The rain started while I was still climbing, a fine, penetrating drizzle. I had to be careful not to lose my direction—after all this effort I would have hated to end up back at my starting point. I made it up to a narrow ridge, seemingly higher than any other. To make sure it was the watershed I was aiming for, I walked along it for a while and found that both side spurs were sloping downward. This is it, I decided, and began the descent. It was midday now and the fine drizzle persisted. After a while I found a trail to follow down into the valley. In the late afternoon I reached St. Anton, the well-known ski resort. It was empty which was a bit disappointing—it would have been easier for me if I could have mingled with tourists—but it was at least comforting to know it was the exact spot I had aimed for—my sense of orientation hadn't deserted me.

By now I could hardly walk. Originally, I had planned to cross another mountain chain but with the state my feet were in I had to abandon the idea. Instead, I went to the station to board a local train passing under the Arlberg and got off at the first stop after the tunnel. There were no complications, and I had probably saved myself a whole day of hiking, but I knew I was taking too many risks—now was the time to be doubly careful. The weather had cleared somewhat and in the twilight I could see the mountain range to my left which I believed formed the border with Liechtenstein. It was too hazardous to go to a hotel here, the border was too close. The best thing would have been to continue walking at night but I was exhausted and, considering the state of my feet, this would have proved impossible. I found a rocky overhang in the woods near the road and made up my mind to spend my last night of wandering there. Once again I slept badly, woke early in the morning and continued to make my way along the ever-widening valley.

I couldn't be on the road now and had to avoid being seen until I reached Feldkirch. Once there I hoped to go unnoticed, mixing with the locals until I'd had a chance to reconnoitre the terrain. By-passing all farms, I made it to Feldkirch, an old town cut by the tributary I had been following all morning, one that emptied itself into the Rhine. Ideally, I intended to follow this river until I got close to the Rhine to make the crossing into Switzerland the same night.

Feldkirch, with its arcaded market-square, was an attractive and busy place, and I felt that nobody was looking at me too closely. To the west of the town there was a park on a small hillock. Recalling my crossing into the Sudetenland, I chose lunchtime to install myself there on a bench while having a snack from my iron rations. Ahead of me was a plain several miles wide with mountains closing it off at the far end. On my left was the tributary to the Rhine and, beyond, a hilly part with farms that I took to be Liechtenstein.

The part of the plain that interested me was an open stretch of fields about half a mile wide with a cluster of farm buildings to the right. Beyond the open fields and buildings the whole area was woodland all the way to the mountains on the horizon. According to the map I had studied, the Rhine was close to the mountains and I estimated the distance to be between two and three miles—a whole night would be ample time to negotiate it. My present problem was that I couldn't stay in the park indefinitely without drawing attention to myself, it was too small and offered no hiding place. The nearest woods were a good half-mile from my vantage point. I either had to recross the town to hide on the far side of it or cross the open stretch in front of me and wait for nightfall somewhere on the edge of the woods.

My feet were so swollen that each step was extremely painful and my decision was made with that consideration—the shortest distance to walk. It was probably the wrong one but my goal was so near and my impatience to reach it overpowering. Undoubtedly, my poor physical condition, plus the fact that I was alone, didn't help me keep a cool head. Fully conscious of the risk I was taking I started out. After all, I had taken a few chances lately and got away with them.

12

I reached the woods without a hitch and began looking for a likely spot to hole up in until nightfall. There was little undergrowth on the fringe and I hadn't penetrated the woods for more than some two hundred feet when suddenly, behind me, a sharp voice commanded, 'Halt, hands up. Don't move, don't turn around.' I stopped in my tracks, surprised and stunned. The voice came from so close behind me there was nothing I could do. That's that, flashed through my mind, all my plans and efforts for nothing. I just felt terribly tired, too tired to react or think. Was there only one man behind me? Did he have a revolver or submachine-gun pointed at my back? Or maybe nothing at all? Then I heard the same voice ordering me to turn left and start walking. I sensed somebody right behind me but couldn't turn to see who he was.

'Follow the path,' said the voice again. There was a wooden bridge to cross, it spanned the river I had intended to follow. Soon we came to a customs house. When an official standing in the doorway approached and ordered me to enter the building I still hadn't seen my captor.

The interrogation was short and superficial, the customs officer seemed to handle it as a routine job. An hour later a police car came to collect me and took me to the city jail. I was put in a large, underground cell with some two or three dozen prisoners—drunks, foreign workers and the like. Still too stunned to want to talk to anyone, I kept apart. There were no bunks to sleep on: the men around me were standing, sitting or sleeping stretched out on the floor. Much later the noise subsided and, sitting with my back to the wall, I dozed off intermittently.

In the morning the door opened and names were called out. The cell gradually emptied and then my name was called. At the reception

101

desk I found the same man as had picked me up at the customs house. Another was waiting at the entrance and they delivered me to the Gestapo headquarters, a private villa on the outskirts of the town. The questioning started right away. There was no way to avoid telling the truth about my call-up for a labour brigade, they had my ID card and could check it in Prague. Moreover, this was a plausible reason for my attempt to escape—otherwise, they might have started wondering if there wasn't something more serious behind it. What interested them was how I had made it as far as Feldkirch without even a permit to enter Germany. I explained how I had crossed the border but didn't mention anything about the bike, just said that I had walked, always sleeping in the open. Nobody thought of asking me the date I started out. I insisted I had done it all on my own, had not been sent by any organization, nor did I carry messages for anybody in Switzerland. Then I spun them a story that as there was no chance to study in the Protectorate for the duration, my cousin Richard had offered to finance me for the University of Zurich.

The interrogation was proceeding smoothly, no raised voices, no trying to trip me. All my declarations were accepted at face value as if none of it concerned them. Actually, everything I said was very close to the truth and the main thing was they couldn't produce anybody to contradict me. At least it was the truth as long as Helena hadn't been arrested and given me away. The session lasted most of the morning and when it was over I wasn't returned to the city jail but to a proper prison in another part of town and assigned to a cell on my own.

The next morning a guard brought me a box filled with short cores of cardboard and a pot of foul-smelling glue. I was told to glue a certain number of cartridges per day and, after the first day, found I could easily meet the quota. For this I was given a reward of three cigarettes and three loose matches—the guard had to be called to strike them. At last I was participating in Germany's war effort, even if the cartridges seemed destined to kill nothing larger than a partridge.

My cell was clean, sunny in the afternoon, with a work table, a stool and an iron cot—in short, a rather pleasant room. The window was high up but I could see the sky and if I stood on the stool it offered a beautiful view, the same range of mountains I had seen when sitting in the park. If I hadn't reached Switzerland at least I could see it through the window—a somewhat ironic consolation.

My neighbour was a young, stocky Russian with whom I walked in the prison yard during the thirty-minute recreation period, secretly exchanging opinions and experiences: in principle, we were not permitted to talk. The prison guards didn't seem very strict, rather easy going in fact, and were probably left over from the Austrian regime. My companion wasn't dissatisfied either with the life we were leading. To my surprise he told me that this existence was in some ways a better one than he had had in Russia. The food was good and a couple of times we were even served rice, something unobtainable in civilian life—it may have come from confiscated contraband.

On two occasions I was called to the interrogation room of the prison. I went in with apprehension but it was more or less a repetition of the questions I had already answered. The time I spent in the Feldkirch prison was a curious experience. Unconcerned and uninvolved, I felt as if life was flowing beside me, as if I were buried but could still follow what was happening. I had been defeated and admitted it, so I had no aspirations and no demands. Of course, there was the hope that the war would eventually end—a spark of hope still existed in me that I would go free one day—but at the same time it was only a kind of subconscious desire to see the war over. I was now only a passive observer and expected events to come to me.

Every morning I was pleased to see my Russian friend, to talk to him at recreation, but I never tried to communicate with him otherwise. I was completely apathetic and knew I was at the end of my tether. In a nutshell, I had ceased to be an individual wanting to be in charge of his own destiny: somehow that drive had left me.

Had I had any previous experience of prisons I would have known that this tranquil and undemanding life couldn't go on forever. One morning, instead of bringing me the cores, the guard told me to get ready for transport. There wasn't that much to prepare but there was no time to say goodbye to my neighbour as the guard was in the doorway. He led me to the ground floor where a dozen prisoners were already assembled in the corridor. Of this group the only one I can still remember is a man in his late forties, a war invalid without a leg, who spoke to me and asked why I was in prison. When I told him, he said in his case it was because he was an active Catholic and I didn't question him further. Later that night I understood that he was active all right but not necessarily in religious matters. In the transit jail in Lindau, where we were waiting to be joined by another transport, he tried, in spite of his handicap, to climb into my bunk.

Incidentally, this was the only occasion during my time in prison that a homosexual tried to make a pass at me.

In the early hours of the following morning our group, and many more who had come from other prisons, were marched to the station. We boarded a railway car that looked like an ordinary carriage with wooden passenger benches, except that on this one the windows were barred. The car was filled to overflowing with prisoners, Germans, Greeks, Spaniards and Serbs, every nationality one could imagine. We were travelling eastwards through the lovely countryside of southern Bavaria, coupled to a normal passenger train which stopped fairly frequently to pick up more people. Towards the evening we arrived in Munich but we didn't disembark at the main station—we were shunted instead to a small one I didn't know. Guards surrounded the train while we formed a marching column. The guards who had accompanied us from Lindau counted all prisoners and those there to receive us did a re-count. It was a sight I was to witness many times over.

We marched through the darkened, cobblestoned streets with seemingly as many guards as there were prisoners. The prison wasn't very far from the station and once there we were sorted out and I ended up in an enormous hall in the basement. The floor was covered with people either sitting or lying down—there were no mattresses or bunks. Those who had some possessions used them as pillows. As we, the new arrivals, were deciding where to settle ourselves, we were approached by those already there who wanted to sort out everyone according to nationality as each language group tried to keep together. The common language was German but many of the prisoners spoke it haltingly. Those who knew it better acted as translators to explain to the others what the guards expected from them.

On the whole, the guards left us pretty much alone and, except to call out the names of those who were to leave the cell, there was no need to communicate with them. Occasionally, a guard's pronunciation of a name was not understood by the person called, which created a bit of confusion, easily settled with a kick in the pants, but most of the prisoners knew how the Germans pronounced their names. Some of the inmates had been in the cell for weeks, others stayed only overnight. A far corner was occupied by Byelorussians who told me they had been there for three months, but that seemed to be the exception. What fascinated me about them was that instead of

104

any current type of footgear they had footcloths wrapped knee-high and, over these, soles cut out from tyres, all tied together with criss-crossed strings.

A large proportion of the occupants was Italian, but nearly all the nations of Europe were represented. There was even a man who wore a strange uniform with '*Freies Arabien*'—Free Arabia—sewn on his left breast. I had never heard of this organization before, nor have I since. Most of the prisoners wore civilian clothes but there was a handful in striped uniforms, in transit from one concentration camp to another.

I kept wondering what was in store for me, would it be the Dachau concentration camp near Munich? The answer came after two days when I found myself part of a transport passing through Salzburg and disembarking in Linz. This could mean either the Mauthausen camp or, more likely, Prague. The idea of Prague didn't appeal to me at all. Why would they want me there? Had Helena got herself arrested? Did they need me for further interrogation or, worse still, confrontation?

After the now familiar head-count and recount I ended up in the city jail. In contrast to the Munich prison, it was a relatively modern building and, as in Feldkirch, the guards were older men and quite friendly. The cell I was assigned to was bright and already had two occupants, a young Czech and a Russian in his late forties or early fifties who had lived for a time in Paris and said he was a colonel in the Red Army. I didn't ask him but supposed he could have been a military attaché—ordinary Russians didn't live in the West, I knew. The Czech had served an eighteen months' sentence for a labour offence and was hoping to be sent to Prague to be released, but he didn't know for sure.

The Russian was being transferred, I think it was from the Mauthausen camp, and had an idea he was *en route* to Berlin for additional interrogation. He was well educated, spoke fluent French and German, and I suspected he might be a member of the Soviet Secret Service although, naturally, he never said so. In contrast to my neighbour in the Feldkirch prison, this man was a dedicated Communist. We discussed politics, Russian and European history plus a wide range of other subjects. He was well read and well informed about the pre-war situation in West European countries. I took a liking to him in spite of our different and often opposing views.

During the talks he made a prediction which sounded far-fetched at the time but has turned out to be nearly correct. The colonel prophesied that in Europe, Soviet or Communist power—he used both terms interchangeably—would stretch all the way from Hamburg to Trieste. Did he really know or was it just bragging on his part? The accuracy of his prediction has amazed me ever since. After the war I often wondered if he could have been Leopold Trepper, the head of the Red Orchestra, the famous spy ring. If he was Russian—but then, Trepper was Polish—and came directly from Mauthausen, his head would have been shaved, but I remember him having normal-length hair. In that case he could have been a prisoner with special status, kept separate from the other inmates. All I have since read about this spy ring, which operated mainly in France, Belgium, Switzerland and Germany, seems to confirm my theory, but of course, I'll never know. It wasn't customary among prisoners spending only a short time together to introduce themselves formally by their full name. Besides, in those days the name Trepper would have meant nothing to me.

My temporary stay in the Linz prison had a beneficial effect on my state of mind. Gradually, I shook off my mental lassitude and fatalistic passivity. My conversations with the colonel, the clean cell and plentiful, if not tasty, food, made me take more interest in what was going on around me. My feet had time to heal and I decided to try to escape should the opportunity present itself.

Early one morning our guard came to the door to tell all three of us to get ready for transport. Again, a crowd of some two hundred men, hemmed in on all sides by guards, was marched through the streets to the station and put aboard several cars waiting on a siding. This time the prison wagons were different. Ours had a narrow corridor passing through the middle with individual cubicles about four by four feet on either side. Each cell had a small, barred window that could be partially lifted, a folding seat and collapsible table. In peacetime a cubicle was undoubtedly meant for one person, but there were three of us tightly pressed against one another in each of them now.

Somehow the colonel and I had managed to stay together and the third occupant turned out to be a deserter from Bavaria. It soon became evident that the train was moving northwards towards Prague. So that was it, I was being sent back for further interrogation.

The tiny cell wasn't very comfortable and both the colonel and the deserter were tall and heavily built. We rotated positions, alternately sitting and leaning against the door or the window. The late August day was extremely hot and as the journey progressed the atmosphere

106

became stifling. Around noon a guard came in to open the window, I suppose more for their comfort than for ours: in the corridor it was likely to be more suffocating than in the cells. The breeze blowing in from the open window felt really refreshing.

While in Linz the colonel had discussed with me the possibility of an escape. As a Russian he didn't think he would have much hope of not being recaptured fairly soon, even if the breakaway itself were a success. Now that it was evident the train was heading for Prague he thought I should take advantage of any possibility as I was familiar with the city and knew so many people there. 'If you are really serious about giving it a try the best time will be in the station,' he advised me, 'or you could bolt from the column when we march to jail, they won't be able to aim well in the blackout. But I suppose you know the consequences if they catch you again.'

Under normal conditions a train in motion offered the best chance, but with the barred window and the guards watching it was impossible. At any rate, I had resigned myself to the coming interrogation and was resolved that under no circumstances would I admit to having anything to do with Helena's activities. At the worst it would be her word against mine. The other two under arrest who knew me, the woman we had accompanied and the farmer, were probably dead by now.

After crossing the border into the Protectorate the prison wagons were coupled to a regular passenger train, a long one, since our car always came to a halt some distance from a station. As the train was nearing Prague it grew darker and, at stops closer to the city, it was possible to make out the silhouettes of women furtively approaching the wagons, softly calling out names and asking if anybody aboard could give news of their whereabouts. In spite of the bars the half-open windows were a help as the women were passing in pencil stubs wrapped in scraps of paper for the prisoners to write messages which they promised to forward. The transport must have been a regular one if they were so well organized. As the train started up again I called out my name and home address to the nearest silhouette, asking her to let my family know that I was arrested and would probably be held in the Prague jail.

It was completely dark by the time our train pulled in at the central station which, of course, I knew inside out. It was probably one of the most sumptuous stations in Europe, with a large and ornate art nouveau entrance hall. The access to trains and exits led through wide passageways under the tracks with individual flights of stairs branching off to each of some ten platforms above. This arrangement, common in many railway stations in Central Europe, gave little thought to the comfort of passengers who had to carry their suitcases up and down, but then, when these stations were built, there were porters to do the carrying.

After the train had come to a complete stop our cars were immediately surrounded by a detachment of *Schutzpolizei*. A short while later—the time it took to clear the platform of regular passengers—we were led out cell by cell to form a marching column several steps away from the wagons. On the platform I could see there were many more of us lining up than the number entrained in Linz: other wagons must have been hitched on. With the columns of five abreast formed we were, as usual, counted and re-counted. The head count was right, the guards from the train handed us over like a shipment of merchandise to be signed for by the boss of the *Schutzpolizei* and the order was given to march. All was done with the usual shouting and clubbing with gun butts. The guards were nervous because it was dark and many prisoners got hit simply because they didn't react fast enough to the orders.

Instead of leaving through the underground exit from the farthest platform where we were lined up, the formation, with guards in front, behind and on both sides, was led into the access tunnel. Going downstairs into the passageway I realized, from the sound of the marching feet ahead, that the column was turning right and up the stairs on to the first platform. That meant we wouldn't be leaving by the main hall of the station. At the top of the stairwell I knew we would have to execute a 180-degree turn to reach the only other likely exit, the one used by postal trucks and where I imagined we would be loaded into prison vans. The Prague jail was far from the central station and at night it would be risky to march us all that distance.

My hunch about the exit was confirmed as we started up the dark stairway. We were about in the middle of the long column, the colonel on my left, the German deserter on my right with two other prisoners beside him. Behind the colonel, in the next rank, was the young Czech from our cell in Linz. Once they reached the first platform the guards on our left would have to space themselves further apart to execute the outside turn. The opportunity for an escape must have occurred simultaneously to the Russian and myself as, without a word, we exchanged places while continuing up the stairs.

As our row reached the top and came out on the platform, the gaurd in front on my side was already engaged in the turn and the view of the one still on the stairs was probably blocked by my former cellmate. This is it, I decided, and instead of making the turn I continued to walk straight on down the platform, neither speeding up nor slowing down. There was a tingling sensation down my back—I was half expecting a shout to halt or the impact of a bullet.

Ahead of me, a cluster of Czech railway employees was watching the prisoner transport from a respectful distance. One of the men held a lantern with the regulation blue blackout light which shone on their brass buttons. A strange detail to register at such a moment, but important, as I felt I had nothing to fear from them: quite the contrary, they were afraid of having anything to do with me. When they saw me walking towards them they dispersed in a hurry in all directions as when a stone is thrown among a flock of sparrows. Behind me I could hear the marching feet and the shouts of the guards while I continued on at the same pace to the end of the platform, then stepped over the rails of the shunting yard and went towards a small merchandise exit some five hundred yards away. There was nobody at the open gate and I walked straight out on to the street.

13

It took some moments for the fact that I was free again to sink in: at first it simply felt as if an enormous load had fallen from my shoulders. Free I might be, but without papers, without money, without ration coupons and knowing I couldn't go home. How long would it take the guards to discover my escape and raise the alarm? Normally, they would count again before loading the prisoners into the vans, that meant the alarm could be raised very soon. I had to get away from the station as fast as possible, but where was I to go? There was a park nearby and I made my way there to think about my next move. My position was still extremely vulnerable. Unshaved, with my clothes in tatters, I couldn't help looking conspicuous and there were spot checks to think of—my appearance alone would prompt the police to ask me to show my papers.

At the moment of my escape I had been perfectly conscious of the chance I was taking but some irresistible force propelled me to go ahead as if the decision were no longer in my hands: anyway, there was no time to reflect or hesitate. Once I had made up my mind to grab the first opportunity that offered itself I had, of course, been planning what my moves would be but I had no way of knowing ahead of time where or when I would make my break. Now it was obvious that the number one priority was to find shelter. It might take the guards another ten minutes to advise the police to start a manhunt.

The names of two people came to my mind at once, Lala and Helena. To get in touch with either of them I would first have to ask a janitor to let me into the building. It was customary to lock the main entrance after nine or ten in the evening: only very few apartment houses in Prague had individual, exterior bells. Although Lala's flat was close to the street level, the windows gave on to a courtyard. Helena's apartment was a better bet, but at the moment I didn't know if she was still free and, more important, if her place was being watched.

The best solution would be to find shelter with somebody who wasn't quite so obvious as these two, maybe an old girlfriend—I had had some short-lived affairs that were unknown to most. On the other hand, since they had been mainly superficial encounters these women might not be willing to stick out their necks for me. No, I had no right to expose them to reprisals unless, fully aware of the danger, they spontaneously offered to help. In any case, they could be a consideration for later, not for now. In the final analysis I came to the conclusion that in spite of the risk, the first person to contact would have to be Helena.

I decided to spend my first night of freedom in a park, but not where I was at the moment. There was a better one, about a fifteen-minute walk away, where dense undergrowth covered a steep hill. The night was warm so sleeping out would be no hardship. In the blackout, the walk there went smoothly. I selected a hidden spot and sat down with my back against a tree-trunk. The slope was too steep for me to lie down although this was an advantage because then I couldn't fall deeply asleep. Between scheming how to contact Helena and occasionally dozing off, I decided on my first steps.

To begin with, the chances that she was being watched were minimal, the Gestapo couldn't spare enough people to keep tabs on every suspect. If she had already been arrested her apartment would be locked though in that case I had an alternative. Helena's flat wasn't far from the home of another former girlfriend of mine who lived with her widowed mother in a villa set in a fairly large garden. Her mother, who knew me well, was a family friend and I was sure she wouldn't give me away. If it came to the worst, I could hide in their garden and think of another solution.

My watch had been taken away from me on my arrest—my knapsack and extra clothes too—but when I heard the screeching of the trams I judged it was around five in the morning. I had to be at Helena's before full light and after the janitor had opened the main door. If her flat was locked I would still have time to reach the villa in semi-darkness. Using side-streets I arrived there while it was still dark. The main entrance was already unlocked and I met nobody on the stairs going up to her apartment. I knocked several times on her door during what felt like an eternity, until I heard her voice on the other side, 'Who is it?'

111

'Please open.' I hoped she would recognize me. The door opened immediately and closed as quickly after me.

'What are you doing here, where have you been all this time?' While I was answering her questions at length she made us some breakfast. I was hungry, my last meal had been the previous morning, before leaving Linz. Helena's reaction wasn't quite what I had expected.

'You're an irresponsible idiot. You knew perfectly well I wouldn't give you away. And I know that the farmer has been executed. There's no news about the woman but she must be dead too, so not a soul knows about you. In any case, there is nothing to worry about, the arrests have stopped. Nobody was taken after you left and I doubt there's still any danger.'

Well, one preoccupation was over for me, but that didn't necessarily solve my present predicament. After breakfast she suggested I have a bath: I suppose I smelled to high heaven because my last bath dated back to Feldkirch. The bath did me a lot of good, at least I got out feeling ready to tackle the future.

I was now an escaped prisoner. Sanctions for an escapee seemed to vary a great deal, I had heard. Those who got away from a concentration camp were returned to the same one to be hanged, but prisoners who escaped from one police force and were captured by another could often get away with it, probably due to inter-service rivalry. Since I had escaped from a transport there was a fair chance that not much would happen to me beyond a severe beating and some solitary confinement. Helena agreed that at any rate, for the time being, the most dangerous moment had been at the station.

As to the question of where to hide, we both knew it wouldn't be a good idea to stay at her place for more than a very short time. For one thing, there were several other tenants on her landing who would soon realize that somebody else besides Helena was living there. Moreover, she was still working with her organization and I considered that that would be riskier for me than if I stayed at the home of somebody who wasn't politically active or, for that matter, wasn't involved in anything illegal at all. If I were found with her it could lead to the uncovering of Helena's group. Before she left the flat she said she would contact Lala and in the meantime I should lie down and have a good rest.

I slept the entire day, but it wasn't a wholly restful sleep. Due to the mental strain I woke up now and then and the drive that had motivated me so far suddenly evaporated. When Helena came back she told me that she had been able to speak to Lala and he would meet me the following afternoon at the foot of the steps of a nearby church. By then he would have arranged for a place for me to stay. Before going to sleep she outfitted me with clothes belonging to her husband. He was a bit shorter—this showed mainly in the length of the trousers—but otherwise the fit wasn't too bad. She also gave me spectacles to disguise myself more but the lenses were too strong and I wore them only on my first day out. She said she wouldn't wake me in the morning and I should stay put until it was time to meet Lala.

When I woke up Helena had already gone. She had left me a bit of money on the pile of my new clothes but otherwise no message. Hours had to be got through and I didn't know how to occupy myself. There were plenty of books in the apartment, but I simply couldn't concentrate on reading; the day seemed endless.

Lala was already waiting when I arrived at the church. There was a little park in front and we went to sit on a bench near where some children were playing. He was in high spirits, not the least perturbed and joking. 'I would never have recognized you if I hadn't known you were coming.'

Of course he was referring to the glasses I was constantly taking off because the thick lenses bothered my eyes. We discussed how to organize my hideouts and Lala offered again to take me in, at least for a few nights. He didn't believe there was any risk involved but I finally got him to admit that too many people knew about our friendship. He was trying to ridicule my fears and, as it turned out, he was right. He thought I was exaggerating both my fears and my importance.

'Do you really think the Gestapo is going to organize a hunt just for you? I wouldn't worry, they have better things to do, you're probably one case in a hundred. But if you won't come to me, how about Elly?'

'That's fine with me, but do you think she will agree?' I asked after a moment's hesitation.

'Yes, I know she will, I've already spoken to her.' Elly had little reason to have fond memories of me. She lived nearby, a woman in her early forties whose husband had got away to England at the beginning of the war: she and their boy of ten had been left behind. It was a mixed marriage, he was Czech and she Sudeten German. I had met her at my favourite café on the river about eighteen months earlier. She was quite good-looking and young-looking too, so much so, that when she told me her age I was genuinely surprised, she looked at least ten years younger.

Elly and a woman friend of hers living in the same apartment house used to organize parties to which I was often invited. After one of these I stayed on and we began an affair which lasted until she discovered that I was also sleeping with her girl friend from the floor above. While the two affairs were going on I had challenging as well as intriguing moments, often wondering what excuse I could give if I happened to meet the wrong woman on the staircase. The degree of suspense was heightened by the fact that Elly's friend was married to a musician with irregular working hours and I had to plan my visits with perfect timing.

Elly took this discovery very badly and our relationship ended there. Somehow Lala knew she was still fond of me and remembered her when he was sorting out likely hiding places. Naturally, because of my bad conscience, I felt a bit uneasy when he told me where I'd be staying and there was the fact of her young son too but I hadn't much choice. When I got to Elly's flat I could feel, however, that she was genuinely pleased to see me. Right away she belittled her chances of getting into trouble: as a German she would be the last person to be suspected of harbouring an escaped prisoner. My stay with her gave me a breather to organize my subsequent hideouts.

It was while I was with Elly that Lala and I realized it wasn't going to be easy to establish a string of hiding places in advance, even though we knew a lot of reliable, trustworthy people. To plan for a long submersion about a dozen places were needed so as to rotate them after a stay of two or three days. Apart from the consideration of safety, I felt that staying longer in one safe place wouldn't be good for my nerves nor those of whoever was putting me up. I could already see the difficulty if children were involved, so my ideal host would have to be single, living alone and preferably someone who would be out of the house most of the day. Given the choice between staying with a man or a woman, I preferred a woman. In general, I thought they had steadier nerves and more guts. If we'd had a previous affair, the past relationship would create a sort of understanding—not that I wanted a woman to sleep with, this wasn't my foremost interest at the time. It was rather the fact that, apart from my close friends, I had always felt more at ease in female company.

Elly's flat was on the third floor and gave me a feeling of claustrophobia, of being cornered if the place were suddenly visited by the police. A good hideout should be on an elevated ground floor or should at least have a balcony and, even better, a second exit. Of course, it was impossible to fulfil all the ideal conditions and I was grateful to anybody who took me in. As a matter of fact, there were never more than one or two safe places programmed ahead and I often didn't know in the morning where I would be staying that night. Most of those who put me up were former girlfriends and I was often sorry that my past amorous activity hadn't been more abundant.

Another and no less serious problem was the scarcity of food. Since I was without ration coupons, I was depriving the person who put me up of his or her own meagre rations. Lala was a godsend in this respect too, and shared the food he was getting from his mother, but I didn't want to meet him more often than was absolutely necessary. We usually saw each other on neutral ground—in the street or a park— after I had phoned him at the studio from a public call-box. The idea was to shield all my contacts from each other so as not to involve more people than necessary. From stories told me during my stay in prison I had come to the conclusion that more people were in jail because they had been implicated by someone else than because of detection by the Gestapo. The larger the circle of people in the know, the easier they made the task for the police.

Incidentally, it was only after the war that I found out how right Lala had been with regard to my relative importance to the Gestapo. It took the police a full three days from my escape to visit my home. When they called, only my sister, Lida, was there. According to her story two men rang the bell and asked if they could speak to me. She answered that I wasn't at home.

'In that case we'll wait for him,' one of the men declared. Lida showed them into the living-room and offered them a cup of coffee substitute. They asked to see my room, went through my desk and cupboard, but found nothing that could give them a lead. When their search was over they installed themselves in the living-room once more, still prepared to wait. After a couple of hours or so they got impatient and asked my sister exactly when she expected me to be there. She told them she couldn't say.

'And when did he leave the house?' one of them wanted to know.

'Oh, some months ago,' answered Lida, pleased with herself and trying not to show it.

This was the only time the police visited my home. Their visit coincided with the delivery of a puzzling letter my stepfather received the same day, informing him that I was arrested and held in prison in Prague. It must have come from the woman I had called out to from

115

the train. This created confusion: on the one hand, my family had information that I was under arrest and in the city and on the other, the Gestapo was searching for me. Given the circumstances, Loiza thought it best to contact my half-sister in Leitmeritz to warn her I might show up there and that the police were on the lookout for me. To find out more, Utta decided to come to Prague. Through her stepfather, Dr Burian, she was able to get a medical certificate saying she needed to undergo some tests at a Prague hospital and with this she got permission to cross the border into the Protectorate.

Her first step was to contact Lala who admitted that he knew where to find me. When visiting my family she managed to smuggle out some of my clothing and underwear and gave it to him for me. In this way I replenished my wardrobe for the coming cold weather.

It was at Helena's flat that I first had to face the problem of how to kill time, not as serious as finding shelter, but I can still remember the interminable hours I spent waiting for something to happen which, when it did, lasted only a few moments, and I was again reduced to waiting for the next event. I suppose this is a predicament for most people on the run and, if they don't learn patience, it often leads to their recapture. There wasn't much I could do to occupy myself. Outings were cut to the strict minimum, no going to cinemas or cafés, of course. Meeting with friends was too risky. In fact, the less I saw of people the better. The centre of the city was for all purposes out of bounds, somebody might recognize me and my moving from one hideout to another was usually done by night—at least for this the blackout was a great help. Walking was preferable to using trams but there were times when taking a tram couldn't be avoided. Holed up indoors and unable to concentrate on reading for long periods, the next best thing was the radio, even if the repetitious and obnoxious propaganda was hard to stomach.

Although Lala was a great help in supplying me with an important part of my needs in food, it wouldn't have been fair to depend wholly on him. One of the biggest problems was to get enough bread. A friend with whom I used to play cards owned a bakery but the shop was in the centre of the city, just the part I tried to avoid. I thought it would be more practical to get ration coupons from him so that I could buy bread close to wherever I happened to be staying. Soon after my escape I spoke to him and he agreed to supply me with a few coupons at a time. He suggested I come to the bakery, preferably when he had a lot of customers in the store and could pretend, should anything go wrong, that he was too busy to look at the faces of the people he was serving. I was to hand him a large denomination bill so he would have to go to the back of the shop to get change and between the returned bills he would slip me enough ration coupons to last for a few days.

After one of my periodic visits, and as I was about to leave, I felt somebody gently pulling at my sleeve. I turned and recognized my young cellmate from Linz—so he had been released as he hoped. Without saying anything we both left the shop and outside he recounted the sequel to my escape. The guards had indeed counted the prisoners before getting them into the vans at the station but for some inexplicable reason the count was good so my getaway was only discovered at the last recount at the prison. There all hell broke loose, enraged guards beat everyone from the transport, but nobody would admit to having witnessed an escape. Marching columns were reconstructed to see from which row someone was missing all to no avail. The formation had been too irregular to start with and, naturally, nobody admitted that it was his marching neighbour who was missing with the result that the guards were plainly at a loss to pinpoint the time and exact spot of the escape.

As a punishment the transport was made to stand to attention the whole night in the reception hall of the jail: the men were assigned to their cells only in the morning. My former cellmate's release came two days later. For showing up late at work several times in a row he had served an eighteen months' sentence. I asked him if he knew what had happened to the Russian colonel but he could give me no news. After the final roll-call they got separated and he never saw him again. We didn't talk for long, I could sense he was anxious to be on his way—he must have realized the chance he was taking just being seen with me.

There was another accidental encounter about this time. It happened between two moves when, for a reason I can't recall, I wasn't supposed to arrive at my new place before a certain hour. It was raining, so for shelter I was forced to ride on trams—less risky than loitering. At a transfer point I noticed Primus standing several feet away, staring at me. Knowing how scared he was of doing anything illegal I didn't want to approach him first so waited to see if he would make a move. Primus hesitated a few seconds, glanced around and came over to me. He said he knew I was on the run and, without my asking, took out his wallet and handed over a wad of bills, telling me it was lucky we had met just then when he could give me something. It surprised me, not because he was a tightwad—quite the contrary, Primus was always very generous—but that he took the risk of acknowledging me. I must admit, at that very moment I would have preferred another gesture like finding a safe place for me: money wasn't the greatest of my worries right then. As it later turned out his present was of great help and financed me over a long period. Our meeting was very brief with only time to exchange a few words before his tram arrived and we parted.

These two unexpected meetings weren't the only ones I had. I knew a lot of people in Prague and it would be only a question of time before an informer heard about me. Finding volunteers willing to offer shelter was becoming increasingly difficult and my sense of responsibility was weighing me down. Slowly, I was forced to the conclusion that it would be better for everybody if I were to leave the city. All in all, I had been hiding in Prague for less than a month but this was certainly long enough for me to know that, at any rate, I wasn't ideal submarine material.

14

In a way, the question of where to go next was solved for me by an unforeseen event—an uprising. It had broken out at the end of August 1944 in the mountains of central Slovakia, about three hundred miles to the east of Prague, in the region where I used to go skiing before the war. The objective was to prevent the *Wehrmacht* from using the mountains as a bastion against the steadily advancing Red Army and also to show the world that the Slovaks wanted to unite once again into a single country. Some Czech elements soon joined the uprising and the Allies began parachuting in supplies.

Conflicting reports as to the success or failure of the revolt were reaching us, depending on whether one listened to German or Allied broadcasts. In view of my precarious situation I decided to try to join the partisans. If for some reason I was unable to make contact with them or, as the German broadcasts proclaimed, the uprising had been crushed, I would fall back on an alternate plan—to hole up in the mountainous region on the border of Moravia, Slovakia and Poland.

I knew the Beskyds, part of the Carpathian range, quite well from my early aborted escape attempt into Poland: from a more recent skiing trip I even had a specific farmhouse in mind. My friends and I had spent a short holiday at this farm and I hoped the owner and his wife would remember me because together with two other skiers I had taken a snow bath every morning.

The advantage this area offered was that it was only some seventy miles from where the uprising was taking place. If the German report of failure proved correct, I would stay on there, make friends among the farmers and wait for the arrival of the Russians. The Beskyds were a little more than two hundred miles away, in the direction of my proposed itinerary. To join up with the insurgents, I would have to cross the Moravian–Slovakian frontier again but this didn't bother

119

me too much: the farmhouse where I hoped to stay was approximately ten miles from the border so I could take my time and choose the best moment for crossing. Anyhow, I felt I had become quite adept at this, discounting my last attempt.

Getting to the mountains was a more difficult hurdle. It would be hard to walk the whole way so I planned to divide the trip into two parts. The first, by train, would bring me close to the Beskyds and corresponded to about two-thirds of the total distance: the rest would have to be done on foot. I considered taking the train a slighter risk than walking, even if I was exposing myself to possible police checks. Should that happen I'd pull the emergency brake and jump out, as the train I proposed to take would be a night one.

The last hideout I used was a country home belonging to my mother's friend Hilda. It was about twenty miles to the east of Prague and in the right direction so it seemed to me a good starting point. Another advantage was that it could be reached by a local train leaving from a small station and one less likely to be controlled. On a Saturday afternoon, among crowds of weekenders heading for the same popular resort, I took the train to Hilda's house. It stood in a fairly large, fenced-in garden among pine woods, away from the road and with no immediate neighbours, a perfect spot for my purpose. For a whole week I lived there without venturing outdoors, switching on a light or cooking a meal. On the last day Hilda arrived with the warm clothing I had left with her and some food for the trip.

The following morning I set out very early while it was still dark and made my way along minor roads to a medium-sized provincial town. I got there in the evening, shortly before the arrival of the train that was to take me to the mountains of eastern Moravia. Everything went off without a hitch—there was no check at the station when I boarded, nothing during the trip, nor when I left the train. It couldn't have been easier and in one night I saved myself a ten-day hike. I got off at a junction and could have taken another local train to bring me closer to my objective but I didn't want to tempt fate again and decided to walk the rest of the way.

It was a beautiful, crisp morning. I was in high spirits because the dreaded train trip had proceeded so smoothly. The first leg of my walk led me through a rich, densely-populated, farming region. There was a lot of local traffic—horse-drawn, people on bicycles and on foot—most of it heading to a small town which was also my goal. After a while a farmer driving a cart reined in and invited me to climb aboard.

He was a chatty fellow so I let him talk but from time to time had to say something too to keep the conversation going.

'You aren't from here, are you? My guess is that you come from Prague,' he ventured. My accent had evidently given me away. The Czech spoken in north-eastern Moravia is different from that of Bohemia. His remark didn't particularly reassure me as I wanted to blend in with the local population. He started questioning me about the situation in Prague, which he said he had once visited. He wondered how people in the city were coping with food rationing. In his region, he told me, it wasn't a major problem but they had quotas to deliver to the authorities and he made it plain he wasn't too pleased about this. Coming close to the town, I jumped off the cart and thanked him for the ride.

'Hey, wait a moment,' he said and rummaged in his bag to give me a piece, or rather a square block, of raw bacon dusted with ground paprika and a slice of light rye bread, something I hadn't seen for a long time. City bread was dark and the texture like putty—press it with a finger and the mark stayed forever.

I skirted the town and from then on was on fairly familiar ground—the foothills of the Beskyds. There was a decided change in the look of the countryside, it was getting poorer as I progressed. Forests became more numerous until they covered most of the land and farms were often clearings surrounded by woods. Instead of the road, I now used paths and when these came to an end I walked through the woods, avoiding the inhabited clearings. When it began to get dark I saw that I had badly underestimated the time it would take me to reach the farmhouse. Since I couldn't very well arrive there in the middle of the night I prepared a bed of evergreen branches and spent the night in the woods, my second one *en route*, from when I left Hilda's house.

I finally arrived at the farmhouse the following afternoon. The farmer didn't remember me but his wife did—after a reminder of the snow baths. As a precaution I used the name of one of the boys from our previous visit. Could I stay at their place for a few days? They agreed but I had to promise to register in the morning with the police in the valley. They were known to put up holiday makers, their land was small so they supplemented their income in this way. I assured them I would, hoping to find some pretext for not having to do so. By postponing it for a bit I would be gone by the time they discovered the lapse. There was an additional complication, I would have to sleep in

121

the attic but that suited me. A German woman with a young child was already occupying the room our group had used. As I later found out she was married to a Czech and they lived in an industrial centre to the north. She was staying at the farm because she was afraid their town might be bombed: her husband joined her at weekends. The woman was a friendly, plump creature and I didn't think her presence represented any real danger. She spoke Czech with a strong accent and for my part I pretended I understood some German but didn't speak it. As a reason for my stay I explained that I suffered from tuberculosis and had just spent some time in a sanatorium—with a few days left before reporting for work I wanted to be in healthy, mountain surroundings. As for my ration coupons, I told the farmer I had used them all up but was willing to pay for my meals at the current black market prices. This he agreed to with the understanding that his German guest was not to know about it.

After breakfast I pretended I was leaving for the police station but as soon as I was well out of sight I headed in the direction of the border to reconnoitre. Going through the woods I came across a young man piling wood at the edge of a clearing and I started talking to him under the pretext of wanting to buy some eggs. I noticed him first sizing me up and then he nodded, he could let me have half a dozen. We went together to his house where he gave me the eggs and invited me in for a chat and a smoke. The cigarettes he had were Slovak. I told him I would like to buy some if he had any to spare but he hadn't.

'Would you know where I could get hold of some?' I inquired.

'Well, that's difficult as I can only get them for myself occasionally,' he explained. Cigarettes were an excellent item for barter, they had been rationed almost from the beginning, the ration getting smaller and smaller. Just then I was more interested in getting in touch with the smuggler who would show me the way across the border. I didn't want to insist on the subject of cigarettes but when I was leaving he pointed out a house on the other side of the valley.

'You see over there, that farmer might have some. Tell him I sent you.'

I made my way across the valley and met an elderly man in front of the house. The place looked somewhat neglected with firewood carelessly stacked and tools lying about. I said, by way of introduction, 'Your neighbour sent me. I've run out of cigarettes, could you spare some?'

For a moment he didn't answer and just looked me over thoughtfully. 'I don't have any for myself. You're from Bohemia, aren't you?'

'Yes, from Prague.'

'And how is life there, do you get enough food?' Well, it wasn't great I told him and said how lucky he was to live where he did. 'You people here don't know what rationing means.'

We started talking about this and other things—he too was taking his time. Then I mentioned my cover story of the sanatorium and the fact that I would be returning shortly. I smoked, I told him, even though I wasn't supposed to, but if I could get hold of a larger quantity I would use it for barter. Cigarettes bought more in Prague than here.

Wondering if I was getting anywhere with him, I made a move to bid him goodbye. As we shook hands he said, 'Well, if you are still going to be here for a bit I'll see what I can do. Anyway, come around tomorrow if you can.' This I promised to do feeling I now had a foot in the door.

When I got back to the farm where I was staying I told them the police employee who handled registration wasn't there and I would have to go down again. The next day I retraced my steps to the smuggler. All he gave me was a single packet of ten cigarettes. I guessed he was being cagey but then I wasn't about to make him any confidences either, at least not for the time being. There was another day of coming and going with me still putting off my farmer host. This situation certainly couldn't go on. On my fourth visit I decided to lay my cards on the table.

'Do you have the cigarettes for me?' I bluntly asked.

'No, it's too risky. You might get stopped, there are border guards all over the place. They'll want to know where you got them and I'll be in trouble.'

'In that case,' I ventured, 'why don't you show me the way into Slovakia and I'll buy them for myself.' Now it was out. He looked at me for what seemed a long time before answering.

'I was wondering about you when you told me you were from Bohemia. There have been a few of you passing through lately trying to get to Slovakia. Now they are coming back.'

'Why is that?'

'The Germans sealed off the region, so they couldn't get through to join the uprising. If that was your intention too you'd better forget it.'

123

'But I have to try, I can't return home. The Gestapo is after me.' So there it was, I had delivered myself into his hands.

'You can't go home, is that it?' he repeated as if he wanted time to let it sink in. Going to his cupboard he took out a bottle of slivovitz, of Slovak origin as well, I noticed, and a couple of tumblers.

'Have a glass,' he said. 'And where are you staying now?'

'Here and there, nobody really wants me, I have no papers, you see. Often I have to sleep in the open but it's getting too cold for that.'

'Well, I can't have you here,' he said after a while, 'I'm too close to the border and the guards pass by sometimes.' Then, as if it were an afterthought he added, 'Come back tomorrow, I'll see if something can't be arranged.'

Walking back to the farm I asked myself if I had done the right thing in divulging my situation to the smuggler. He might very well alert the police: they could be waiting for me tomorrow. Well, it was done now, he did seem trustworthy and I had to find an ally somewhere.

Before lunch the next day, telling them I was going home, I said goodbye to my farmer host, his wife and the German woman, then returned over the familiar route to the smuggler in a strange mental state, half full of hope that my situation would now improve, half in fear that I was walking into a trap.

'I have news for you,' he greeted me, leading me out towards the woods. There were two men standing behind a thicket as if they were waiting for us. I froze.

'Don't worry,' said the smuggler, 'I know them.' They didn't look like farmers but they weren't border guards either, more like factory workers or plain city people, both a few years older than me.

'Tell him what you know,' said the smuggler addressing the two. They had just fled from Slovakia after taking part in the revolt. It was crushed, the Russians didn't or couldn't help, more or less the same story as the Warsaw uprising. Now they were heading home. The old fellow suggested they take me back with them to near Brno but they didn't think they could, they might have to go into hiding themselves. However, unlike me, they had papers and hoped to manage.

'But you can have our guns,' one of them offered. 'We can't take them along.' I didn't think the rifles would be of much use to me on my own, so we wrapped them in old burlap sacks and buried the bundle in the woods some distance from the house. I asked for details of what

124

had happened in Slovakia but they couldn't tell me much—they thought the Germans had known about the uprising before it really got started and were prepared for it. From the conversation I understood it was the smuggler who had helped them to cross the border some time ago. While we were digging the old man went to the house and brought back provisions for their journey. A little later the men set off.

The news about the uprising was a let-down though I had half expected it: I would have to reconcile myself to staying where I was. On that point the old chap had an idea. He knew of a young farmer by the name of Ondrej who had met and married an ethnic Hungarian while doing his military service in southern Slovakia. All this happened before the war, he explained: the marriage hadn't lasted very long. It seems the girl couldn't get used to life in an unfamiliar and isolated place, so she left him. Since then he had been on his own except for a niece who came every second day or so to keep house. With no near neighbours the smuggler thought Ondrej might appreciate having someone to give him a hand.

He pointed out the route I should take, saying it should be less than an hour's walk. I thanked him for his help and suggestion—it certainly sounded like an ideal location. On my way there I planned how best to present my case. I made sure that I arrived at the farm late in the afternoon and, walking up to the fellow working by the barn, asked if he was Ondrej. He nodded.

'I'd like to talk to you, but finish what you're doing first.'

'It may take a while, you'll have a long wait. What's it about?'

'I have time, I'll come back in an hour or so.' We left it at that and I went off to explore the surroundings since it suited me better this way. It would be getting dark fairly soon and he might at least let me stay overnight if things didn't work out. The farm was certainly isolated, the closest house was about half a mile away and was probably where his niece lived—there were no other buildings in sight. A perfect spot, but how was I to persuade him to let me stay? I wandered around until dusk. Ondrej was indoors when I got back.

'I came to see if you have any eggs for sale,' was my feeble opening, 'I could give you cigarettes in exchange.' The smuggler had let me have a few packets plus a bottle of slivovitz which I had in my knapsack and intended to bring out later when I saw how the conversation was going.

'At the most I've a dozen or two, nothing worthwhile,' he

125

answered. The old story, he was sizing me up, not committing himself. To keep the conversation going, I offered him a smoke.

'Oh, you have Slovak cigarettes,' he remarked seeing the package.

'I've just come from there,' I lied. 'I'm not a black-marketeer, I want the eggs for myself.'

'Things don't seem to be going too well,' Ondrej reflected, half in statement, half in question. I passed on what little I had just heard.

'But how did you get here, you're from Bohemia, aren't you?' It was the standard question and needed no answer.

'If you're hungry, stay for supper—it will only be eggs and potatoes.'

I quickly accepted: it was the opening I had been waiting for. When we were half-way through our meal I reached into my knapsack for the slivovitz.

'Maybe you don't have any food but I see you have the essentials, liquor and cigarettes,' he remarked with a grin. We finished supper and went on talking until the bottle was half empty and both of us were feeling the effect.

'If you like, you can sleep in the hayloft, it's too late to go anywhere. I'll get you up in the morning.' When I woke, I could hear Ondrej busy outside. Looking through an opening in the roof, I saw that the sun was already high, so I dressed quickly and went down.

'Hello, so how did you sleep up there?' he asked.

'Like a log, but why didn't you wake me up?'

'I thought you were tired. There wasn't any rush, was there?' True, there wasn't, but I still had the difficult conversation ahead of me.

Ondrej had thoughtfully left something for me on the table: after breakfast I came out and helped him with some chores. I wondered if I was much of a help—I had no idea about farmwork—but he accepted my efforts with good humour. He was a friendly person, probably in his early thirties, easy going and joking a lot; tall, blond and of such a strong build that all work seemed effortless. The livestock consisted of three cows, a couple of goats and plenty of chickens. As I later learned, he had two fairly large fields of oats that he worked with a pair of cows. It was a primitive farm with no running water and the lavatory was an outhouse: no wonder his bride hadn't adapted to this type of life.

Supper that evening was the same fare as the previous night and we finished the slivovitz, still without my broaching the subject uppermost in my mind, although I had fully intended to. The following day was the same except that I met his niece, a girl of about sixteen who cleaned the kitchen, did his laundry and, fortunately, mine as well. We had nothing to drink, an omission I intended to remedy. There was still no mention of my leaving and I was content to have it that way—life here was so much better than in Prague.

15

Two nights later, over a new bottle picked up from the same source, I finally admitted I was in trouble, saying nothing about my being an escaped prisoner so as not to scare him off, only that I had been conscripted for work in Germany and had come to the mountains to hide. Ondrej said he suspected something was wrong but hadn't wanted to probe. The fact that I had come from Slovakia was already an indication. However, he didn't mind my staying for a while. He enjoyed our evenings together as it was a change to have somebody to talk to. With my half-confession I thought it wiser not to admit to my own name and kept the one I had assumed when coming to the area.

Ondrej agreed to pretend I had been sent to him temporarily by the Labour Office as I had been suffering from TB and was not yet fit enough to work in a factory: it wasn't a very convincing explanation for my being there but we couldn't come up with a more plausible one. If I was to be of any help I had to move around the farm and the fields, not stay hidden in the loft, so there was no way to avoid being seen by some of the neighbours. We hoped that with a bit of luck my presence would pass without comment. The police station was down in the valley, a good hour and a half's walk, and the locals had almost nothing to do with it. Ondrej said it was undermanned and mainly concerned with the illegal border traffic. Later on, whenever there were visitors I tried to keep out of the conversation without appearing too unfriendly.

While I was with Ondrej the Soviet armies were coming closer, at certain points to the north-east they were only some hundred and fifty miles away. In the evenings we listened to news broadcasts from everywhere, anything we could pick up, then compared reports to figure out how long it might take them to reach us. It didn't seem there would be any fighting in the Beskyds themselves. The Red Army would probably advance through the Moravian Gate—a stretch of rolling country to the west of us—forcing the *Wehrmacht* to retreat to avoid encirclement. In time of war this was a good place to be with the food situation so much better too. Even after the obligatory deliveries of farm produce Ondrej was left with enough. It may have been a monotonous diet but we never went hungry.

He and the surrounding farmers were taking advantage of this relative surplus to trade with townspeople who came to visit them on Sundays. As money had little value the transactions were done on a barter basis, most often with cigarettes for currency. One of the more regular buyers was a man by the name of Kupka, a Czech employee from the Labour Office in the nearest town. He was on good terms with the country people and seemed to know the ropes for smuggling whatever he bought on the farms. He usually paid in cigarettes, didn't quibble over prices and bragged that he could get half a dozen pigs into town at one go if only the farmers weren't too scared to let him have them.

I had heard of Kupka but we met only after I'd been at the farm for perhaps a fortnight. At first, I kept out of the way: I wasn't too keen on seeing him, he had an official position so was more of a threat to me than the occasional neighbour. Ondrej assured me he was all right: he knew that Kupka had sometimes intervened when a farmer's son was called up for forced labour. Anyway, I couldn't avoid him forever, he was in the habit of coming irregularly, staying for supper and sometimes overnight. Kupka often arrived with a bottle and during an evening of drinking would talk against the Germans in a very outspoken way. As the evening wore on he would grow bolder, promising to get a few men together to make up a guerrilla band as soon as the Russians came a bit closer. He wanted to round up those 'shepherds'—a derogatory Czech term for Germans—open their bellies with a butcher's knife and brand their women and children with swastikas, just like cattle.

On one visit Kupka took me aside and spoke again about forming a partisan group, saying he knew of a few other young fellows, eager and absolutely dependable. One had been a sergeant in the Czech army and could show us how to handle weapons. Was I interested in joining them? He insisted he'd be willing to buy the guns if only he knew where to get hold of some.

I just kept quiet: to me he was a big mouth, and somehow his talk never sounded convincing. If I let him know about the two buried guns I was sure he would do something stupid, get himself arrested and compromise Ondrej and me. I hadn't told him much about myself, or rather my cover story. I admitted only that I'd had some minor trouble with the Prague Labour Office but all that was settled now because of my stay in the sanatorium. Kupka thought I was being too optimistic and offered to settle the question for me once and for all.

'Just give me your labour book and I'll have it fixed up officially at the exchange,' he promised. 'Better be on the safe side.' The labour book was a pocket-sized, passport-like booklet that had to be produced along with identification papers to prove that the bearer was lawfully employed—that is, had an authorized job. To get rid of him I said I would have to write for mine, that I didn't have it with me. Of course, I no longer had one, not even in my rightful name, and hoped he would forget the whole thing. No such luck, the next time he asked me right away if I'd received it yet.

This insistence made me uneasy. I asked Ondrej to tell Kupka that I had left. My lack of trust seemed to upset Ondrej and we almost had a scrap over it. He kept repeating that my suspicions were unfounded, he was sure all the fellow wanted was to be helpful, but since I insisted, he agreed, in the end, to give him the message. From then on I arranged to be nowhere in sight whenever Kupka was expected. However, he soon returned unannounced. He was happy to find me back, he said. He had some important information to pass on from a conversation he had overheard in his office. The SS was planning a clean-out operation in the area. According to Kupka, the authorities had got wind of the fact that more and more men were hiding out in the Beskyds and they feared another uprising like in Slovakia.

'When I heard it I immediately thought of you. If you're interested I could arrange a new hideout with a couple of guys who're keeping away from the Germans.' My answer was that I would think about it and let him know. After Kupka left we talked it over. I was somewhat sceptical about this new development but, on the other hand, it could be true. Ondrej thought it better to accept the offer.

'If they find you here we'll both be in trouble. When this blows over you can come back. It won't last long, they can't spare the troops just to flush out a handful of people.' He repeated he felt there were absolutely no grounds for distrusting Kupka: even if he happened to be a braggart, he was dependable. Whenever possible he was willing to help and no farmer who had black-market dealings with him ever had any problems. Kupka showed up two days later. I told him I had decided to accept his proposition.

'I'll come and fetch you the moment I have it organized,' he promised.

'If you have too much for your knapsack, leave some things here. You'll be back as soon as the round-up is over. Your new safe place is fifteen miles away over the mountains, so travel light,' he suggested.

Naturally, I wasn't too happy to be leaving, the farm was a perfect spot and I was lucky to have found it. The new hideout might not be as good. Moreover, I felt uneasy and didn't relish delivering myself into the hands of Kupka. I considered myself a loner and shied away from situations where I couldn't decide on my own what moves to make. However, if Kupka's information was correct, there wasn't much else I could do. To stay on indefinitely would only endanger Ondrej and maybe his niece as well; going to another of my contacts wouldn't be of much help if the SS started combing the entire region. In another area I would have to start all over again and there was no guarantee I could do as well. I felt nervous and apprehensive, so much so that I had a dream, a real nightmare—I was arrested again. It was so vivid my own screams woke me up. Kupka reappeared a day later.

'Everything is fixed up,' he announced, 'get your things.' The young girl had done my laundry and now Ondrej quickly prepared a meal for us plus something for the trip. We had to count on at least six hours' walking.

It was a clear and nippy evening as Kupka and I made our way down into the valley on paths I now knew well. We scarcely exchanged a word. Further down, the cart track we were following led over a wooden bridge and on towards a road. Against the railing of the bridge, leaning on it, I could just distinguish the outline of a figure. The man seemed to be watching the stream below and turned as we came up to him.

'This is a friend of mine,' said Kupka. 'He knows the road better than I do. He'll lead us part of the way.' My suspicions were immediately aroused, he hadn't mentioned anything about a friend before, that was odd.

'I've brought along a gun in case we run into a patrol,' said the stranger. 'Do you want it?' holding it out to me.

'No, I don't think so,' I replied. If we suddenly got stopped I didn't feel that a revolver would make much difference. The fellow put the gun back inside his coat and remarked, 'As you wish. We'll follow this road for a couple of hundred yards and then turn off into the woods.'

My strong feeling of unease wouldn't leave me: I made up my mind to scram at the very first opportunity. Just then Kupka excused himself saying he had to piss and jumped across the ditch. His friend and I had gone on for another twenty or thirty steps when two figures with revolvers leapt out on to the road from behind thickets and somebody else pinned back my arms.

An ambush! My first reaction was to be furious with myself, how could I have been so stupid! I should have run away the moment I saw the man on the bridge. My wrists were handcuffed before I could make a move.

'Does he have a weapon?' I heard one of them asking in German. Kupka's pal came up and frisked me. I was told to advance with a man on either side, one behind and a fellow in front still with his revolver pointed at me. Around the bend a dark car was parked on the side of the road. They ordered me into the back with two of the men and we drove off. I guessed I was being taken to Vsetin, a town about twenty-five miles away, probably the nearest Gestapo head-quarters. Not a word was said during the whole drive. My brain was working feverishly. Kupka was an informer, how could I warn Ondrej? Why hadn't I been arrested on his farm? Obviously, they didn't want to discredit Kupka but let him continue to spy. When would they arrest Ondrej?

Their silence was fortunate, it left me free to prepare myself before interrogation. I would have to say who I was, they would find out anyway: I had been fingerprinted for my ID card and again by the Gestapo in Feldkirch. What about my stay in Prague? How did I get from there to the mountains? Where had I stayed before meeting Ondrej? How had I got hold of clothes? I mustn't mention a single name. What about money? I'd have to get rid of it. No, I'd say I had always had it on me, nobody asked me to hand it over when I was arrested at the Swiss border. The questions and my answers were running back and forth through my head. The handcuffs were hurting, they were too tightly set, cutting off the circulation in my wrists, but I wouldn't ask them to loosen them.

With my mind wholly taken up with the interrogation to come, the drive seemed short. When the car stopped somewhere in the centre of town I was told to get out, led past a guard standing in front of the entrance and brought to an office on the second floor where two men were waiting.

'Do you speak German?' one of them asked. I nodded.

'Stand here in front of the desk,' said the man who seemed to be the boss. The two men who brought me up from the car were dismissed. We were now three in the room, the boss, the man at my side and myself. A picture of Hitler was staring at me from the wall behind the desk.

'Your name, age and place of birth.'

'Are you German?' the boss asked in surprise when I had given the information.

'No, Czech.'

'What were you doing in the mountains?'

'I was hiding there, I have no papers.'

'Why don't you have your papers? Do you mean you've left them at the place where you were?'

'No, I am an escaped prisoner.'

'What's that?' he exclaimed. 'You had better tell me the whole story. Sit down,' he ordered after telling the other man to take off my handcuffs. I felt that my best, and really only, tactic was to tell him everything that could be checked. It was important to give the impression that all my answers were straightforward as if I had nothing to hide.

'Have a cigarette,' he said, handing me the matches. I thought that his cigarettes and Kupka's 'currency' must be of the same origin. The boss seemed to have decided to use the soft approach. So much the better I thought—if only it continues this way.

Starting with the flight to the Swiss border, I told him of my arrest in Feldkirch and the transports in the direction of Prague. I described my escape at the station exactly as it happened but naturally without mention of the role the Russian colonel had played. To explain my clohes I invented a story that I had hidden what was too bulky and might have slowed me down when I set out for Switzerland. As I later had time to realize, it was lucky that my interrogator didn't jump on the fact that I had left in July, carrying unseasonal clothing, but he let it pass.

'Where did you hide them?' the boss interrupted me.

'On the racetrack, below the stands.' My choice of the racetrack wasn't so far-fetched, it was on the exit road in the direction I would have taken and all horseracing had been stopped a long time before.

'How far is the racetrack from the station?'

'About a two-hour walk. I don't know the exact time it took me, I had no watch.' I was afraid he might butt in with more questions. To my relief he told me to continue.

'Then I waited around there until morning, went back to Prague and to the place where I knew I could buy ration coupons from black marketeers.' He didn't seem to know the city: I explained the location, a well-known spot in the passageway near the Crown snack-bar where I had occasionally bought a few coupons in the past. One just had to approach any of the characters hanging around. It was also a dangerous place because it was known to the police who raided it fairly often and many of the doubtful types were actually informers.

'Go on with your story,' the boss ordered. Once I had my ration coupons, I told him, I started out on my trek to the Beskyds, sleeping in deserted barns, haystacks and woods. The length of my supposed walk from Prague had to correspond roughly to the time I'd spent hiding in the city. Here and there I threw in the names of some towns I was supposed to have crossed or skirted but I couldn't name all the villages, as I'd walked only by night. My advantage lay in being able to describe a trip I had done many times by car whereas the German had no idea of the geography of my itinerary. Suddenly he came out with a question I had been expecting for a long time.

'Where did you get the money to buy the ration coupons?'

'I always had it on me. Nobody ever asked if I had any money or told me to empty all my pockets and only my sides, chest and arms were ever frisked.' This was a blatant lie, but I figured he had no way of verifying it. As if to prove my statement I reached into my back pocket and gave him what was left of the banknotes from Primus. The two men looked at each other, obviously feeling uncomfortable, and didn't pursue the matter. So far, the interrogation seemed to be going well, no discrepancies and nobody to contradict me—what luck that I was alone. The difficult part was still ahead, however—my stay at Ondrej's.

When it did come up I stated that he seemed a decent but uncomplicated person who accepted my cover story, that is, about having tuberculosis and my recent discharge from the hospital. He was so trustworthy he hadn't even asked to see my papers and believed me when I told him I had registered with the police. A confrontation with Kupka could have shown a discrepancy in my allegations but his name wasn't mentioned. Had there been a confrontation, my prepared argument was that Ondrej had introduced us, he had never hidden me from him. However, the entire proceedings were conducted as if Kupka had never existed.

When the interrogation was over it was already getting light. The assistant, silent as ever, handcuffed me again and led me to a sort of cell on the same floor. It looked exactly like any other I had been in—actually better than some—with bars on the frosted glass window and a reinforced door with a spy hole. There was a small table, a stool and an iron bed with a mattress but no running water or washbasin and a chamber pot under the bed. I assumed they considered me an important catch since I was alone there. Without doubt they intended to keep me away from other prisoners to prevent me from communicating with the outside world.

Late that morning I was taken out of my cell and led into the same room where once again I had to face the Gestapo boss. He seemed sleepy and tired from a tough night. Next to him a man was sitting at a typewriter. I was asked to repeat the whole story I had told him but in greater detail. This time I was expected to furnish exact dates and descriptions of the places where I had slept on my trek to the mountains, where I got food, the hour I bought the ration coupons, what the man looked like and so on. Once again I explained it was difficult for me to furnish the names of all villages where I'd slept: I'd arrived before sunrise and left in darkness. As for where I'd bought food, I offered to show him the shops if they would take me to them.

So far, the boss hadn't detected any contradictions, even if some of the explanations sounded far-fetched, especially the one about getting hold of my clothes at the racetrack. His assistant dutifully typed everything I said, from time to time perhaps correcting the sentence structure. The interrogation proceeded in a quiet and businesslike fashion without a raised tone or threats. Within a couple of hours we had finished. What bothered me most were my handcuffs. They were kept on most of the time I was being questioned and in the cell as well—even when I was eating—and were only removed when I was taken to the lavatory, but then the door was left open. Sitting on the john with a guard looking at me made me feel rather foolish. My captors certainly seemed worried that I might try to escape again. On my third day in Vsetin the boss asked if I knew how to type and when I said I did he told me to write down my story in my own words with all the details I could remember.

'You have the whole day to do it, take your time.' With that he took off my handcuffs and, before leaving, offered me a cigarette. The guard sitting in the corner of the room reading a newspaper looked bored and rarely glanced at me. I typed for most of the day and was only able to relax during my meal. All the time I was conscious of the fact that the story I was putting down had to coincide in detail with my earlier statements. When it was finished the guard called in the boss who told me to initial each page and sign the last one. Another cigarette was my reward. The guard handcuffed me again and I was taken back to my cell.

The next day and the day after I heard nothing from anybody. Meanwhile I was racking my brains for a way to warn Ondrej but couldn't see how since I never had even a glimpse of another prisoner. As I hadn't been sent to the local prison, it was clear that the Gestapo intended to keep me isolated from all contacts. Kupka had to be an important informer for them to go to such lengths to protect him. Occasionally I heard shouting so knew that there were other prisoners in the building and wondered where they were kept.

On the third day after my last written statement I was again brought before the Gestapo chief. He motioned me to sit down in front of his desk and there was the same offer of a cigarette. They must appreciate my attitude I thought, although at the same time I was apprehensive of the moment when the kid gloves would come off. Next to the boss was the man who had typed my first declaration.

'We'll go over your testimony once more but this time you must try to remember absolutely everything.' I could see that he had the initialled papers in front of him, plus the text of my first statement. Every step after leaving the station had to be gone over while he insisted again on times and locales, what I had paid for the ration coupons, how many and so on. I had to repeat the places where I had slept and describe the weather. Questions were raining on me at such a rate that at moments I was sure I had made a mistake, but if so, neither man noticed. While alone in my cell I had had time to reconstruct my story in my mind down to the most minute details. Their ignorance of the geography worked in my favour: when I named a locale it was a place where I had actually been at some time and I pretended not to know the names of others, either because of darkness or saying I had skirted them. My confidence grew as the interrogation progressed. I hadn't been caught out in a single contradiction. After several questions and answers, the boss would dictate the gist to the secretary. This went on for most of the day. Again I had

136

to initial each page and sign the final one. Back in my cell my handcuffs really started to bother me but even if the Gestapo didn't trust me, at least I was never abused.

My statements must have sounded logical because that was the last time I was questioned. However, what worried me most was the knowledge that Kupka was still informing and Ondrej trusted him. On the whole, I was much calmer now than at the beginning of my arrest, in spite of cursing my bad luck in falling into the hands of an informer and my own stupidity in not having seen through him. Looking back, the way he talked, the ease with which he was able to pursue his black-market activities should have made it clear that he had connections with the police. Ondrej and I had grown careless and before long I would have been discovered one way or another. As for my immediate future, I hadn't the slightest idea what would happen: most likely I would be sent back to Prague.

16

Free travel was evidently the only perquisite the Gestapo was prepared to offer their charges: about a week after my arrest a guard came to my cell and told me to get ready for a trip. He stood in the doorway watching my preparations then escorted me to another Gestapo officer already waiting with a prisoner and hand-cuffed the two of us together. We were driven to the railway station where a wagon sat on a siding. The conductor opened a compartment and locked it behind the three of us. The other prisoner and I, still attached by handcuffs, settled ourselves on one bench while the guard sat facing us. After a short wait we felt our car being coupled to a train and start to move. Several stops later passengers began filling up the corridor, staring enviously at the three of us through the glass door. Our guard was in civilian clothes and I suppose we looked to them like regular travellers. There was an attempt or two to enter the compartment until an irate man tried to force the door.

'You have no right to keep the whole place for yourselves when we have to stand out here,' we heard through the glass. In reply, my companion and I lifted our hands to show the handcuffs. The disgruntled passenger gave us a surprised look and quickly left: from then on our door was avoided as if we had the plague. Once in a while a furtive glance was cast in our direction when somebody passed along the corridor. The guard kept his eyes on us as we weren't permitted to talk. I never found out who my co-prisoner was: he looked very young. All I remember of him was his carrot-red hair.

Our train reached Prague late that evening and pulled in at the station I had escaped from—what irony, I had come full circle. We were marched over to the Gestapo headquarters, a stone's throw away. Inside the former bank building I remembered the large ornate staircase in the hall. The guard from Vsetin released the handcuffs, turned us over to the man on duty and I was taken into a nearby room to wait. Within minutes a man came in.

'So, you are the one who got away. I wondered when we would be seeing you again.' Then a second joined him to have a look at me. My escape must have caused some uproar and this didn't augur well for my future. The two started joking about me in pronounced Viennese accents and both looked surprisingly like caricatures of Jews in anti-Semitic magazines: I wondered if they hadn't been chosen precisely for that reason. After a while another plain-clothes man arrived and took me down into the cellar which, in early days, had probably served as a safety deposit vault. There were about a dozen cells separated only by bars—like jails in American westerns—completely bare and without windows; all were empty. With no one to talk to, I lay down on the tile floor and tried to sleep.

When a uniformed guard opened the door, I had no idea of the time of day. He told me to follow him. We walked up a flight of stairs to the entrance hall and took a lift. I must have been in this lift once before, I thought, when I was hauled in at the time of the Heydrich affair. I was taken to a large room on the first floor. Long benches in rows stretched most of the width of it, some already occupied. The men were sitting five feet apart, all facing in the same direction, with a Czech policeman on guard. Prisoners were not allowed to talk to each other or turn around. They simply had to stare ahead at the whitewashed wall in front. As somebody later told me in the van, in prison jargon this room was known as the cinema: it served as a waiting-room for before and after interrogations. The procedure was to bring in the prisoners from the two jails in the morning and have them wait there for vans to return them in the evening—a sort of clearing house. There were no backs to the benches and the bench board was rather narrow. After only a couple of hours it became extremely uncomfortable and often a prisoner had to sit there a whole day without being called for questioning at all. This was my experience that first day in the cinema—something of an anticlimax to have waited all those hours in suspense without finding out what was in store for me. There were moments when I felt I would willingly expose myself to a beating just to know.

During those endless hours on the bench I had plenty of time to think. The joking remarks of the two Gestapo men the night before had made me realize that this time my situation was serious. Well, if I had to die now there was nothing to be done about it. I was sorry for myself, thinking I was rather young, although there was a certain satisfaction in knowing I had taken advantage of life's pleasures for as long as I had—at least that nobody could take away from me. The idea of death itself didn't frighten me much, it was too abstract. The overall sadness I felt was more like regret, looking for the last time at something familiar, something I enjoyed.

Every so often someone came to the door to call out a name: a prisoner stood up and left for questioning while another was returned to the bench, often with a face showing signs of beating. Considering the state in which some of them were brought back it seemed ridiculous for me to be in a rush. It would be hard to say which was the more difficult to put up with, the dragging hours of sitting or the waiting in suspense. All inmates dreaded both but either was preferable to the interrogation itself.

Men arrested at any time during the day were also delivered to the cinema. The seasoned inmates referred to these new arrivals as 'fresh from civilian life'—a literal translation from Czech: as they were not yet broken in to this interminable waiting they got restless and exposed themselves to abuse. All in all, I spent a number of days in the cinema and was once witness to the following exchange between a newcomer and the policeman on guard. The man, who happened to be sitting just in front of me, raised his hand as a sign that he wanted to say something and the guard nodded to go ahead.

'Sir, would you please be so kind as to tell me what time it is?' he asked in a most respectful tone.

'What,' exclaimed the guard, his face twisting into a smirk, 'are you pressed for time? Are you by any chance catching a train?' At this sally the old hands all burst out laughing.

But to go back to my first day in the cinema: by the time it was growing dark outside the waiting-room was completely full. Some of the late arrivals who couldn't find room on the benches—the space of five feet had to be strictly adhered to—were ordered to stand facing the wall. At last the policeman told everybody to stand up. A schupo guard called us out into the corridor where we were made to form a marching column, taken down the stairs and loaded into police vans waiting at the entrance. By the time the doors were shut we were packed in like sardines. That was the moment to talk to each other and exchange information, but the trip was short, at the most a quarter of an hour.

When the doors were opened we found ourselves in the courtyard of the main Prague jail, St Pancras. With shouts and clubbings the prison guards herded us into the reception hall to be counted. Then an order was given to empty all our pockets and we were frisked. Those who had anything left in theirs, even spectacles or a handkerchief were beaten up. All orders were given in German, the guards didn't care if they were understood or not. After this the old-timers were returned to their cells and the new arrivals left standing. This waiting could last several hours, even late into the night which was how it was when I checked into St Pancras. Finally, our sorting out began: I was taken to the top floor and shoved into a cell. The door slammed behind me and I had to grope my way through bodies lying on the floor.

'When were you picked up?' asked a voice in a whisper. New-comers were popular as everybody was eager to hear the latest news, especially how the war was going. There was disappointment when I said I was only a transferee from another prison. I found a free spot near the door and settled down with my jacket under my head—there was no blanket but it wasn't cold. A low-wattage bulb was left on all night and once in a while I heard a click at the spy hole.

A bang on the door woke me—it was time to get up. I discovered we were six in this cell which was the size of the one I had occupied alone in Feldkirch, approximately seven by fourteen feet. Next to the door was a lavatory but no washbasin; opposite the door, high up, a barred window. The long wall had a collapsible cot fixed to it and on the other side a small table and a stool. The cell senior hurried to instruct me on what to do when it came time for roll-call: he alone had to stand facing the entrance while the rest of us turned towards the window wall. As soon as he called us to attention we were to make kneebends in unison with our arms extended forward and keep it up until the door was again locked.

Cells were being opened all around us. From next door I heard in a clipped military tone, 'Ein Saujude angetreten'—one dirty Jew present. Somebody told me the man was a German Jew from Breslau, a former officer and veteran of the First World War. Then it was our turn, the senior calling out 'Achtung. Sechs Schweinehunde angetreten'—Attention. Six dirty dogs present—while the rest of us began kneebends.

My cellmates represented a cross section in age, social background and reasons why they had ended up in jail. The senior was a middle-aged school-teacher accused of listening to foreign broad-

141

casts. Another was a butcher who had killed a pig illegally, the third a peasant from a village in central Bohemia who had done something similar. The fourth was a former university student who had left his job in Germany without authorization, while the last, a fireman from somewhere near Prague, was alleged to have formed an underground organization with other firemen to prepare an uprising.

The daily schedule was simple. After roll-call breakfast was served, a bowl of black, substitute coffee without sugar and with an individual loaf of bread, a sort of bun about three inches in diameter which had to do for the whole day. It was of a sticky consistency but this had a certain advantage—after each bite it was possible to press the loose crumbs back into the loaf so that nothing was lost. After breakfast the prisoners scheduled for interrogation were brought to the reception hall and the rest led into the courtyard for exercise—alternately running and doing kneebends. When the guards were in a bad mood or if Germany had lost another battle the exercise was changed to running once or twice around the yard in a bent-knee position, an exercise that left even the young inmates completely exhausted. I don't know how the older ones managed it. The guards stood over us and if anybody touched the ground with his hands he was immediately clubbed with the gun butts held ready for the purpose. Prisoners who fell from exhaustion were beaten until they got up again. It was useless to plead, the guard would shout, 'What, you say you can't? You just don't want to, you swine!' and hit all the harder. Sometimes an older inmate had to be carried off by his fellow prisoners. No wonder these recreative outings were dreaded.

On our return to the cell there was a general clean-up: the floor had to be washed two or three times a week, without soap, of course. Once a week our growth of beard was shaved and, since this was done with the same blade for several dozen men, it was known as skinning. Showers were also once a week. The cake of soap the size of a match-box was greenish with a lot of sand and was referred to as UWA DÜ after the initials stamped into it. Rumour had it that it was made from the fat of gassed concentration camp victims but whatever the ingredients, it was impossible to clean oneself with it. By the autumn of 1944, it was common knowledge, at least in prisons, that large numbers of prisoners were being sent to gas chambers and the bodies cremated.

After chores came the so-called free period. We took it in turn to sit on the single stool while the others paced or just stood: leaning against the wall or squatting on the floor was forbidden and the bed was folded back against the wall during the day. There was another place to sit down—on the lavatory seat. This was used in preference to the stool because it was in the corner next to the door and at a dead angle to the spy hole. Without a washbasin, our drinking water had to come from the lavatory: this wasn't as bad as it sounds—the lavatory was kept spotlessly clean.

I wouldn't know if this routine and treatment resulted from the personal initiative of the warden, an SS captain, or if it was ordered by the Gestapo to break down the physical resistance and morale of the prisoners. In any case, St Pancras was markedly different from the prisons I had known until then. When I told the inmates how I had been treated in Feldkirch they were incredulous and remarked that, from my description, it sounded like a health resort.

During our free period the main subject of conversation was when our first meal would be when we got out of prison: the theme of food was such a popular and persistent one we could discuss it for hours. Among the dishes, roast pork or roast goose with sauerkraut were by far the favourite choices. Knedlik, a type of dumpling, was most often mentioned as a side dish. The roast pork had to have the skin left on, scored into little squares and golden brown, sprinkled with caraway seeds. The goose had to be darker, with crisp skin; the knedlik should be light with big holes, like French bread. It had to be thinly cut, preferably with a thread; some wanted a clear gravy, others liked it thickened with flour. The favourite for dessert was a plum knedlik, similar to a Chinese won ton, stuffed with a whole unpitted plum, thrown into boiling water, then served swimming in melted butter, sugar, cottage cheese and cinnamon. The butcher was an expert cook and used to explain to us in great detail his tricks for making this dessert successfully. Obviously, the richer and heavier the food, the more popular it was with us.

Another good subject to pass the time with was guessing how long the war would go on. Often the most fantastic rumours, or 'latrines', as they were known, were circulated. These usually originated from the new arrivals during the trip in the vans from the Gestapo head-quarters to the prison. Anything new was immediately communicated to neighbouring cells with the aid of our eating bowls placed approximately opposite each other on either side of the wall—a whisper on one side had enough resonance to amplify the sound on the other. The best spot to do this was above the lavatory, safe from the spy hole.

Lunch, consisting of porridge or potatoes with a nondescript gravy, was distributed at 11.30. The cell senior lined up our six bowls near the door and, while kneeling, passed them on to the trusty out on the catwalk who ladled in the food. Everything had to be done at breakneck speed because the guard could lose patience and slam the door before all the bowls were filled. Meanwhile, the other cellmates had to be facing the window doing kneebends as they did at roll-call. If a prisoner happened to be absent for interrogation his portion was put aside for him but he then lost his evening serving of watery soup as only one bowl was issued per inmate. The evening meal was distributed at about five o'clock, except for Sundays when we got nothing. The soup wasn't very filling so it was important to keep a bit of bread from breakfast to soak in the liquid.

Some men had food package privileges but nobody in our group did. It was customary for prisoners receiving food packages to share them with their cellmates. The cell senior wasn't necessarily the oldest but in most cases the man who had been the longest in a particular cell. Unlike the concentration camp system, being a cell senior in a jail carried no special advantages, it could even be a disadvantage. A senior was responsible for seeing that each man received his portion of food and, in the case of a shortage, was expected to share his own with those who didn't get their ration. His only privilege was the use of the cot but that had to be given up if there was an old or sick inmate in the cell. Guards didn't care who the cell senior was as long as he spoke German. Ours, the school-teacher, was both the oldest and the one who had been there longest. A prisoner's length of stay most often depended on how many others were involved with him and how long it took the Gestapo to interrogate them all and bring the case to a close. Thereafter the most likely outcome for the prisoner was a transfer to a concentration camp. In the teacher's case, if I remember well, there was quite a bit to unravel: he had been translating the BBC English broadcasts for a score of his neighbours.

Nobody had any way of knowing how long he might be kept in prison before being shipped elsewhere. In the majority of cases there was no court verdict and the Gestapo didn't bother to inform the person concerned what the punishment would be. Prisoners were sometimes allowed to write to their families when they were about to be sent elsewhere—but without knowing their destination—and they

144

were at times permitted to write from a new camp or jail.

To illustrate how things were handled, the following incident is worth mentioning. One of our fellow inmates, the fireman, returning one evening from interrogation, joyfully told us he was to be released the following morning. The man in charge of his case had told him a decision had been reached that the accusation against him was unfounded. This seldom happened and all of us were very happy for him. Our cell had a special possession—a small piece of lead from a pencil, hidden in a crack between two floorboards. The knowledge of its existence was passed from occupant to occupant and the original owner long since forgotten. One of us—it may have been the student—had a banknote hidden in his clothing. We all scribbled a phone number or address on it so our families could get news through the fireman after his release: some of the men in our cell had been in jail for nearly a year without a chance to advise their families of their whereabouts. Everybody was in high spirits but had we known at the time where he was really being sent our hopes would have suffered a terrific letdown. Some time later the fireman and I met again and recognized each other immediately, even with our shaved heads. He was released from St Pancras all right, but not to go home. We couldn't help having a good laugh about it.

One day some new arrivals were put into the adjacent cell. When our neighbours 'telephoned' us with the latest news from the outside I discovered that Eric, Loiza's cousin from Vienna, was among them. From Eric I heard that Feli had been arrested. The charge against Eric was the one I had expected—*Rassenschande*—but aggravated by the fact that he had fiddled with Feli's papers. He could so easily have avoided his present troubles by marrying her before the Germans took over Austria instead of always postponing the wedding. Later on I had a chance to get to know Eric better. What seemed to have bothered him a great deal was to be imprisoned on the site his grandfather had donated to the city on the understanding that it was to be used for a park.

17

My turn for questioning came about a week after my arrival in St Pancras. I had barely taken my seat in the cinema when I heard my name called out and went to the door. There stood a heavyset man in his late thirties whose blue eyes scanned me from head to foot. With a gesture, he indicated I was to follow him to the lift. Was he to be my interrogator? On the top floor we got off, still in silence, and went into a large office, rather luxuriously furnished with an oriental carpet, paintings on the walls and an impressive mahogany desk, all probably taken over from the original owners of the bank. A secretary was typing at a smaller desk near the window. She looked up when we entered. 'He will be here right away,' she said and continued typing.

I was still waiting near the door when a middle-aged man with duelling scars came in through another entrance and quickly crossed the room, completely ignoring the interrogator. He stopped in front of me, shouting in my face, 'That was a lot of crap you told our people in Vsetin. You'll see, we'll straighten it out here in no time,' and began pummelling me with his fists. His sudden action stunned me, I hadn't expected a big shot to take part in physical punishment. I stood there, neither trying to avoid the blows nor raising my hands to protect my face. By the time I had recovered from my surprise his blows were getting less harsh until they stopped altogether. The methods of the Prague Gestapo were certainly different from what I'd experienced before.

After he had finished the thrashing, the scar-faced superior lost interest and made a sign to the interrogator to take me away. We left the office, went down a flight of stairs and along a corridor where he ordered me to turn and face the wall. I heard a door open and close and he disappeared, leaving me to stand there for what I thought was

146

about a couple of hours. All this time people were walking by me but since I couldn't see their faces or anything other than the blank wall in front of me, the shouting, the cries and sounds of blows coming from all directions were that much more impressive. It seemed as if everything was carefully staged to condition the prisoner.

At last the door opened and my interrogator—much later I found out his name was Bauer and his title *Kriminalrat*, criminal counsellor —told me to enter. There was another man in the room with him. 'You heard what the boss said so I advise you to tell us the whole truth this time.'

And so it began. First we went over my trek to Switzerland. That was easy, I just repeated everything I had already stated and written in Feldkirch and Vsetin. He listened without comment or interruption; the other man was taking notes, hardly ever looking at me. Anyway, this part of the story didn't seem to interest them very much, but, as I expected, the atmosphere changed when I started recounting my escape from the station. From then on I was frequently interrupted. The storm really broke when I reached the part about leaving my clothes in a spot I proceeded to describe. From my betting days I was familiar with the track but I would have had trouble pinpointing an exact place had they decided to take me there.

'Do you think we are so feeble-minded as to believe this invention—what do you take us for?' With that, both men started pummelling me as if I were a punching bag. I had to go back to the moment when I left the station and resume my story. When I repeated my testimony about hiding my clothes, Bauer stopped me.

'We won't get far this way. Bend over that chair.' I did as he ordered. His companion began whacking me with something like a riding crop.

'We'll stop as soon as you tell us the truth about where you got the clothes.'

'I have no other story to tell you, it's the truth,' I was trying to answer between the blows. How long the beating lasted I have no idea nor do I recall how I got back to the cinema. The only thing I clearly remember is that that night the cell senior let me sleep on his cot.

Next morning I was again called for questioning. I was made to wait in the cinema until the afternoon when Bauer came to fetch me. Walking to his office he advised me, in an almost fatherly tone, 'You'd better be more reasonable today.' Even before the interrogation started I was made to bend over the chair, then my wrists and ankles were tied together with leather thongs so I couldn't move.

'You can begin telling us your story again,' Bauer ordered. Word for word I think, I repeated my version: by that time I would have managed it even in my sleep. Blows were raining on me without interruption until I heard something tear: it was the seat of my pants that gave. This must have somehow dampened their ardour and the thongs were released but I had to go on with my recital. When I was brought back to the cinema, sitting on the bench was torture. According to my cellmates, my back looked like steak tartar. My companions didn't ask for details, they were used to it, practically everybody looked like that after at least one of his interrogations, usually the first. It was essential to break the prisoner's morale as quickly as possible and this was probably best achieved by sheer physical terror.

The Gestapo was not above using a prisoner's wife in order to obtain a confession. They either threatened or sometimes, if the case was important enough, actually brought in the wife and beat up the husband in front of her. Normally, they would get the information they wanted before that point because, if the police had gone to the trouble of arresting the woman, they wouldn't release her after the confrontation: she had seen too much and could talk about it.

Torture may have been used to extract information about associates as yet unidentified, not as a punishment proper—at least I never came across anybody able to recount a first-hand experience of that sort. There were too many concurrent cases to be solved and torture, as such, meant a waste of time. If the Gestapo wanted to punish, the person was simply sent to a concentration camp with an annotation on his file: the guards there took special care to see that it was carried out.

The following day I was left in peace but I knew I wouldn't be left alone for long: my story about the hidden clothes was too far-fetched to be credible yet I had to stick to it. To change it would have been a fatal mistake so during my next interrogation I declared to Bauer, 'I can't give you another version because there isn't one. I've told you the truth. If you let me, I'll show you the place where I hid the clothes.' Determined to bluff it out I continued, 'You want me to give you names of people who helped me. I never asked anybody for help. I knew what would happen to them. Kill me if you don't believe me but I can't change my testimony.' Somehow my outburst quietened him down. Either he had decided to believe what I declared to be the truth or he realized I wouldn't change my story: without accomplices he couldn't confront me with a conflicting account.

From then on Bauer allowed me to continue my version without too much interference—he probably had more important cases awaiting him and little time to waste on me. After that session I was called in once more to sign a written declaration which was no different in content from the one I had signed in Vsetin.

My cellmates were curious to hear how things had gone. I gave them the gist of my declaration but of course refrained from divulging the true story. Their attention was soon diverted by other things and I went back to sleeping on the floor. From my own experience—regardless of what one might imagine to the contrary—the longer one sleeps on a bare floor the worse it becomes, hip bones get sorer and sorer. Less than a week after I had signed the declaration, a guard came at breakfast and told me to get ready—that meant another transport.

In the reception hall there were about fifty of us lined up for the trip. After the checking-out formalities we were counted and taken to vans parked in the courtyard where more guards surrounded them, a seemingly unnecessary precaution as the loading was being done within the prison walls. Inside the van we were free to speculate on our probable destination. Instead of the main station we ended up at a smaller one—the starting point for northbound traffic, which seemed to indicate Terezín—and were put into an ordinary wagon on a siding away from the regular passenger trains. Much later the wagon was coupled to a normal train. At the station closest to Terezín, the one I knew from my trips to meet Franta, our wagon was shunted off.

When we marched by the ghetto I was back on familiar ground, though somehow, the fence cutting it off from the road looked higher and more imposing now. Leaving the ghetto behind us, our column crossed a bridge and continued straight ahead down a cobblestoned way with tall trees on either side. In the darkening sky it was just possible to make out the outlines of the Small Fortress. The end of the road was blocked by a large wooden gate; thirty-foot-high brick walls rose above the moats, their tops covered with tall, rough grass. Although it was known as the Small Fortress, those brick walls seemed at least half a mile long.

Once the column passed over the moat, the gate was swung open on a tunnel about fifty feet in length. Inside the tunnel several guards stood in front of a door in the right-hand wall. The only illumination came from the electric light shining through the window beside the door of the recessed guardroom. On the far side of the entry tunnel our column was ordered to halt in a sort of square which was partly enclosed by elongated, one-storey buildings and, at the furthest point, opened on to a larger space with a few trees and two taller houses. Some twenty guards armed with sticks came towards us.

'Empty your pockets, everything out of your pockets,' they shouted in German, hitting out at those who stood on the edge of the column. We quickly did as we were told: the ground was soon covered with handkerchiefs, cakes of soap, eye glass cases, bits of string, toothbrushes, even a tin of sardines. When our pockets were emptied we had to advance another thirty feet, leaving our possessions behind us.

'Form rows of ten.' For not executing the order fast enough there was more clubbing. The next command was to about-turn to face the tunnel entrance. Over the mouth of it and following its arch was written in Gothic script on a whitewashed background ARBEIT MACHT FREI—something like Work Gives Freedom. Meanwhile, the gate had been opened again. Work battalions of different strengths—*Arbeitskommandos*—were marching in, surrounded by guards shouting at them to hurry. Columns of inmates in grey uniforms with round caps ran past us. The left breast of each jacket had a coloured mark crudely painted on it—most often an inverted red triangle—and the trousers had a painted stripe down the outside seam. Some wore a spoon stuck in the top buttonhole. Whenever a detachment passed a guard, regardless of his rank, a prisoner in front shouted, 'Caps off!' All turned their heads towards the guard, at the same time smacking their caps against their right thighs. Once past him, a new order was shouted, 'Caps on!'

One after another of these eerie, ghostlike columns went by us in the twilight, halted not far away and immediately formed up to be counted. From the speed with which they proceeded, it was easy to see they had had practice: the column, in straight lines and five men deep, was ready in no time. The counting, called *Appell* in German, went quickly and the formations were soon dismissed. Once more the guards turned their attention to us. By now all our pockets should have been emptied.

We were made to pass one by one through a double row of guards, each wielding a hazelnut stick about an inch and a half thick, the kind normally used for herding cattle. As a new arrival passed between the

150

guards in the line-up, he was hit over the head and shoulders. At the end of the row each man had to stop in front of another guard to be frisked. If a pocket lining hadn't been turned out to his satisfaction it meant a further beating and the rest of us made doubly sure that all pockets were really turned out, that we hadn't forgotten a single one. Just watching what happened to those ahead of us was enough, no written instructions were needed. Suddenly, the guard doing the frisking exclaimed, 'Look, we have a poet here. So, you want to write poems.' He was holding up a pencil for everybody to see. The guards forming the rows rushed to surround the culprit, hitting him until he fell, then kicking him.

'We'll teach you about writing poems,' they shouted. Those of us still waiting to be frisked were furtively getting rid of more incriminating objects. Finally, the poet was allowed to get to his feet. As the rest of us were advancing towards the row of guards, I noticed a few lumps of sugar on the ground. Fortunately, the SS were getting bored by the time my turn came and I passed without trouble.

It was now dark and searchlights were turned on us until the last man had been checked. We had to move again, passing through another tunnel with a mirador above it and into a pentagonal courtyard where, to the left, were four or five huge newly-built cells. The whole transport was put into a centre cell which was completely empty except for two lavatories and some washbasins by the entrance. The weak light-bulbs were hardly adequate to illuminate the cavernous space. There were puddles here and there on the concrete floor caused by the rain coming through a row of leaky skylights.

Some of us chose to sit along the walls, others walked in a large circle around the cell, avoiding the puddles and causing the fine cement dust to swirl in the air. We had come to know each other a little and small groups formed discussing the usual subjects: how the war was going, how long we had been in jail, food and so on. Some of our group had already experienced life in the Small Fortress and told the others what to expect. Their description didn't sound very encouraging.

When the time for morning roll-call came we were told to line up outside in front of the cell. No eating bowls had been issued so there was no breakfast: there had been no supper the previous evening either. Decidedly, the camp authorities were following to the letter the well-known maxim of so many totalitarian regimes, 'He Who Doesn't Work Doesn't Eat.' Later that morning we were marched to the

151

Kleiderkammer—the clothing-room—and stood outside in ranks to be called in one by one to exchange our civilian clothing for the grey uniform. My neighbour's came with a little round hole in the back of the jacket, a hole with singed edges, half an inch in diameter, just below the shoulder blades. It was easy to guess the fate of the previous wearer. In addition we were each issued with an earthenware bowl, a spoon, two footcloths, a pair of wooden clogs, a blue striped shirt and underpants, a thin blanket and one sheet. From the clothing-room we proceeded to the showers. There, before being able to wash, our heads were shaved. After going through all this treatment it was rather difficult to recognize the men I had talked to the evening before.

Now that our transport could be considered a full-fledged part of the camp population, everyone was looking forward to a meal. Unfortunately, our hopes didn't materialize—we still had to be assigned to different cells according to the type of work expected of us: this caused us to miss the midday meal.

My new cell was just beside the one where our transport had spent the previous night. Except for three tiers of wooden bunks along the walls, it was identical to the old one, even down to the puddles. Most of the bunks were already spoken for, with bedding and eating bowls on them, so newcomers had to find space on the floor. There weren't too many free places to choose from: either close to the lavatories where the smell was nauseating or near a puddle underneath one of the skylights. I opted for the latter which turned out to be a mistake.

Each cell was under the supervision of a senior, called *Zimmer Kapo*, who was responsible to the SS guards. His main duty was to line up the inmates for the morning and evening roll-calls. He had a helper, the *Stubendienst*, a sort of janitor, and both were exempt from any other work. The rest, some four hundred men, were loading coal at a railway junction about twenty-five miles from the camp.

That evening we received our first meal—a piece of dark-grey bread of a consistency even more putty-like than the bread in the Prague jail and a bowl of soup served from wooden buckets carried into the cell. We lined up in Indian file, each with our bowl into which a prisoner ladled the precise quantity of liquid: on that occasion it was called barley soup. After wiping out the bowl with a piece of bread, we were given black substitute coffee sweetened with saccharine. The distribution was always done in alphabetical order and each day a new letter came first. Ladling out was considered an art and had to follow a precise procedure. When the server dipped the ladle into the bucket he had to turn it with a fast movement three times clockwise, three times counter-clockwise, quickly scoop out the liquid, and the ladle had to be full to the brim. If these rules were not observed the prisoners had the right to ask the cell senior to replace the server, who was permitted to feed himself only after everybody else had had their portion but the privilege of wiping out the bucket was his. The stirring of oatmeal or barley soup wasn't as important as with potato, cabbage or turnip soup—in that case the server could cheat and the person served end up without a single piece of solid food.

At the beginning of my stay in the Small Fortress a slice of bread of about ten ounces and a matchbox-sized bit of either margarine or jam was served with the morning coffee. Later, the breakfast bread was abolished and the margarine distributed with the evening meal until this too was cut out. As a result, we went out to work with only the hot coffee substitute for breakfast, unless one had enough will power to keep part of the evening bread for the morning but very few could: besides, there was always the danger that somebody might steal it.

That second morning, after roll-call and breakfast, we lined up into marching columns in front of the cells. By now each of us knew his approximate place in the line-up so it went faster and there was less confusion and little time lost. A prominent, that is, a prisoner with special privileges, in black uniform with highly polished riding boots, took overall charge of the line-up and counted us. When everything was in order he reported to the SS guard supervising the procedure, who double-checked. Everything was written down on sheets on a clipboard and the different work columns started to march towards the gate.

In principle, the SD was in charge of the administration while the SS supplied guards to go out with the labour battalions as well as to control the perimeter of the Fortress. Since both sections wore the same uniform it was difficult at first to distinguish which branch a particular man belonged to.

We soon found out that marching in wooden clogs was an art. The foot cloths, if not properly wrapped, slipped down and this in turn made us lose our grip on the clogs. Another difficulty was that each row had to walk as closely as possible to the row preceding it. The reason for this closed formation was that a short column needed fewer guards but it meant we had to step into the exact spot the foot of the man in front had just left. A lost clog usually resulted in a mix-up which the guards sorted out by hitting the nearest prisoners with their gun butts. Since the last row suffered most from this treatment, the oldtimers tried to keep to the front of the column.

The prominent didn't go out to work with the battalion. His only task that we knew of was to line up the prisoners and make the preliminary count. He didn't live with the rest of the inmates, I was told he had private quarters somewhere in the camp. He never exchanged any words with us so we didn't know who he really was except that he was German. There were also prominent prisoners of a different kind in the Fortress but the ordinary inmates rarely saw them. They also lived in private cells: usually they were known personalities or their immediate relatives. They were not expected to work either, wore civilian clothes and their heads were not shaved. There were only a dozen or so in the camp and they may have been considered a sort of exchange material in case an important German fell into Allied hands.

Our first destination was the railway station in Leitmeritz, some four or five miles from the camp. Our work battalion marched out from the fourth courtyard, through the tunnel below the mirador, and into the square where we had been frisked on arrival. There a squad of guards surrounded us, the camp gate opened and we marched out, passing by the Terezín ghetto and into open farmland. Since we weren't yet used to marching in wooden clogs, our column extended too much, making the guards shout '*Aufgehen, aufgehen*' ['Walk up, close up']. When the column shrank until we were touching the behinds of the preceding row with our bellies, this didn't suit them either and they yelled, 'Don't fuck him in the ass.' With these conflicting orders our part of the marching formation extended and shrank like an accordion.

After crossing the Elbe, we had to march through the town though there, in front of the population, the guards behaved better. We crossed the town square, passing the house where I was born. At first this gave me a strange feeling but later I grew apathetic as if I had lost my identity. The person born there seemed to be somebody I had known only fleetingly in the past. At first I wondered what my sister, Utta, would say if she saw me among the prisoners or whether she would even recognize me: later I stopped looking for her.

A special train was waiting for us at Leitmeritz station. After a thirty-minute ride it brought us to the shunting yard. That journey, but even more so the return, was one of the best moments of the day. The train was heated, it was a shelter from the weather and we were resting. Moreover, on the way back there was the added pleasure of anticipating the hot soup awaiting us. At least for a while our bellies would be filled.

Our work was to load coal into freight cars. Shovels were issued, then we were separated into groups of between ten and twenty men, each group assigned to a coal pile. Depending on the guard overseeing us, the work had to be done with more or less speed and there was no time to pause or rest. The shovelling had to go on for the whole day except for a brief respite at noon, but without food. The tempo with which we had to fill the cars would have been hard labour under normal circumstances—for underfed men unused to this type of work it was debilitating.

Some guards were better than others and let us cheat a bit: as long as we went through the motions they overlooked the fact that the shovel was only half full. Of course, others knew this trick and wouldn't tolerate it. Sometimes a guard would single out a particular man, watching his every move. It was not uncommon for a prisoner thus picked on to become desperate and throw himself under a passing train, an action hardly appreciated by his fellow workers who had to carry the body back to the camp on their shoulders while keeping step in the column. There existed an inflexible rule, the same number of prisoners checked out of the camp in the morning had to return, alive or dead, at the end of the day. If anyone was missing it meant only one thing, an escape.

An attempted escape—if it was one—happened only once during the time I was in the coal-loading brigade. That day, when we got off the train on the return trip and formed into columns, the count was short by one man. A few of the guards went back to search the cars and found the missing prisoner asleep on the floor or perhaps just pretending to be. He was hauled out by the enraged guards and beaten into such a state that he had to be carried back. I didn't know the man nor learn what finally became of him—nothing mattered as long as it didn't happen to me. A year or so before my arrival, I was told, two prisoners who did escape were brought back a couple of days after their getaway. Wearing cardboard placards with a crude verse, '*Ha, Ha, Ha, Ich Bin Schon Wieder Da*' [I am back again], they were hanged in front of their fellow inmates.

During my time, in March 1944 I think it was, three young chaps escaped one night by loosening the window bars of a cell in the fourth courtyard. It remains a mystery to me how they could have done it in a cell of some four hundred or more without anybody noticing: they must have had accomplices to distract the attention of those around. When the absence was discovered, the rest, out of fear of reprisal, began banging on the door, shouting to the guard in the mirador who gave the alarm. One of the escapees was wounded and captured. With two other men and one woman prisoner he was shot the next morning in the presence of the assembled inmates of the yard as a warning that at the next escape every tenth man of the cell from which it happened would be shot. The other two men made it to Prague where they were soon picked up and sent back. Rojko chose seven other prisoners and ordered them to stone the unfortunates who had been tied to a ladder. When he noticed that one of the pair was still alive, he picked up a heavy stone and smashed the man's skull.

After each full day out in the rain and cold, we were utterly exhausted. There was still the roll-call to get through. We all longed for it to be over quickly with no frisking to make us lose time before going back to our cell to be fed and have a whole night of rest. A wonderful prospect, peace until morning—no guards, no beating, no marching, no shovelling, no rain. The cell became synonymous with heaven.

⋙ 18 ⋘

I hadn't been in the Fortress for long when dysentery broke out. As soon as we were returned to our cells there was a mad rush for the lavatories; the queues grew longer every day, men impatiently shifting from one foot to the other while those by the lavatories banged on the door. After a while some dropped out, it was too late. The stench in the cell became unbearable, not only from those who had soiled their pants in the line-up but also from the men who had dirtied themselves at work—no facilities were provided in the shunting yard.

Some who were desperate lowered their pants in a corner, but for that they were beaten up by the others. Of course, there was no toilet paper or paper of any kind. Footcloths were sometimes used and washed in one of the basins. Two lavatories and six handbasins were never adequate for four hundred men, even without an epidemic. There was nowhere to dry the footcloths, they had to be worn wet to work the next day: if left in the cell they would have been stolen. Soiled underpants were more of a problem. Those who washed theirs had to wear them and hope for fine weather. The grey drill uniforms, worn in all seasons, were soon soaked through on a rainy day.

Shortly after the dysentery outbreak I became ill myself. My clothes never had a chance to dry. Out at work they got wet and at night the puddles underneath the skylights, fed by the constant, late-autumn rains, spread until they reached the floorspace where I slept. In the beginning I tried to push against the sleepers lying around me but later, exhausted by work, the water no longer woke me. Eventually I developed a temperature and gradually began to lose the little strength I had left. Worse still, in spite of the enforced physical exertion, I lost all appetite, stopped lining up in front of the food bucket and gave my portion away, keeping only the bread.

157

Conditions in the cell were such that I hadn't formed any close friendships: friends supported each other both morally and materially and, given the circumstances, it could even be dangerous to be a loner. A young man sleeping next to me took my bowl and brought me my portion of bread. After a couple of days of this the cell *kapo* let me visit the dispensary. When I got there, there were already too many waiting and the guard in charge, seeing how many we were, chased us all away.

In the state I was in I wouldn't have lasted for long and knew I probably wouldn't make it on the march to Leitmeritz the next day. Anybody falling out of line and unable to keep up risked being shot. Unbelievable as it may sound, something completely unexpected happened at roll-call the following morning. My name was called out, I was told not to join the labour battalion and to stay in the cell. So apathetic was I by that time I wasn't even grateful for the reprieve. Later, a guard came to take me to the *kleiderkammer*. There the orderlies took my bowl and spoon away, I returned the sheet and blanket and undressed as ordered, quite unconcerned about what might happen next. I waited until another trusty came with my old clothes, the pants still split from the beating in Prague. Then I was brought to a cell where several prisoners, in civilian clothes like myself, were waiting.

They were all wondering where they would be sent but I didn't care—I just stretched out on the floor and half rested, half dozed. As the day progressed the cell filled up until I had barely enough space to lie full length. At some point I vaguely remember a guard coming in and distributing cards and a few pencils, saying we had permission to write to our families. I must have put down what was uppermost in my mind—some warm clothing—and addressed it to my sister in Leitmeritz. When writing the card, it didn't occur to me that I had no idea where I was being sent or if I would be permitted to wear what I was asking for.

Late in the afternoon we were ordered out of the cell to form a column. As night was falling when the guards marched us to the station they were edgy and during a mix-up in front of the cars I got close to an SS officer known for his brutality, one we called Horse Head, who was using his gun butt left and right to put some order into us. When I was hit I must have lost consciousness because the next thing I remember was that the train was already in motion and a fellow prisoner was asking me if I felt better.

The transport went back to Prague, to St Pancras prison. For some reason I ended up in solitary, at least that's what it seemed to be. The cell was underground, without a window and I was alone but to me it felt more like a resort hotel. It had a cot, was warm and dry and there was no work. For days I sat at the table and slowly recuperated. I hadn't the slightest clue as to why I was there or why I had been brought back at all. Maybe I had been returned to be confronted with Ondrej, or could it have something to do with Helena?

I had been in the basement cell on my own for more than a week when the door opened and a guard shoved in two men talking to each other in German. Since they had just been arrested I had to tell them what was expected of them—the rules of the house, so to speak. Somehow, they gave the impression of knowing each other from civilian life. However, it would be highly improbable for two men arrested in a connected case to be in the same cell unless there was a special reason. This made me wary and put me on my guard. To their question as to why I was there I mumbled something non-committal and let it go at that.

'He's a rough-looking type,' commented the older man to the other in French, 'just look at his face and the way he's dressed. Doesn't he look to you like a common criminal?' Listening to them talk I decided not to let them know I understood. Actually, I didn't like them either, regardless of whether I trusted them or not. Their behaviour was unusual, people didn't act like that in jail. The next day I was on the verge of telling them it was pointless speaking French in front of me—I spoke it better than they did—when a guard came in and brought the older one a food parcel. This only re-awakened my mistrust.

I was still groping in the dark as to why I had been returned to the jail when one morning I was ordered out of the cell. The prison vans had already left, so it was too late for an interrogation—this was really puzzling. The guard led me through a labyrinth of underground passages into what I thought might be the Justice Building in front of the jail. Could it be a trial, I wondered? My case wasn't important enough for that and I rejected the idea almost immediately.

Most inmates I had met never had a trial. They were simply imprisoned and no prisoner was ever told for how long. Quite a few didn't even know why, none knew where they would ultimately serve their punishment and, of course, the great majority had no idea what awaited them. Later, when I was back at camp, an inmate working in the administration office told us that some of the prisoners' files carried an annotation—J, KA or XYZ. It was known that J meant Jew since not all Jews were sent to the ghetto: those who were with us were there for punishment. KA stood for *Kein Ausgang*—no outside work—which could mean somebody not supposed to do heavy work, or someone with a record of an attempted escape. Nobody could figure out XYZ—there were about a hundred of them. The significance of these initials became clear only in the very last days of the camp's existence. After the war it became known that there were at least two other categories, NN—*Nacht und Nebel*—night and fog—person to disappear without trace; RU—*Ruckkehr unerwünscht*—return undesired. After my guard had unlocked and re-locked several heavy doors, we emerged from the underground passageways into a building of long corridors with many doors. The guard stopped in front of one and ordered me to enter. A man was sitting behind a desk in the small office.

'Go into the next room,' he said in German. It was all very mysterious and made me uneasy. From what little I could see of the other room through the half-open door, it looked like a place reserved for torture. The three of us went in and there my fears dissolved immediately for, in the middle, stood a large, old-fashioned camera. The man had me sit down on a stool, hung a placard around my neck, click, and that was all, except for finger-printing.

Back we went through all the underground passageways to my French-speaking cellmates. Would this be the beginning of a new interrogation? I couldn't believe that I had been brought back to Prague just for a photograph and finger-prints—in any case they could easily be obtained from my identity card on file. Ondrej was on my mind a lot and I was sure it had something to do with him. It worried me that he would have to suffer for helping me and, more than that, by trusting Kupka he might endanger others as well, but there was no way of warning him.

The ostracism I'd had to endure from my cellmates didn't last long for the same day, after my picture-taking session, we were given a new inmate, a young German in trouble with the draft authorities. From what I understood, he hadn't presented himself for his medical when called by the draft board: whatever he had done or omitted to do wasn't very clear, but here he was, in jail. The two of us hit it off well and at last I had somebody to talk to. One thing, however, was again puzzling me, was this supposed to be a German cell? If so, what was I doing in it? Was it simply because my interrogations had always been conducted in German?

One morning a guard opened the door and pointed at me, 'Get ready, bring your things.' I quickly said goodbye to my friend but couldn't resist the opportunity of addressing myself in French to the other two inmates. Unfortunately, the guard chased me out before I had a chance to enjoy their reaction.

My stay in St Pancras had been beneficial: it gave me time to regain my strength and I was once more thinking of an escape, firmly determined not to go back to the Small Fortress or another camp. Sooner or later the camp meant death whereas, by trying to escape now, I might have a slightly better chance of surviving. The opportunity would present itself during the transport if, as on my earlier trip there, the wagons used were normal passenger cars. Either I could bolt from the column when we were being marched through the station or wait until the guard was distracted, break the window and jump out when the train wasn't moving too fast.

This time there were about two hundred of us going through the formalities prior to transport. Since I was now familiar with the procedure I was able to avoid anything which could land me in trouble. At last we were ready to board the vans but at that moment an SS officer came into the hall to call me out of rank.

'You got yourself into quite a mess,' he told me after I had followed him into his office, 'but I have a message for you,' he said looking at me intently. 'Your sister has been given permission to visit you in the Small Fortress.' The importance of the message didn't register with me at that moment, all I felt was disappointment. Now my planned escape attempt from the transport would have to be postponed in order not to complicate things for Utta. Getting out of the Fortress seemed impossible and the work battalions were too well guarded.

It came to me only later, when in the train, that a visiting permission was an unheard-of privilege. None of the inmates I had ever spoken to had had a visitor, either in Prague or in the Small Fortress. So far I had received the same treatment as everybody else, why was I now being singled out? I hadn't done anything to warrant this concession. How had Utta managed to get the permission and, anyway, how had she found out I had been arrested again? The card I had written on the day of my transfer from the camp to St Pancras had completely slipped my mind.

When my companions found out I had been in the Small Fortress

161

before, they avidly asked me what it was like and what to expect there. I tipped them off as best as I could while at the same time wondering about myself and the forthcoming visit. A fleeting idea came to me that the whole story of the visit was a hoax, but no, that wasn't likely either. I still couldn't grasp the news. For one thing, I wasn't particularly looking forward to the event: on the contrary, I was a bit apprehensive. I hadn't seen myself in a mirror for a long time but was conscious of the fact that I must certainly look quite different from when we had last met. My French-speaking cellmates had left me in no doubt on this point.

When our column marched through the entrance tunnel and into the square, the scene hadn't changed at all.

'Empty all pockets,' the guards shouted at us. With the tip to my travel companions, our pocket linings were already turned inside out. The inspection seemed to take less time than on my first arrival, in spite of the larger transport. It was still light when it was finished and, instead of being sent to a cell, we went straight to the *kleiderkammer* to have our clothing exchanged.

While we were waiting I heard my name called out. Ahead of the other prisoners I was brought inside and issued with a special uniform. The jacket seemed to have been made from a dark-blue winter coat and looked like those I had seen before on trusties—even the red triangle on my left breast was painted with greater care. Compared to the majority of inmates I looked pretty smart. Then the SS supervising the issue of clothing handed me a large white oil-cloth apron and told me I had been assigned to work in the camp laundry. Whatever this job might entail I was sure it would be better than loading coal. Indeed my prospects were suddenly looking brighter. Still ahead of the rest, I was taken to the showers where the trusty barber, maybe on instructions or because I was first in line, used a new blade on me. What a difference to my first introduction to the camp, not a single blow, no endless waiting in the rain—I simply couldn't get over it.

From the showers, where I was collected by an important-looking SS, I passed my former travelling companions still lined up by the clothing-room and suspected that their curious stares were fixed on me. I felt like a heel but at the same time was glad not to have to share the kind of life awaiting them. The inmate philosophy prevailing in the Small Fortress and probably in similar camps had already infected me: if we have to perish, it might as well be you first. Even though I still didn't know why I had been singled out and was bewildered by this unexpected turn of events, the important fact was that I was luckier than they were. In camp life, compassion was a rare commodity not to be too generously dispensed: only those equipped with a healthy instinct for self-preservation could hope to survive.

This frame of mind was exploited to the utmost by the camp authorities. The inmates themselves kept the camp running. As a rule a prisoner, a *kapo*, commanded a work battalion. He was responsible to the SS guards for fulfilling any set task and to this end was permitted to use any means at his disposal; in turn, he received most of the punishment if the work wasn't accomplished. A *kapo* would be executed if the culprit of sabotage within his brigade wasn't found and he was also held responsible if anyone escaped from it. In order to save his own skin, he drove his fellow prisoners more ruthlessly than many guards. The mentality of a *kapo* was, of course, a peculiar one. He was ready for anything, the worse the working conditions, the more ruthless he became: as a matter of fact, some of the *kapos* were common criminals. Nevertheless, many aspired to the post.

It has to be admitted that a *kapo*'s advantages were appreciable. As a rule a *kapo* had to supervise the work battalions outside the camp—the *Aussenkommandos*—but did not have to work with the detail. Similarly, the cell *kapo* was responsible for the inmates in his cell. There were *kapos* who ran the whole camp—it was like a pyramid. The top *kapo*, the *Oberkapo*, drove the *kapos* under him and they in turn drove the inmates. In this way the camp authorities supervised everything with the least effort, the least manpower and maximum efficiency.

To illustrate the *kapo* mentality I can relate an experience of my own from shortly before I was sent back to Prague. That morning we arrived at the work site without our *kapo* and were standing around with nothing to do as it was always his job to issue the shovels. Any moment the guards would be down on us. Since I spoke German it was decided I should be the one to report his absence and the guard appointed me *kapo* on the spot; this suited me, I had already begun to feel sick, and feeble. Two days later our old *kapo* reappeared and, when he discovered that I had taken his job, invented ways to make my life miserable. I tried to make him understand I had only been standing in for him, that our detail had chosen me to speak to the guard so none of it was really my doing. Either he didn't believe me or, what is more likely, was determined to show the others what would happen to anybody who dared to usurp his position. Later that evening I found out I wasn't the only one who spoke German in our group but the German-speakers had preferred to have me take the job; out of fear of him they had offered it to me, a newcomer who didn't know the ropes.

Even if the prisoners could be said to have helped their captors with the internal running of the camp, guards were still needed to patrol its outside perimeter and especially to supervise the *Aussenkommandos*. With the chronic shortage of able-bodied Germans, this duty was handled by older or disabled SS but, as there weren't enough of them, the SD headquarters in Berlin had to draw on other nationalities. In the Small Fortress we had Ukrainians and Crimean Tartars who had been offered release from POW camps in exchange for guard duty. These two contingents wore practically the same uniform as the SS. The behaviour of the foreign guards was inconsistent: sometimes they could be brutal, on other occasions, especially if one spoke Russian to them, they were essentially correct.

In addition to these two nationalities there was a detachment of Hungarians, that is, ethnic Germans with Hungarian citizenship, in uniforms reminiscent of those worn in the days of the Austro-Hungarian Empire. Most of them were older men who were unfit for combat. They were the friendliest of all and looked somewhat forlorn themselves in the wretched surroundings. Towards the end of the war yet another category of guards was assigned to duty, the so-called *Volkssturm*, German conscripts somewhere in their fifties. All these guards were housed in one of the two taller buildings set in the large open space in the centre of the Fortress, where a few trees and patches of grass provided the only touch of greenery. The other tall building housed the camp commander, the SD administrative guards and their families.

19

Cap in hand as regulations required, I walked beside the officer along the length of the low buildings that ended on the entrance square. We were passing, as I found out later, the very nerve centre of the camp administration, the commander's office, the guard room with the telephone switchboard and the teletype, and entered the *Geschäftszimmer*—the administration office—the last door in the row. The room was large and square with two or three doors leading off. The officer directed me towards one of the doors and, in this inner room, stood Utta. She looked at me intently seeming to have difficulty in recognizing me, but then she quickly hugged me. We were alone in the room, but somehow neither of us could speak in a coherent way. I wanted to know how she had found out where I was. My question surprised her. 'But you sent me a postcard from here, don't you remember?'

I certainly didn't—most of that day when I left the camp for St Pancras was a blank. After getting my card she had gone to Prague to speak to the Gestapo, to ask for permission to visit me there, which was refused. However, later she was promised a visiting permit for the Small Fortress. Utta talked very fast as if she wanted to anticipate all my questions while we were alone, but I just couldn't take it all in. We were both too upset for our conversation to be logical. When I tried to ask her how she had managed to get permission to see me at all, the SS officer came into the room and she didn't answer. From then on we talked about inconsequential matters. I found out that my family and Lala knew where I was. Towards the end of her visit Utta asked the officer if she could give me a few personal items she had brought with her. A sleeping bag and a box of cube sugar were permitted, the rest had to go back. As it happened, both things couldn't have suited me better.

165

When Utta's visit was over, the same officer, instead of turning left towards the horrible fourth yard where I had previously been held, took me a different way. Passing various workshops on our right-hand side, we came to a widening of the alleyway and I could see the entrances to some cells. At the first of these I was handed over to the cell *kapo*. The officer left after telling him I had been assigned to work in the laundry. Speaking to me in German the *kapo* said his name was Hans Hofer and that I could choose any bunk I liked, there were plenty free. He seemed a friendly chap, about eight years my senior and, as he had nothing special to do, quite disposed to chat with me. The first thing I wanted to find out was the name of the SS officer who had been my escort. Hofer was surprised that I didn't know it was Schmidt, the second in command, and proceeded to fill me in on the hierarchy and other aspects of the Fortress.

I told him I could already place Jöckel or Pinda as I had always heard the commander referred to—loosely translated from Czech it meant Little Prick. Jöckel was an enormous hulk of a man in his early fifties with a protruding pot belly, fleshy face, small, dark, close-set eyes, brown hair and a Hitler-like moustache. He used to wander around the camp, appearing at the most unexpected moments, always carrying a riding crop which he didn't hesitate to use on the prisoners, often for no apparent reason. Pinda had a daughter who sometimes accompanied him on his rounds.

Schmidt was Pinda's opposite in looks. In his early or middle thirties with reddish-blond hair and blue eyes, he wasn't especially tall but always looked smart in uniform. If Schmidt was less visible than Jöckel it was probably because he was busy running the camp from his office. The third in command was the Austrian, Rojko, whom I already knew by sight from his visits to the fourth yard. He was rather short, ruddy faced and dreaded because of his unpredictable reactions.

Once Hofer saw how little I really knew of the camp he explained that I would have dealings with Wachholz in the *kleiderkammer* and with Mende who looked after the laundry. Wachholz's speciality was hitting prisoners over the head with a steel ruler, keeping time like a metronome, while talking to them in a quiet, even tone—I was later to see him lose his composure whenever someone broke their bowl or lost a spoon. When it was necessary to speak to any guard, prisoners had to address them as *Herr Kommandant* while standing to attention, cap off and held in the right hand pressed against the thigh.

166

The courtyard I was now in was known as the second and our cell was reserved mainly for Germans. At first glance I realized how much better it was than the huge concrete blocks of the fourth. There would be no more sleeping in puddles and there were bunks to spare, built in triple tiers along one of the longer walls. In the central space was a kind of rough refectory table with benches on either side and a round iron stove. To the left of the entrance was an enclosed lavatory, two washbasins and beside these a tall, narrow window giving on to the yard but affording little light to the rear of the cell. The cells on this yard were of the older type known as casemates and were actually a sort of vault built into the earthen rampart. The floor was made of wood and the ceiling was vaulted to support the mass of earth above it. Our yard was the smallest, with only four or five casemates, measuring about twenty by thirty-five or forty feet. Each pair of cells shared a common entrance hall from which two doors, only locked after the evening roll-call, led into the cells proper. A small printshop was housed between our cell and the neighbouring one. The second courtyard was separated from the third, the women's yard, by a tall wall.

Hofer told me that some inmates from our yard worked at so-called inside jobs, as electricians, plumbers and various trades; others were waiters in the SS canteen or batmen. The majority, however, formed part of the *Aussenkommandos* which explained why the cell was empty except for ourselves, the orderly, and a man on crutches.

I already knew part of the layout of the first courtyard—the showers and, from my attempt to visit it, the dispensary. Hofer said that the punishment cells were near the dispensary and the kitchens were at the far end. The inmates housed in that yard were, in the main, the holders of the most sought-after work—anything to do with administration, the kitchens, food-stores and the clothing-room. The Jewish cell was also in this yard, next to the Russian one, across from the *Hofverwaltung* and too close to Rojko. Due to the exceptionally poor living conditions in these two cells the mortality rate was high. These men were usually assigned to outside brigades along with those of the fourth yard.

In the course of our conversation I found out that Hofer and the orderly were former SD guards from the Prague prison and had been caught accepting bribes to smuggle in food parcels. The orderly, Frühauf, was younger and a rather taciturn individual. Somehow I never got on friendly terms with him.

167

Gradually, my new cellmates returned, but by roll-call we were no more than thirty. We were able to sit at table and converse normally over more abundant food which went further here because the food buckets for most cells were of a uniform size. Given the unusual way I had been assigned there, I didn't feel any overt mistrust—the men freely discussed the day's events, commented on the behaviour of the guards and inquired about my background and how I came to be in jail.

The prisoner who struck me most and eventually became one of my two closest friends in the cell was a young priest by the name of Ferdinand Frigge. He was originally from the Rhineland but before his arrest had been administering a parish in north-western Bohemia on the border of Saxony. Before his prison days he must have been very corpulent, but when I met him he had lost it all. The only traces of his former portliness were bags of loose skin hanging from his belly and breasts which made him look somewhat ridiculous when undressed. Frigge used to walk up and down the cell in the evenings reading from a breviary he had somehow managed to smuggle in. The reason for his imprisonment was that during a discussion with a fellow priest he had compared the Nazis to a gang of criminals and murderers and had been denounced for his remarks. Once we became close, Frigge confessed to me that he and the others in the cell had been wary of me at first and this I fully understood.

My other friend was Heinrich Schumann who was, perhaps, a couple of years younger than me. A deserter, he had been set to work in the SS canteen as a cook. He had been hiding out in an apartment in Prague when the police came to arrest him. While they were searching the place, on a fifth floor, he slipped out and, using the key they had forgotten to remove, locked the door from the outside. He raced down the stairs and on to the street while, from above, the Gestapo men shouted to passers-by to stop him. Of course nobody did—on the contrary, they simply made a wide detour. Schumann was from Magdeburg, spoke no Czech and all his contacts were German as well, so it didn't take the Gestapo long to locate him a second time. The men he had made fools of beat him up so badly his body bore scars like the stripes of a zebra.

The oldest man in the cell was in his early sixties so, due to his age and general culture, any dispute among us was submitted to him for judgement. Korda, a wealthy businessman, had transferred some of his foreign holdings to his Jewish wife who had escaped to the States.

There were two Jesuits who were quite friendly but kept mostly to themselves. They were often a target for jibes because some of the inmates thought they were homosexuals, a suspicion which I believed was unfounded—they were merely very close to each other and shared everything they could scrounge.

The man on crutches was a former pilot from the old Austrian Imperial Army who had lost both legs in a plane crash in the First World War. He was Czech and may have ended up in our cell because he was a former Austrian officer—in view of his invalidity he couldn't be expected to work. He was an inveterate joker, often telling us dirty stories in his heavily-accented German. His favourite targets were the two Jesuits and Father Frigge whom he once asked how he was able to manage without ever sleeping with a woman. 'It's strange how everybody always asks me that question. No one ever wants to know how I can manage on the salary I'm paid,' Frigge promptly replied.

The pilot was popular with everyone but nobody wanted to sleep near him—even to most of us who could wash only once or twice a month, he smelled to high heaven. I don't know whether this was because he couldn't use the showers or because he had difficulty with the lavatory.

Inexplicably, two Flemish-speaking Belgians were also in our cell. Nobody could make out their German so, if they had a problem, they explained it to me in French and I translated for the others. Another colourful character was the man the Germans called a *'Bibelforscher'*—Bible researcher—and he may well have been a Jehovah's Witness or a conscientious objector, something not tolerated by the Nazis. Shortly before the end of the war he fell victim to what we called the sheep sickness, an illness which affected certain inmates. For a while, before we became aware of his illness, he used to spend a lot of his free time on the lavatory holding his eating bowl to his ear and talking to himself. From then on he was known as the 'Telephone Operator'. The symptoms of sheep sickness were drooling and behaving as if one was mentally deranged. I well remember one evening when this man returned to the cell looking curiously at his hand from all angles. During work he had chopped off his fingers and was inspecting his hand as if it no longer belonged to him. He died soon afterwards, either from loss of blood, infection or as a result of the sheep sickness. I never knew his real name or anything about him.

Until the big clean-outs from the prisons in Prague and evacuations from other jails such as Dresden, our cell was a rather close-knit

169

community. Without a doubt, this was due to the better living conditions where we were less crowded and had more to eat. Moreover, as many of us were working inside the camp, we had more opportunities to steal—in camp parlance, to organize—than those on work details outside the Fortress. Organizing was sometimes outright stealing from camp stocks or trading for whatever was in short supply.

Following roll-call the morning after my arrival, I reported to the laundry *kapo*. No more long marches in all weathers, my new place of work was right across the courtyard from the cell. The laundry was a bright room about twenty by fifty feet with tiled walls and a terrazzo floor. A huge drum in galvanized sheet metal stood on the left-hand side by the rear wall next to an oversized window of etched panes giving on to the women's yard. To the right, against the far wall were the driers—several frames mounted on rails that could be pulled out from a closed housing. Opposite the racks, on the right front wall below a window also with etched panes, was a big, sturdy table. It was a modern installation which had been completed not long before I arrived and was a sort of showpiece of the camp.

Until I joined it, the laundry detail had been made up of three men. They might have considered me a welcome addition but the reception I got from my future co-workers was reserved. Under normal circumstances the allotment of choice posts was the prerogative of the head *kapo*—a former general in the Czech army—and his clique. Naturally, the best jobs went to army officers and the SD administration interfered only rarely, unless of course a man's file was marked with restrictive initials. In my case, and contrary to the usual practice, I was thrust upon the laundry *kapo* by the assistant camp commander, Schmidt. The *kapo* and his crew had every reason to be wary and suspect me of being a stool-pigeon.

The laundry *kapo* was a priest and a theology professor from Prague University. He was a dour, humourless, middle-aged man, referred to by the others as Lustyk: this could have been a play on words as, in German, *lustig* means merry. Over six feet tall, with his shaved head and long arms he looked like a gorilla and had the strength of one. The drum operator was just the opposite, a short and quick-witted man of about thirty, always full of fun and telling dirty stories to annoy the *kapo*. The third man was a colonel in the Czech army, middle-aged and nondescript. I took over his job of fetching and carrying the laundry—a job which could be hazardous. The *kapo* may have decided that if I had been placed with them for any ulterior motive I had protection or maybe he just thought that if anyone had to get into trouble it might as well be me. The first of the crew to thaw out was the drum operator, Antonin Zima, whom everybody in the yard called by his nickname Tonda. Given the physical condition in which I arrived, he believed I couldn't be a stoolie. In his opinion, a stool-pigeon would have been in far better shape. Personally, I doubt his reasoning was valid, a weakened prisoner might lend himself more readily to the role. After we got to know each other we often discussed this point, funnily enough with me defending our *kapo*'s initial reaction. The question of whether or not I was an informer was rather more important than it might appear. It wasn't only a question of not being able to talk freely in front of me; all three lived in the neighbouring cell and could have talked as they liked after work. It was whether or not they could safely continue to 'organize'.

Tonda must have been quite persuasive in his arguments because, a couple of weeks after I started to work in the laundry, I took part in my first organizing expedition. A few days before, I had been asked by the *kapo* to help him carry clean laundry either to the clothing-room or to the women's yard for ironing and mending or sorting out for baling. A visit to the women's quarters was a pleasant diversion as I later found out. The lack of food had a negative influence on the men, but the reverse was true of the women who seemed to have acquired a pronounced streak of lewdness as if the food situation had no adverse effect on them whatsoever. They never missed an opportunity to feel me or touch my bottom if the female guard was not around. I often wondered if the women took the same liberties with Lustyk—he always insisted on being one of the carriers.

On the day of my first organizing expedition, the cook's aprons and kitchen towels were ready for delivery. With the *kapo* taking the front end of the wooden stretcher, we carried the freshly laundered and folded washing into the first yard, at the end of which were the kitchens. Hidden among the exclusively kitchen laundry were clean shirts and soap for the cooks. Although we had to pass a few guards loitering on the corner of the entrance square and the administration office, nobody made a move to inspect what we were carrying, but the tricky part was still ahead of us. Under the eyes of the kitchen guard, we had to deliver the contraband and collect one or two loaves of bread hidden among the dirty kitchen things. All went smoothly and from then on I was considered one of them and no longer suspected of being an informer.

The laundry crew, working twelve-hour shifts six days a week, managed to wash shirts, underpants, footcloths and sheets for a prison population of some three thousand although inmates could change their underclothes and the single sheet only every ten weeks. In addition to this we were also expected to wash the clothes of those who died in the camp, that is to say, whatever they had worn on arrival and turned in at the *kleiderkammer*. This clothing was later baled and shipped to Germany for redistribution in the bombed-out cities.

Our working conditions were among the best in the camp. The laundry was always warm and we could wash with hot water—at least at moments when we would not be surprised by a guard. Mende, the SD in charge, paid us a visit maybe once or twice a week and never stayed for long. The other guards left us alone, they came to the courtyard only for the roll-calls. Our underwear could be changed as often as we liked, a privilege that, in the last stages of the war, became a matter of life or death. For now, however, the greatest advantage of the laundry personnel was that we could move more or less freely through the sections of the camp that mattered without being stopped by an over-zealous guard asking snoopy questions— the white oil-cloth aprons were recognized as a badge of office. All one had to do was carry something, look busy and move fast. There were only a handful of other jobs that provided such freedom of movement.

Although I still didn't know the reason why I had landed up in the laundry, I considered myself very lucky to have fallen into such a berth. A recent arrival usually had to start at the bottom, for instance in the fourth yard, with all the risks that that entailed. The first months in any camp were crucial: chances of survival increased considerably once the prisoner made friends and learnt the ropes. For one thing, in the *Aussenkommandos*, knowing how to work when under the close supervision of the guards was important: it was essential to work as little as possible in order to conserve strength and, at all costs, avoid exhaustion. What really mattered was not the output but how busy one looked. This was an art acquired with experience. Not all guards were simpletons to be fooled by a clumsy pretence. It was also important not to stand out in any way because drawing attention to oneself could be fatal. There was one golden rule—keep away from the guards as much as possible. They were given a free hand and in general were unpredictable.

Sometime in December 1944, an odd individual arrived with a transport from the east and ended up in our cell. Witnesses told us he had come into the camp as a sort of auxiliary guard, armed with a submachine-gun. His head was shaved but, in contrast to the rest of the transport in their striped-pyjama uniforms, he was smartly dressed with a grey, battledress-type jacket, black riding-breeches and jack-boots. However, immediately after his arrival in the Fortress, he was issued with the same grey uniform as inmates working in outside brigades. Of course, the gun had been taken from him right away. We couldn't detect any preferential treatment on the part of the camp administration but he boasted that the guards from the transport had trusted him enough to give him a gun and that he had helped to bring the prisoners from Auschwitz to the Small Fortress. For obvious reasons he wasn't very popular and we kept out of his way as much as possible. His name was Jupp and he came from the Rhineland. He claimed to have been in concentration camps for the previous eleven years, which meant that he had been arrested soon after the Nazis came to power. From his appearance we judged him to be around thirty at the most.

Jupp used to talk to us about conditions in Buchenwald and Auschwitz. We found it hard to believe there were whorehouses in some of the places where he'd been interned but his stories were very vivid and he couldn't have invented everything. He claimed the *kapos* and trusties could visit the brothels twice a month and the women were prisoners themselves. Jupp never told us why he was in prison but we guessed he was classified as an habitual criminal. This was difficult to reconcile with his age if he had been designated as one at the age of nineteen but we had no other explanation: his mental development ruled out his being in the camp for political reasons.

I don't recall to what battalion he was assigned, only that he wasn't working inside the camp. But I do remember him arriving triumph-antly in the cell one evening after Christmas when the German counter-offensive in the Ardennes was in full swing, boasting that the *Wehrmacht* had turned the tide and would push the Allies out of Europe. There was dead silence in the cell—he must have been the only inmate in the whole camp to wish for a German victory. As an *Aussenkommando kapo* he certainly made himself a lot of enemies among the prisoners in the relatively short period before the end of the war.

❧ 20 ❧

The initial success of the panzers in the Battle of the Bulge threw us into deep gloom, until it became clear that the attack had failed. But the confirmation of the failure of this last German offensive reached us only much later; all we knew for a while was what the official German communiqué said. Most of the news originated from prisoners who worked as servants for the guards or as waiters in the SS canteen. Often a report came to us so garbled that it didn't make sense at all. One day the news spread that the British had landed on the Baltic at Szczecin, Poland, although we knew the Russians were already poised on the Vistula to the east. These false reports were often the result of wishful thinking but, in spite of the occasional 'latrine' we usually had a fairly good idea of the progress on different fronts.

With the start of the final year of the war, conditions in the Small Fortress began deteriorating drastically—at least in our courtyard. Until the New Year there had been a certain monotony to everyday camp life: one day resembled the next, one week hardly differed from the one before. Suddenly, all that changed. In a single day the population of our cell increased from a fairly constant number of twenty-five or thirty to a hundred or more. With that influx, the friendly atmosphere was doomed to disappear. Our cell soon began to resemble the one I had first been assigned to in the fourth yard. Personal items like an additional pair of footcloths, a spoon or a few cubes of organized sugar would vanish. The lavatory, until then very clean, became dirty and smelly. If not eaten right away, the bread ration had to be carried in one's pocket. We had to be more careful of what we said in public. This didn't mean that there were many criminals or informers, it was just that the overcrowding made our living conditions unbearable and brought out the worst side of everyone's character.

174

Most of the newcomers were genuine political prisoners, especially among the sizeable number of Austrians. There were men who, after the war, became members of the government in Vienna—one was a Vice-Chancellor—or held important administrative posts. The man who, for a while, slept next to me was the first Austrian Ambassador appointed to Prague. Most Germans from the Reich, as opposed to the Sudeten Germans, were professional men, doctors, lawyers and a couple of university professors from Saxony. I suppose they were shipped to us because the prison in Dresden was overcrowded and with the territory occupied by the Reich shrinking daily, there were fewer and fewer camps left to which they could be shipped. At the most, there were two or three soon-identifiable criminals in the new lot. These men alone couldn't have been responsible for the deterioration in the atmosphere since they couldn't make a move without being observed by someone. Now there wasn't room for all of us to sit down at table, or space to lie in the bunks without being touched on both sides. The sleeping conditions were especially bad—when one person turned, the whole row had to follow suit. The flea plague was beyond control. Every evening, in the old days, we used to walk barefoot so that the fleas jumping on to our legs from the floorboards could be picked off easily. With the larger number of inmates the flea hunt became difficult to organize methodically because more time had to be spent on food distribution and other tasks. The bedbugs, too, were more difficult to get rid of. Before the crowding there had been enough space on the bunks to empty a whole tier then, systematically, usually on a Sunday, examine each crack in the one just vacated: now there wasn't a free place to transfer to.

One of the more disagreeable side effects of over-population was the bad air. Our cell, buried deep within the fortification walls with at least twenty feet of earth above the vaulted ceiling, had probably been used originally as a storeroom for explosives. As a result of the poor ventilation, the sickness rate increased rapidly. There were some isolated cases of the sheep sickness, but later infectious jaundice spread alarmingly. Shortly before they died, the colour of the infected men's faces became more orange than yellow: they gradually lost all strength and, for a time, there were several whom we had to carry out into the yard for roll-calls. Too feeble to stand alone, we lined them up against the wall of the cell hoping they wouldn't topple while the counting lasted. The rule that all live prisoners be outside for roll-call was never changed. Unfortunately, this prolonged the counting time and afforded more opportunities for a beating. And these were only a foretaste of the sicknesses that were to befall us later.

While previously transports of new prisoners had arrived at more or less regular intervals, in the last year they would arrive at any time. The cooks, as a rule, prepared a quantity of soup corresponding roughly to the number of inmates counted at the last roll-call but with these sudden, irregular arrivals they were confronted with an unexpected number of men to feed. When informed that a batch of new prisoners had just arrived, the kitchen *kapo* would call out to his helpers, 'Pour another five gallons of water into the kettles, we have a new transport,' and the slices of bread got thinner too.

On the other hand a transport could sometimes bring a real bonanza if it came from a prison where food parcels were permitted. As the men were required to empty their pockets on arrival and put down whatever baggage they were carrying, we often sneaked to the entrance square to pick up pieces of salami, bacon, sugar cubes or even toothpaste or a cake of soap. Later, this scavenging became impossible: the administration posted a guard until the place was cleared by the cleaners and the booty sorted out.

As a humane gesture, Jöckel decided to let the whole camp profit from these windfalls. All foodstuff, regardless of what it might be, was separated from the personal belongings and thrown into the soup kettles. The result, called a *Pinda Topf*, where Pinda stood for the name of the camp commander and topf, for pot, made it a sort of potluck indeed. There were pieces of smoked meat, bits of cake, maybe the wrapper of a chocolate bar or even a tube of toothpaste. On the whole, except for the risk of biting into something like a razor blade, it was a popular, nourishing meal. In the latter days, when most of the transports came from the evacuated concentration camps in the east, the prisoners carried nothing from which we could benefit, they brought only lice.

Among those who showed up in the German cell around this time was cousin Eric, to whom I had last spoken through the wall in the Prague prison, but whose whereabouts I'd known nothing of after my departure. He looked like a scrawny kitten, an oversized head balanced on a thin neck. With him was Feli's presumed father: both were terribly starved. They told me that the food situation in St Pancras had become steadily worse after Christmas. I took care of them as best I could but this wasn't easy as I already had a few friends to help out. However, I had made a lot of contacts in the organizing

176

field and one of them was indeed unusual—a direct link with the outside.

It required good maintenance to keep the laundry drum running practically non-stop. There was an inmate, a mechanic-electrician who circulated freely within the camp—his badge of office was a toolbox—and he showed up fairly often in the laundry. When he needed any spare parts and the necessary replacement wasn't to be had in the camp storeroom, the administration got in touch with a man who owned an electrical shop in Prague. This civilian came to the Fortress every fortnight or so. I heard of him from our mechanic who told me the man was prepared to smuggle food parcels into the camp for a steep but not exorbitant price—considering the risk he was willing to run he could hardly be blamed for the mark-up.

It was through the same man, incidentally, that a note reached me from Lala saying that he was married and that my place had been reserved as godfather to their first child. I mentioned the outside contact to Eric, warning him that the smuggling of each little parcel would cost him a lot of money, not counting the black-market price of the food itself. However, he was a wealthy man who I felt could well afford it. Starving after nearly a year of imprisonment, Eric eagerly accepted the offer and gave me a list of items to be purchased by his land agent. Although a native of Vienna, most of his holdings were in Prague, properties inherited from his grandfather, the mayor.

It took a little while before his first package came through, together with a note stating the cost, but soon afterwards a second and a third parcel came, always accompanied by a bill. In the family, Eric was known as a tightwad and even Feli's presumed father, Major Uhman of the Imperial Austro-Hungarian Army, complained to me in private how little he'd received for declaring officially that Feli was his daughter. When the fourth parcel arrived, Eric took me aside to ask if I couldn't re-negotiate the smuggling fee. 'Please tell your contact that the money I am paying wasn't earned on the black market, it's still the good, old, gold-backed currency.'

There and then I pointed out to him that the smuggler couldn't care less when or how the money had been earned, gold-backed or not and that he and a few others were risking their necks so that Eric could have something more than just the camp soup. However, my refusal to ask for a reduction of the amount he was originally quite willing to pay didn't discourage him from pestering me to re-negotiate until, to get some peace, I stopped the flow of parcels altogether. That didn't please him either and he refused to speak to me from then on. Eric survived the camp all right but, as if there were some justice in this world, when the Communists came to power after the war, his property in Prague was confiscated. What he lost was definitely worth more than all the parcels he could have had for the rest of his life. I guess what galled him most was that he felt obliged to share the food with Major Uhman.

The Major was a likeable old chap in his early sixties who enjoyed talking to me about the Vienna of his youth. In many ways he had known the same sort of life as my stepfather so I liked listening to his stories. On one occasion we were talking about his arrest in Vienna and his transfer from there to the jail in Prague. The Major complained how hot it had been on the train on the second day from Linz to Prague and, as if that weren't enough, somebody escaped from the transport. He described how he had been beaten up when he couldn't identify the men in his line when the guards were trying to reconstruct the row from which a prisoner was missing. 'I was with people I'd never seen before and didn't pay any attention to them. What was more on my mind at the time was what could be awaiting me in Prague.'

'Do you have any idea who it might have been?' I inquired innocently.

'No, not exactly, but I suspect it could have been a young fellow with blond hair. He was wearing shorts. That's why I noticed him when we were making up the marching column on the platform but I couldn't see him when we were counted in the jail. Why do you ask?'

'Because I might know him.'

'Well, if I could, I'd give him a good kick in the ass for the beating I got.'

'Then why don't you do it? He's standing right in front of you.' Uhman looked around, not catching my meaning until I confessed that the blond young man in shorts was me. Of course, I still had hair in those days—that is, when he noticed me in the transport.

With the considerable increase in the number of prisoners more workers were added to the laundry brigade and two shifts were instituted. Instead of working a straight twelve hours we had to work alternate twenty-four-hour shifts, Sundays included. Even so, compared to loading coal, my work was easy. It consisted of picking up the dirty laundry from the *kleiderkammer* and sorting it into batches, hanging on the drying racks what came out of the washing-drum and helping with the folding, which was done on the large table. The sheets had to be stretched by the *kapo* and myself before folding and Lustyk used to get angry with me if I didn't hold them tightly enough and he was able to jerk them out of my hands. Even if the work in the laundry was easy by camp standards, it was extremely tiring over a twenty-four-hour stretch. Sitting down was forbidden and risky and once almost cost me my life.

It had been a particularly busy shift that day and at three in the morning we had been on our feet some twenty hours. Apart from the normal batch of laundry there was a consignment of clothes to prepare for bombed-out cities. This shipment had been delivered in the evening but the table was still full of the prison laundry being folded by the *kapo* and the colonel. I was sitting on the floor in a corner beside the table with my back to the door, smoothing out footcloths and putting them into piles. The drum was washing a new load when two guards entered the room, the noise of the machine drowning out the sound of the door being opened. Tonda also had his back to the door so it wasn't until the guards were in the middle of the room that the *kapo* noticed them and called out the mandatory '*Achtung.*' I jumped up but it was too late—they had already seen me. The two men were Mende and Horse Head, the SS guard I had come across on my transport back to Prague.

'So, that's how you work, sitting on the floor!' exclaimed Mende coming over and hitting me in the face with his fist. I didn't answer.

'That's sabotage. Here we make short shift of saboteurs, you should know that,' shouted Horse Head. Both of them were completely drunk—their breath left no doubt about it. Horse Head drew his revolver and ordered me to turn around. When I felt the cold mouth of the barrel on the back of my head I was sacred but, more than that, surprised—everything happened so fast. Then Mende said, 'We'll let you go this time but don't let me catch you sitting again.' With that they both walked unsteadily out of the laundry.

Lustyk was so astonished that his second call of '*Achtung*' came only after they had disappeared into the darkness. It seemed to me that the others were even more stunned than I was. The scene they had just witnessed probably looked worse than what I had perceived. It was a few seconds before anyone uttered a word—we stood there like statues. At last Tonda muttered in Czech an approximate equivalent of drunken sons of bitches.

Episodes like this happened quite frequently and inmates were killed for less, it was simply a question of luck. Some time before this I had witnessed an incident that didn't have such a fortunate ending. A prisoner, a Dominican monk, was employed as a street cleaner. I used to see him when I was doing my errands. On this particular day, he was sitting down in a doorway adjusting his footcloths. As I approached an SS guard appeared as if from nowhere. He stopped in front of the man, said something I couldn't catch, drew his revolver and shot him on the spot.

'Get the *Totenkommando*!' he called out to me.

The *Totenkommando* was a death-brigade of two or three Jewish prisoners well known around the camp. Instead of the red triangle, they wore a yellow, six-pointed star on their jackets and were among the few who survived the periodic massacres in their cell. Never overcrowded due to the regular culling, the cell was on my way and I gave them the message. When I came back past the scene of the shooting, the body had gone and one man from the death-brigade was cleaning blood stains from the doorway. Whenever somebody died, the death-brigade arrived promptly with a cart, loaded the body and disappeared just as fast. I don't know where the victims were buried but, in view of the number of dead, the *Totenkommando* became very efficient at their job. Later I saw their work from close quarters when our cellmate, Korda, died of jaundice. It was my twenty-four-hour rest period and I was in the cell. That morning our cell *kapo* had reported one dead to the SS taking the roll-call and the death-brigade arrived shortly afterwards. The height between the tiers was barely enough for a man to kneel with his head lowered. Korda's body was on the third level. One of the men climbed up, got him down to the floor, out of the cell and on to the cart so fast that the whole operation didn't last more than thirty seconds. Of course, the handling of the body didn't measure up to the standard procedure for undertakers. Korda's body was pushed off the bunk and his head hit the wooden floor with a dull sound difficult to forget. There was never any medical check to see if the man was really dead. As far as I knew at the time, the camp didn't have a doctor. The dispensary wasn't much use and the fact that there was a small infirmary wasn't generally known, at least not in our yard. Any doctors among the prisoners were assigned to labour details like anybody else.

The irrational and inconsequential behaviour of the guards can best be illustrated by two other incidents. A cellmate, whose name I've forgotten, exchanged a gold watch with the camp baker for some loaves of bread. How he managed to smuggle in such an item I have no idea: all valuables, even wedding rings, were confiscated on arrival. The baker was caught with the watch and beaten until he told the guards how he had acquired it. The SS descended on our cell and ordered my cellmate to explain how he had got hold of the watch. Thinking that somebody had denounced him, and not knowing that the baker had been caught and had named him, he put his hand into his pocket and, to the astonishment of the guards, pulled out a second watch. I forget what he explained to them but apart from some beating nothing further happened, at least not while he was with us. A few weeks later, however, he was included in a transport to another camp. If I remember correctly the baker was later killed as a punishment for black-marketeering.

The other episode involved me and occurred several months before the end of the war. The foreign guards, especially the Ukrainians, used to sneak into the laundry during the night-shift offering cigarettes for civilian clothes—the going price was ten cigarettes for a decent-looking suit. By then it was pretty obvious the end was in sight so they were preparing to go underground to avoid being handed over to the Soviets.

Since they couldn't buy civilian clothes in stores—there was nothing to be had—the only solution was to get hold of a suit from us. At first there weren't many Ukrainians visiting us at night but, with each advance of the Red Army, more guards became interested in outfitting themselves. Soon Tonda and I were getting our hands on more cigarettes than the civilian population was officially receiving for their ration coupons. There was no control over how many suits were delivered to us for washing and we could sell as many as we found customers for. Ridiculous as it may sound, the suits actually did get put into the washing-drum—orders were orders. Cigarettes were a precious commodity, they could get us a loaf of bread or a cake of margarine but, of course, we also smoked them on special occasions.

This time of affluence coincided with a large earth-moving job in the vicinity of the camp which necessitated the use of explosives. As a precaution, the big frosted-glass panes giving on to the women's yard had to be removed from the laundry. For a few days we could watch the women on the other side and make signs to them, that is, only

Tonda and I did. We were working our twenty-four-hour shift on a Sunday but the women were free from work and permitted to walk outside their cells. I saw some I knew from my laundry deliveries and, on an impulse of generosity, threw a handful of cigarettes to them. Unfortunately, the female guard supervising the outing noticed what was going on and denounced me to the guard on duty. It wasn't long before he appeared in the laundry.

'Which one of you was throwing cigarettes to the women?' he shouted menacingly at the *kapo*. I had no choice but to step forward. My admission was far from being an act of chivalry for I knew very well that Lustyk would ultimately have to tell him who it was. By owning up right away I hoped I might spare everybody, including myself, a beating.

'Come with me,' he ordered ominously. The duty guard that day was Wachholz, the metronome, the clothing-room SD: he must have known me by sight from when I was delivering or collecting laundry. While walking beside him I wondered what I could say when he asked me where the cigarettes came from. We were crossing the entrance square heading towards the administration office. I thought he was taking me to Schmidt but he suddenly stopped and asked, 'How long have you been here?'

'Since autumn, *Herr Kommandant*.'

'Then you should know better than that,' and added unexpectedly, 'You can go back to work, just don't try anything like that again.'

'Thank you, *Herr Kommandant*,' I answered quickly before he could change his mind and returned straight away to the laundry, astonished that I'd got off scot-free. Was it because he knew me by sight and I was no longer just another anonymous face, or did he perhaps know that it was Schmidt who had put me in the laundry? Anyway, I thanked my lucky stars: not only had he not inquired about the origin of the cigarettes, which was strange, but he let me off without punishment. When I got back, my fellow-workers were astonished to see me so soon—they had expected that I would be put into solitary confinement at least—and wanted to know what had happened. When I told them, Lustyk couldn't resist the opportunity to give me a lesson.

'You still deserve a punishment. You endangered all of us by your stupid act,' he said and punched me in the face.

The female guard who denounced me was well known to the

laundry crew as she was often around when we delivered clothing for mending. A hefty and rather plain-looking woman in her late thirties she lived in one of the tall houses where the other guards were quartered, but on a different floor where she had a room to herself. A female inmate was assigned to her as a servant and kept her room tidy but for heavier work she occasionally used a friend of mine, Honza Pospichal, a likeable chap. He was a young lawyer from a provincial town in eastern Bohemia and would probably have been considered handsome but for his somewhat short stature. Honza's official function was janitor of the building: his duties were to keep the stairway clean, cart coal from the cellar, wash windows and the like. He was popular with everyone in our yard because, while doing odd jobs, he could eavesdrop on the latest broadcasts and keep us informed on how the war was going.

One evening, when he brought a bucket of coal up to her room, he found her sitting on a low stool washing her legs, her skirts well above her knees. Honza excused himself and tried to leave but she asked him to change the water. As there was no tap in her room he had to go out into the corridor to get it. When he came back with the clean water he thought her skirt was pulled up a fraction higher than when he left. Putting the basin on the floor in front of the woman, he was turning to go when she called him back.

'I'm rather tired, please wash my feet.' He found it an unusual request but of course obeyed and soaped her already clean-looking feet and legs up to her knees.

'That feels good, now give me a massage.' He rubbed her legs as best he could and after a while she indicated to Honza that it was enough and pointed to the stove, 'There, you take what's left in the casserole.' My friend related all this to us that evening, describing her fat legs with gusto. As time went on he was asked to repeat the massage whenever the opportunity presented itself. At each subsequent session her skirt was pulled higher while the portion left in the casserole increased accordingly. He kept us informed on progress and promised that when he reached her crotch he would give away his issued food ration, he'd be getting enough from her. One day the woman asked him how long he had been in jail.

'Two years, *Frau Kommandantin*.'

'That's a long time, do you like massaging me? Does it excite you?' Our friend had to think fast. On the one hand it could mean an invitation to proceed further, on the other a deliberate provocation to denounce him for disrespect. Honza decided to play safe. '*Frau Kommandantin*, I am only executing your orders.'

'You haven't answered my question,' she persisted, 'does it excite you?'

'If you order it, *Frau Kommandantin*, it will excite me,' he said in desperation, to which she just laughed, adding, 'You are a good one.' From then on she stopped raising both her skirt and the level of the portion left on the stove.

My friend Frigge was attached to a work-brigade digging the foundations for an air-raid shelter for the hospital in Leitmeritz which was run by a religious order. The nuns somehow found out that there was a priest with the detail and started leaving food in places where he would find it. This went on for a while until Frigge hit upon the idea of leaving a message for his sister, his housekeeper in his parish not far from Leitmeritz. He wrote that, through the nuns, she was to send him some of the home-cured tobacco he kept in the loft. His sister did as he asked and from then on Frigge frequently brought back small bundles of tobacco suspended under his jacket; it was well before my cigarette bonanza.

This went on for a time until one day a cohort of guards descended on our cell. It was my day off and the cell *kapo* wasn't around. Since some of them knew me by sight, I was asked to show them where Frigge slept. At that moment I didn't know the reason for the raid but I knew that he kept a few bundles of tobacco along with his breviary in the clothes pile underneath his head-rest. Naturally, they would have found it so, instead of Frigge's place, I directed them to mine; we slept close to each other, only Schumann was between us and neither he nor I had anything they could object to. My few possessions were kept in the laundry and my deserter friend had his somewhere in the canteen. A guard got up on the bunk, went through my things and saw that there was nothing untoward. It was clear the guards had got wind of something irregular and would search Frigge thoroughly on his return from work. I had to warn him.

A couple of hours before his brigade was due back I went to the laundry and told the *kapo* that I was bored in the cell on my own and had come to help them. My offer to work extra hours must have sounded odd but was accepted. I donned my apron, the badge that allowed me to move freely about the camp, and worked to fill in the time. Under some pretext or other I left the laundry and went to the entrance square where the returning brigades were counted. Frigge's battalion hadn't arrived and I couldn't hang around too long, so I left a message with an inmate who knew Frigge to warn him that the guards had searched the bunk but found nothing. He should get rid of the tobacco if he could and under no circumstances was he to admit to anything. After delivering the message, I headed back, hoping for the best. That evening, another member of his brigade living in our cell told us that after roll-call Frigge had been taken away to the administration office. There was no news of him the next day nor the day after nor all the following week. We were afraid that he hadn't been able to dispose of the evidence and imagined the worst.

Two weeks later, to the surprise of us all, Frigge appeared in our cell in the evening. He was in a lamentable state, loose skin hung on him, making him look like a teddy bear whose stuffing had fallen out. Unbelievably cheerful, as always, he explained the mystery of his disappearance. He got the message all right but that day he wasn't carrying any tobacco and, in spite of the beating, he refused to admit to anything until the guards became so exasperated they put him in solitary anyway. They were determined to punish him even without proof. He had no idea how the guards found out about the smuggling but suspected somebody in the hospital must have seen the nuns depositing the bundles of tobacco. Pleased as I was to have Frigge back, I still couldn't resist a bit of teasing so jokingly asked him how he could reconcile his beliefs with lying.

'For self-preservation one can lie. I was only following the example of Saint Peter,' he replied without hesitation.

·§ 21 §·

Apart from the chances of coming down with a fatal disease spread by overcrowding and absence of medical care, another way to lose one's life was in a solitary cell. Ending up in solitary was feared more than a severe beating although those sent there were usually beaten as well. Luckily I never had occasion to experience a solitary cell myself but was told there were two types: the size of either was the same, too short to lie down in with just space enough to crouch on the floor because of course there was no bunk. The difference between the two was that most had a roof but perhaps two or three were without. Those in a roofless cell had to hope for good weather, otherwise they died from exposure. Frigge had been fortunate, his cell had a roof and the season was early spring. The usual length of time spent in solitary ranged from three days to two weeks, enough to make it worthwhile and for the unlucky man to remember it for the rest of his life.

A prisoner could be put in solitary for an infraction of the camp rules, not necessarily a proven violation either, as was the case with Frigge. There was no rule of thumb—as always, it was simply a question of chance. If a prisoner happened to be in the wrong place at the wrong time he was in trouble, or sometimes got away with it but, of course, we tried not to tempt fate. It was like ending up in a bad work-battalion, in a wretched cell or at the end of a marching column: somebody had to be at the tail-end so it often fell to those who were new and didn't know what to watch out for.

New transports arrived constantly. From the original camp population of around three thousand, we were close to double that number by the end of January 1945. As a rule a transport would consist of some two hundred men but once in a while that winter a group of five, ten or at the most twenty prisoners would be marched in. These were

186

what we began to call death transports. Nobody knew who the men were or where they came from: only rarely were they dressed in the striped-pyjama uniforms with their heads shaved, more often they wore civilian clothes and had normal haircuts. There was no way to get near them, the guards were always present. Like all other prisoners they had to empty their pockets and leave whatever they carried on the ground in the entrance square. Once they had been led away the clean-up was done by a detachment of the SS rather than by the inmate street cleaners. Prisoners working in the administration told us there was no record of their having ever reached the Small Fortress. The men were taken straight to the execution yard which was separated from the main camp by a tunnel and a gate. This was the usual procedure except for one I know about.

On a late January afternoon, I was returning from the kitchen to the laundry with an organized loaf of bread under my jacket when a group of ten men in civilian clothes, accompanied by a guard, came towards me from the entrance square. Earlier, on my way to the first courtyard, I had passed Jöckel, Schmidt, and Rojko among others, standing outside the administration office. The set-up looked unusual so it didn't seem wise to walk past. On the spur of the moment I decided to turn back and take refuge in the showers.

I was on good terms with the *kapo* there, a Russian, and explained to him why I had come. He agreed to keep the bread for me until I could collect it at a better time. Since I had no business being in the showers I was on the point of leaving when the *kapo* held me back, opening the door a crack to see if the way was clear. Just then the guard with the civilian transport rounded the corner and came to a halt some hundred feet from the showers, right in front of Rojko's office. Now I certainly had to wait. The *kapo* and I watched from behind the door—we both sensed something unusual was about to happen.

In a minute or so an SS officer came to the group and stood talking to the guard. One by one Jöckel, and the rest of those I had seen outside joined them, each carrying a club. The guard barked an order for the civilians to form two ranks of five. The first then had to take ten steps forward and each man side-stepped to a distance of an arm's length. Now came a new order: Undress! There was hesitation among them: it was cold and there was snow on the ground.

'Undress, faster!' the SS shouted while clubs started raining on heads and shoulders until all ten men were completely naked. Now, with one accord, the SS surrounded the two closest to them and the clubbing began in earnest. The men tried to protect their heads with their arms but the blows came down on them hard and fast from all sides, until one toppled, then the next and the SS began kicking them.

'Get up, will you get up, you swine!' Finally both men stood up again and the guards, like demented furies, clubbed them once more. Between the shouts we could hear the clubs hit bone. The naked men fell again and after this had been repeated several times no amount of kicking would make them get to their feet. Methodically, after the first two men, the SS went from pair to pair until all of them were lying motionless on the ground. The snow was stained with blood, their clothing spread around. Once in a while an arm or a leg moved: it was an indescribably horrible sight. I was petrified and unable to utter a sound. The *kapo* and I kept staring at the bodies. The SS, seemingly satisfied with their work, left the scene. The death-brigade arrived and carted the lifeless men into a small room nearby. I sneaked out of the showers and hurried back to the laundry.

'Where have you been all this time?' Lustyk greeted me. Then he noticed my expression. 'What happened, what's wrong with you?' I was trembling and couldn't speak, as if I were choking. Eventually, I was able to tell them what I had just witnessed, but probably quite incoherently, because all three kept interrupting me with questions.

'I'm going there to see for myself,' Tonda suddenly declared.

'You stay right where you are,' shouted the *kapo*. 'Are you out of your mind? They'll be drinking now and you'll get it too.'

When I returned to my cell in the evening everybody knew what had happened. They questioned me but what could I tell them? I had no idea who the men were or what they had done. The soup carriers returning from the kitchen had seen the blood stains on the snow; the clothing had been picked up. I spoke to the shower *kapo* a few days later to ask if he knew anything more: what he could tell me was second hand.

'They were left in the little room for two days with the door locked, then they were carted away, I didn't see it myself, I wasn't in the showers that day.' And so ended one of the most ghastly scenes I have ever witnessed.

In the early spring a transport of New Zealand prisoners of war arrived at the Fortress. The SD knew I spoke French and had sometimes called on me to translate. On this occasion I was sent for by Schmidt to translate for the English-speaking POWs lined up in front of his office. During the transport two prisoners had escaped and Schmidt wanted to know where the men were sitting on the train in order to identify the neighbours of the escapees to determine the time and place of the evasion.

The POWs weren't being very helpful in giving the information: once their refusal to co-operate became only too clear, the guards started hitting them with their gun butts. The men protested that the guards had no right to hit them—it was against the Geneva Convention.

At this Schmidt just laughed. 'This is not a POW camp,' he said after I had translated and, as if to prove it, hit the nearest man so hard that he fell and then kicked him. 'Here we do things according to our own convention.' After this interruption the questioning began again—who was sitting next to whom? Each man was ordered to stand next to his neighbour from the train. The seating pattern slowly began to emerge.

At this point an English voice ordered all the others to stop supplying any more information to Schmidt, whom he then addressed in fairly good German telling him he was a senior officer and would provide all the information permitted under the convention. The guards were taken by surprise and so was I, it was unheard of for a prisoner to talk back.

'Why didn't you tell us you spoke German?' Schmidt asked. At that he ordered the New Zealander into his office and I was sent away. I never saw these men again and thought that their stay in the camp didn't last very long but in this I was mistaken. Their army uniforms were exchanged for the grey prison garb, they had their heads shaved like the rest of us, and were kept in the Small Fortress until April 1945, when they were sent to an unknown destination.

Besides our ever-shrinking bread ration and the problems brought on by overcrowding, there were other unmistakable signs that the war was coming to an end. Some concerned us directly but others were circumstantial. There was one event towards the end of the winter which left a deep impression on us all. One night after we had just fallen asleep, we were suddenly roused by a strange sound, as if sack after sack of potatoes were being emptied into a cellar. We soon realized that the sound was rather that of bombs exploding in the distance, too far away to distinguish each separate explosion. The overall effect was a rumbling noise lasting well over twenty minutes.

The only window in the cell, right beside my place on the bunks, faced in a northerly direction. Soon I could discern a red glare to the left above the fortification walls, a glare increasing in intensity by the minute. The whole cell was awake and a crowd of us pressed close to the window trying to get a glimpse of the spectacle. Some had been through air-raids before but the general consensus was that this attack was of a so far unexperienced intensity.

We were all trying to guess which of the cities in that direction could be under attack. Dresden was the most likely but it was hard to believe the sound could be so intense over a distance of some forty or fifty miles. Soon afterwards a second bombing-wave began and the red glare grew even more intense. The reaction of all was unanimous—everybody cheered although there were men from Dresden among us who, with families there, must have been torn between worry and elation. No, there was one who condemned the bombing outright and that was Jupp.

One afternoon Tonda came running into the laundry calling us out to watch a plane circling over the camp—it was our first sight of a jet and it seemed to fly twice as fast as any aircraft we had seen before. Soon the camp was buzzing with the alarming news that the *Luft-waffe* had a plane capable of knocking the Allies out of the sky. Our worries were dispelled when the grape-vine reported new air-raids on other cities—if this new wonder plane were that effective, how could the Allies still continue their day and night attacks?

Now that the end of the war was coming closer, one of our frequent subjects of discussion was whether or not the guards would try to kill us before leaving the camp. There seemed to be as many guesses and opinions as there were men in the cell. Some were convinced we would be locked in to starve to death, others believed the SS would machine-gun us down, lob hand-grenades into the cells or poison the food. The more hopeful were banking on being evacuated to other camps. Speculation was endless but, for some among us, the end came in a way nobody anticipated.

By some time in March—or was it the beginning of April—it was becoming clear that the fighting was approaching our area. One morning more guards than usual were on duty for roll-call. The order was given that everybody, those working as waiters or servants, those in the offices, the cell *kapos*, in short, all, without exception, whether fit or not, were to form a single work detail. Once the entire yard was part of this *kommando* Schmidt arrived and pointed at me to step out of rank followed by all laundry personnel plus maybe half a dozen others. The rest were sent to join a huge labour battalion forming into a marching column on the entrance square. Shovels were distributed—God knows where they got them all.

At daybreak the camp gate was opened and this gigantic, human snake surrounded by the regular guards plus an additional unit from the SS training centre in Leitmeritz, began slowly moving out to an unknown destination. What was also very unusual was that many SD in the administration—Rojko among them—went out with this battalion. For the few who stayed behind, the camp acquired an eerie, unreal aspect. Apart from the disabled pilot, I was the only one left behind in our cell, and it didn't look much different in the other cells in our yard, where normally a good portion of inmates were employed as inside workers. In the laundry we speculated on the possible reason for this wholesale clean-out. Spirits were subdued, even though we considered ourselves lucky to have been excluded. The whole undertaking didn't look too reassuring and our fears were confirmed in the evening.

Watching those who marched back, we knew that something extraordinary had happened. They lined up in front of our cells, their faces drawn with fatigue and later I learned the full story. They had been sent to dig anti-tank ditches, not too far from the camp, alongside the road from Dresden to Prague. As they had been marched out of the Fortress, the prisoners were given to understand that this would be an assignment unlike any they had experienced before. The normal retribution for breaking the marching rhythm was a bash with a gun butt: now anyone slowing down the march for whatever reason was hauled out and summarily shot.

When the column reached the site, the guards formed a huge circle around the men. A few of the SS began circulating among the diggers and, if they didn't like a prisoner's work or perhaps his face, they would take his cap and throw it outside the circle, ordering the man to go and fetch it. As soon as the hapless victim stepped out he was shot for attempting to escape. I was told that two young inmates had had their caps taken away simultaneously. When they were ordered to break the circle, one of them asked if they could go only after they had eaten their portion of bread. The guard magnanimously agreed, whereupon the two men calmly sat down to have their last meal, then suggested that, as they were going to be shot anyway, why not do it right there. The guard, considering it a great joke, killed them on the spot.

191

Since the dead had to be brought back to camp, the returning column presented an awesome and chilling sight. There were some fifty bodies carried on the shoulders of their fellow inmates. At roll-call the dead were laid out in front of the prisoners—like game after a successful shoot. The anti-tank digging lasted three days. The fear of those leaving in the morning was easy to understand, each wondering if it wouldn't be his turn. In order not to draw attention to themselves they worked like mad and the physical exertion showed at the end of the day—some could hardly move when they returned.

There were two casualties in our cell. One was a relative newcomer whom I didn't know well but the other, a man of about forty, a policeman from Vienna, had been with us for some time. The Major described his death. During the lunch-break, when they were permitted to sit down to eat their piece of bread, an SS man came up to him and, apparently without any reason, took his cap and walked towards the circle of guards. The Viennese, realizing what was going to happen next, ran after the guard and threw himself in front of him, imploring, 'Don't kill me, please. I have small children. What will become of them?' The SS kicked him away and threw the cap beyond the circle. The inmate stubbornly refused to fetch it so the guard kept on kicking him until, in the end, he got to his feet and, crying, stepped outside the circle. He was shot before even touching the cap.

The sight of a prisoner begging for his life was a rare one. Those who knew they were about to be shot were aware that begging for their life would make no difference. The majority of inmates awaited their execution with numbed senses: there was no outburst of heroism or defiance, but no plea for mercy either. Had I been in the situation of knowing that I would be shot in the next instant, I believe my main regret would have been that it was to happen when the end of war was near—at least, that is what I think I felt when Horse Head held his gun against the back of my head. From the treatment we received and the daily brutality, our senses were blunted, almost as if we had been on drugs for a long time. Fatalities no longer evoked the same reaction as they would have done in normal life. It might be an exaggeration to pretend that our feelings were comparable to those of cattle but I suppose a certain similarity did exist: sadness over the death of someone we knew well was over-ridden by relief that it hadn't happened to oneself.

From my cellmates I heard that during the three-day *Aussen-kommando*, Rojko surpassed himself in brutality, shooting men on the slightest pretext; he and Horse Head were the worst of the guards. I saw Rojko from close up only rarely, he had nothing to do with the laundry. Once I witnessed him clubbing and kicking the German-Jewish officer from Breslau, the occupant of the neighbouring cell when I was first in St Pancras. Our *kapo* and I were just passing Rojko's office with a batch of clean kitchen laundry when he was in the act of mistreating the former officer. Either we weren't carrying the stretcher fast enough to suit him or he didn't want us to see him in action. He hit Lustyk with the stick, shouting, 'Don't you know you are supposed to move at a trot? Get going!'

On another occasion he came into our cell unexpectedly while I was standing by the door. He fixed me with his blue eyes. 'Which of you is Krebs?' Krebs, a man who had been with us only a short while, immediately presented himself and Rojko said, 'Come with me.' We never saw Krebs again!

Some time later Rojko appeared in our cell again, this time looking for me. I was sure my last moment had come. As we were leaving our courtyard he broke the silence. 'Why are you here?'

'For illegal border-crossing, *Herr Kommandant*.'

'You liar!' and he looked at me contemptuously. The reason he had come to get me was a much more cheerful one than I had imagined—my sister had come to visit me again. Normally, on the occasion of my sister's visits, it was Schmidt who came to collect me. I suppose Rojko too must have wondered why I had been singled out for this preferential treatment and may have resented it.

As winter gave way to early spring, signs of the end in sight were multiplying. Schmidt was present at one morning roll-call and chose some dozen men from our cell, ordering them to follow him. As I have already mentioned, nearly all of my cellmates were German or Austrian, whereas the largest single nationality in the Fortress was Czech, with a sprinkling of Frenchmen, Poles, Belgians and Russians. All in all, some twenty nationalities passed through at one time or another. Later that evening the same men told us they had been offered immediate release if they would accept being drafted. I think all of them agreed, mainly because they were given to understand the offer was symbolic but in actual fact they had no choice: they also knew they were heading for the punishment battalions, that is, units detailed to carry out the most dangerous missions.

Among those who left us were our cell *kapo* and the orderly, both former SS members—they were needed again because of the shortage of men able to bear arms. Others were soldiers like my friend Schumann, the deserter. I was sorry to see them go, they were all part of my original crowd and we got on well together. The *kapo* had been able to spare us a lot of the trouble to which other cells were sometimes exposed; he understood the mentality of the guards and knew how to handle them. With Schumann I had formed an association advantageous to both of us.

His working hours as a cook in the SS canteen were relatively short and we used to prepare fried potatoes and onions on my free day when most of our cellmates were out on work details. Making this mixture on the iron stove was something I always looked forward to. Schumann would steal margarine and onions while I liberated potatoes and coal. The potatoes originated from the kitchen detail and were smuggled as far as the laundry in the same way as the occasional loaf of bread—it was one of my private deals. Getting hold of the coal was much simpler, it came from just around the corner of the second yard, from the laundry boiler room about a hundred feet away. The fellow working there was a friend who often benefited from our crew's dealings with the kitchen-brigade.

Schumann wasn't too happy about going back into the army but, as he said, a punishment battalion was still better than the camp. Anyway, when leaving, his last words to me were, 'The *Wehrmacht* won't have to feed me for long, I plan to scram the first chance I get.'

The empty spaces on the bunks were soon filled by newcomers and, with these newcomers, came lice. Until then, the only bothersome insects to be coped with were fleas and bedbugs, which we tried to keep under control with somewhat mixed results—at least they weren't dangerous. With lice, the situation was different. These weren't the kind of lice found in hair—that was one of the reasons our heads were shaved—although by now we were all sporting the camp style of the period, one closely shaved strip in the middle, called *lagerstrasse* or camp street, with the side hair left to grow about half an inch, something like the reverse of an Iroquois' hairdo.

The dangerous lice hid in the seams of underwear and prison garb. Every evening scores of inmates methodically inspected all possible hiding places, turning their clothes inside out, but there was no way of controlling the plague effectively. Not all prisoners went over their clothing thoroughly and every day for some were already too apa-

194

thetic. Moreover, on the overcrowded sleeping bunks we were fitted in like sardines in a tin while the lice crawled from one sleeping form to the next. Washing clothes brought only temporary relief, hot water killed the lice but not the eggs.

The only defence we knew of was to wear silk next to the skin which was, of course, out of the question for the prisoners. In the laundry we put aside every piece of silk underwear or the occasional silk shirt found among the clothing being packed for Germany but the quantity, as can be imagined, was pitifully small: only we and our closest friends could hope to wear silk. Some of the men arriving with transports from the east told us the best way to get rid of lice was to bury the clothes, leaving only a small corner sticking out above the ground. The lice would crawl to the part above ground and could then be picked off. The problem there was that internees were issued with only one set of clothing and anyway, the ground in the Fortress was hard as rock—and where could we get hold of shovels?

It wasn't so much the constant biting, or rather itching that was bothersome—flea bites and especially those of bedbugs were worse. Lice, maybe one-eighth of an inch long, were slow-moving, transparent, whitish, pointed ovals with a dark spot in the centre, easy to find and kill by squeezing them between thumbnails. The real danger was that lice were typhus carriers. In the laundry, since we were the ones most exposed to infection from handling dirty clothes, we started to work undressed, wearing just a pair of silk underpants, and this only as a concession to our *kapo*. For extra protection, we shaved our body hair with a razor organized from the shower *kapo*.

As the transports from the east increased so did the cases of typhus. The first to be infected were the men from the crowded fourth courtyard and it didn't seem the camp authorities were doing anything to stem the infection. There was no space for setting up a quarantine and every cell was crammed to more than its full capacity. To make things worse, a special transport of Frenchmen arrived, so two large cells had to be cleared of inmates. These Frenchmen with unshaved heads were in civilian clothes. They even brought Red Cross parcels with them—American cigarettes started circulating in the camp. Although theoretically there was no contact between us, it was soon known that the Frenchmen were hostages—politicians and other public figures with Albert Sarraut who had been prime minister for a very short time in 1933, and an archbiship among them. They didn't stay for long, however—a month or so before the end of the war they were evacuated from the Fortress in Swedish Red Cross buses. The news of the arrival of the buses spread like wildfire. Many prisoners were convinced that the Red Cross would return and take us all away in order to stem the spread of the typhus epidemic.

Of course it was only wishful thinking and nothing like that happened. The camp was buzzing with latrines which even the most simple-minded had trouble taking seriously. One rumour was that a work battalion had seen a column of American soldiers in the distance so there was speculation that the next day we would be liberated. The only change that actually occurred was that transports were organized that left the Fortress. I guess this was the only preventive measure the authorities were taking to control the epidemic. We believed this decision was taken after a high-ranking SS officer—some of the inmates thought it was Ernst Kaltenbrunner, who succeeded Heydrich as boss of the SD and was second only to Himmler in the SS—visited the camp. Whoever it was arrived by car, which in itself was an event. By this time the petrol shortage was so acute that only the most influential had access to it.

Pinda, the camp commander, left by bicycle to meet the officer outside the Fortress and led him in. A witness told us with glee how furiously he was pedalling ahead of the car, his stomach almost touching the handlebars. When they arrived in front of his office, Pinda nearly fell from his bike, but straightened himself immediately and was standing at attention when the visitor stepped out. Of course, we had no idea what was discussed between the two men but it was a fact that his visit and the evacuations from the camp more or less followed each other. Kaltenbrunner, who was tried and hanged in Nuremberg with other Nazi big shots, did come to the Small Fortress, but to tell Jöckel to stop further executions. His order wasn't obeyed either by the Prague Gestapo or by the camp commander himself. All that came to light during Jöckel's trial.

22

Late in March, I think it was, my name was called out at morning roll-call and I was sent to the shower-room together with some fifty other inmates, none of whom I knew. A civilian doctor from Leitmeritz came in and told us to undress, looked at us from a distance of ten feet and within a couple of minutes declared all fit for transport, presumably to Flossenbürg in Bavaria, close to the border with Bohemia. It was a camp with a bad reputation and I would have to start again at the bottom of the ladder with all the hazards that entailed. Naturally, I wasn't very happy with the prospect but, once again, the same unknown quirk of fate that seemed to have a hand in my prison destiny saved me from being shipped out.

Our medical inspection was only another example of the inconsistencies to which the Nazis were given: prisoners could be worked to death or killed on the whim of a particular guard, yet had to pass a medical—if such a farce could be so termed—in order to be declared fit for transport to another camp. These absurdities were so common we stopped paying any attention to them.

In the German cell there were a few men who had actually come before a court and been judged. In some cases the accused were acquitted or condemned to only a few months' imprisonment. However, this didn't prevent the Gestapo from putting them into a concentration camp for an unspecified time, where they might have stayed forever had the war ended differently. This internment classification was known as *Schutzhaft*—preventive or protective internment.

When I was interrogated by the Gestapo I had to sign the bottom of my complete written statement and initial every page and any corrections. I knew of many prisoners who had stubbornly refused to sign anything—the result was identical, they were put into a camp all the same but with the difference that beforehand they were beaten more than those who signed.

There were other inconsistencies, such as the right to receive food parcels or mail, but I don't recall anybody in the Fortress ever getting either. Another incongruity was the dispensary. In theory it was open two days a week after work but, if more than a couple of dozen sick presented themselves, all were sent away. There was no medication to be given out and the most one could hope for was a chit from the guard granting dispensation from work the following day. The list of contradictions was endless.

The first cases of typhus in our yard were discovered round about the beginning of April. Until then the epidemic had been limited to the fourth yard and most of us had no contact with these inmates. Now, prisoners working in the same details with them, men with whom we shared the bunks, were falling victim to it. Each cell had its own method of attempting to stem the spread of the disease. Every evening inspections were organized in our cell. Each of us had to undress while a chosen committee looked for the tell-tale red spots: those found to have them were ordered to sleep on the floor. Many of us, however, were of the opinion that this measure was useless because those showing red spots could have already infected their neighbours. Roll-calls were becoming more and more difficult—the sick were too weak and lifeless to stand up for counting.

The first symptoms seemed to be a headache, apathy and progressive weakening with the sick person often giving the impression of running a temperature. But these various signs were difficult to recognize, since otherwise healthy prisoners commonly suffered from the same ills. General weakness and apathy due to overwork and undernourishment were common: the only concrete indication of a typhus infection remained the diagnosis of the tiny red spots that within a short time spread all over the body. Confusion was heightened by the fact that many of us were suffering from skin diseases and sores, so it became virtually impossible to separate the inmates who had contracted typhus from those who hadn't.

As always, the grape-vine kept us informed about progress on the fronts. The Russians had entered Berlin and, by late April, the Allies occupied the whole western part of the Reich. There were bets as to who would reach the camp first. At any rate, it was now evident to all of us that we were witnessing the last days of the war: but at whatever speed the Allies were advancing it wasn't fast enough, the typhus was spreading faster. Our drum operator, Tonda, fell ill in spite of all the precautions he was taking. The *Aussenkommandos* virtually stopped going out, there were more sick men to be carried back than there were healthy ones to work. The whole organization of the camp was falling apart.

In this general disintegration, somebody came running to tell us that Hitler was dead. Nobody could believe the news but the prisoner had heard it on the radio—a communiqué announcing that the Führer had fallen in Berlin, fighting to his last breath. We were surprised to hear Berlin mentioned: like everybody else we had expected Hitler to continue fighting in the Alps. That evening nobody could get to sleep wondering what would happen next but nothing of importance did, at least so it seemed, although the subdued spirits of the SS were noticeable.

At roll-call the following day some prisoners were taken away, among them the mechanic-electrician, the man I had had dealings with on behalf of Eric. During the morning we learned that more than fifty men from other yards had also been called out from ranks, and word soon spread that they were all in the XYZ category. Now we were convinced the initials stood for early release. Many of our yardmates, having nothing better to do, were in and out of the laundry, all commenting on how lucky these fellows were.

The next we heard was that the new Head of State was Admiral Dönitz who had declared that the war would go on. Everybody was taken aback by this announcement. Dönitz was not a Nazi party member and should have been anxious to end the fighting as quickly as possible—strange that Hitler hadn't designated a Nazi to succeed him. The information was classed as another latrine. Whether true or not and regardless of what Dönitz had to say, the war was over and the only question of importance for us was how to get out of the camp fast, because the typhus was now reaching catastrophic proportions.

During the afternoon of that same day we were startled by a burst of shots. Our first idea was that fighting had broken out in the vicinity of the Small Fortress but the salvos kept repeating themselves at fairly regular intervals and seemed to be coming from somewhere closer, inside the camp itself—from the execution yard, to be exact. Whom would they be shooting now with the war virtually over? Was this the beginning of what lay in store for all of us? A shout from the doorway, and someone burst in.

'They're shooting the ones they called out this morning.'

'That is how all of us will be liberated,' commented our *kapo*.

'Even if they shoot a hundred a day some of us might still be alive when it's over,' said the man who had brought us the news, almost as if he wanted to allay everyone's fears.

'Tomorrow they'll organize it better,' came from Tonda's replacement.

Neither the colonel nor I said anything. I had been observing him since the morning and he seemed listless, leaning once in a while against the table where he was folding shirts. He didn't appear to be his usual self, but the general atmosphere was such that none of the others paid any attention to it. So, at last, we knew the meaning of the letters XYZ—liquidation.

Sure enough, the colonel didn't show up for work on our next shift and the *kapo* told me he had come down with typhus, which left only the two of us from the original crew of four. The colonel was his friend and I could sense he was deeply affected. Lustyk had mellowed a lot in the last months, had become more talkative and enforced less and less discipline. When Tonda and I first began our deals with the Ukrainian guards he threatened to report us if we continued. Lately, that is until shortly before Tonda became sick, we had been able to do our deals quite openly while he pretended not to know anything about it. I guess he never had any intention of reporting us, it would have landed him in trouble as well. Fears that a new batch of prisoners would be singled out never materialized but, around ten o'clock that morning, Mende walked into the laundry.

'You there,' he said, pointing in my direction. 'Come with me.' As I walked towards Mende, I couldn't help but notice the expression on Lustyk's face and, remembering what had happened to the others, I had a kind of hollow feeling in my stomach—so this was to be my turn. We walked by the now-deserted workshops, along by the administration office and turned right behind the SD living quarters: Mende was leading me straight to the execution ground. The closer we came to the tunnel the stronger became my feeling of emptiness. He must have guessed my thoughts and looked me right in the face as if he wanted to say something but, instead, just unlocked the gate. We passed through the tunnel and out in to the execution yard. It was an empty terrain overgrown with grass, surrounded by the fortifications.

Away from the entrance stood the gallows: otherwise the whole place had quite a bucolic aspect.

'I might as well show you where I keep some rabbits. You'll be feeding them,' said Mende. What an anticlimax. To my relief there was indeed a row of cages to the left against the brick wall. He opened the door to each one and showed me how much fodder to put in. The feeding finished, we headed for the gate and I felt much better, I must admit.

'From now on you're going to be cleaning for me. My wife has left so you'll be looking after the place,' he explained as we walked back towards the SD quarters. It seemed odd that he should have chosen as his orderly someone he had once threatened to shoot. We went into his ground-floor flat which comprised two small rooms and a kitchen. He showed me around, said I was to wash the dishes then the floor and left. What interested me most was the radio. I would be able to listen to news directly but not yet being familiar with his habits I just ogled the set without daring to touch it. After a couple of hours Mende came back and told me to return to my cell.

I was about to pass the corner of the administration office and the entrance square when I heard my name called. I turned to see Schmidt but before I had a chance to salute, the unbelievable happened. He came to me.

'Please tell your sister I won't be able to call her. Say hello to her for me when you see her.' At that precise moment, I have to admit, his message didn't make any sense but my reaction was automatic, 'Yes indeed, *Herr Kommandant*.' Like all prisoners I was well conditioned to execute orders without question but why this strange request? Schmidt returned to join a dozen or so SS guards standing talking in front of his office. Was he, along with the other SS, preparing to leave the Fortress? Where would he be going and what for? All of Germany would be occupied in a few days. Did he imagine he could hide somewhere? Now it would be his turn to be hunted. I continued on my way. Why on earth should I give Utta the message, Schmidt hadn't actually issued an order, he said please. My thoughts were interrupted by two inmates standing at some distance from the group of SS. Coming abreast of them I heard one say, 'Some morons will be saluting them until doomsday.' I paid no attention as the remark didn't seem to be directed at me. I found our cell was in an uproar.

'The guards are leaving. It's finished, it's all over, we're going home.' Everybody was shouting and laughing at the same time and it came to me what the prisoner had meant. I had missed out on the most exciting moment, the one I had been waiting for since my arrest. Among all the fantasies of how we would see our liberation what I hadn't imagined was that I would be washing dishes when it came. There was such an effervescent atmosphere in our yard, everybody visiting, talking at once, making plans—it was good to have a future again. In the small cubicle between our cell and the neighbouring one the inmate in charge of the letter-press machine was busily turning out certificates stating that the bearer had been a prisoner of the Small Fortress.

Several men were posted at the entrance of the courtyard to observe the movements of the guards on the square. They kept us informed on what was going on until one ran back shouting, 'They're leaving, they're pulling out.' It was late afternoon on a beautiful May day, the 5th. The moment we had all wanted to live to see had arrived at last. Sometimes, even contrary to good sense, one persists in keeping up hope against all odds and ends up being justified: I guess that is how we, the survivors, felt but, nevertheless, for most of us there had been some close calls.

I went to the entrance square to see for myself and, sure enough, all the guards had gone. Some men were trying to force the locked gate but the assistants to the head *kapo* asked everyone to take it easy, to go back to the cells, they would let us know what went on.

'Nobody is permitted to leave the Fortress on his own. Everybody has to pass through quarantine first.' Later I noticed a yellow quarantine flag over the entrance gate. We heard that medical teams from the outside had moved into the camp and, together with inmates who were doctors, had started to take care of the sick. I was restless and couldn't stay in the cell. We went from yard to yard in small groups to see what was going on. Sights awaited me which I will never forget. Hundreds upon hundreds of prisoners lay haphazardly on the ground, some still alive, others dead: more were being carted out of the cells. All were infected and the still healthy inmates didn't want them inside. Tonda had been taken away a week earlier, but I walked among the stretched-out forms to see if there was anyone I knew. In the women's yard I came across our colonel from the laundry lying on his back staring straight up into the sky.

'So, you've got it too,' I remarked rather stupidly.

He looked at me for an instant as if to make sure he knew me and slowly answered, 'Yes, I caught it.'

'Do you need anything?'

'No, my friends are already taking care of me. I'm supposed to be taken out today.' The colonel had been moved there by the officer clique and I knew they could look after him better than we could. I also learned that the previous night the women's yard had been secretly cleared of its inmates and a quarantine hastily set up for them in the Terezín ghetto.

Towards the evening, the first batches of healthy prisoners were evacuated there too, into the former military barracks. Word passed around that we could go to the clothing-room to collect our belongings. The evacuation went on steadily and my turn came in the middle of the night. Among the men who had been moved earlier I found many I knew from the second yard: they were sitting in small groups discussing the latest events. Nobody could sleep, and anyway, there was too much coming and going. I was told that Jupp, the German *kapo* was dead, killed by the men who worked under him. The news didn't surprise me, he had it coming and I expected that other *kapos* might end up the same way. The moment for settling personal accounts had arrived.

23

In the morning I left the barracks and ventured into the ghetto to find out about Mother, Grandfather Joseph and Franta. Although the ghetto had also been flooded with transports from the east and from Germany, at least here the typhus was under control: recent arrivals in their striped pyjama uniforms wandered aimlessly through the streets looking for anybody they knew. It seemed the Terezín SDs had left earlier than ours and some kind of organization was beginning to take shape. Doctors and nurses from the outside were preparing temporary dispensaries and de-lousing stations while field kitchens were handing out food. In the Fortress we hadn't eaten after the guards left so I was really hungry. I joined a queue and was given a bowl of soup but no spoon. While I was sitting on the ground drinking it, somebody tapped me on the shoulder. It was Hanka, a girl from Prague with whom I used to take the tram to school. She said she recognized me immediately.

Hanka had arrived in Terezín three days earlier, she told me. She looked well and I found it hard to believe she had been in Auschwitz and after that in Dora, an underground factory in central Germany where the women inmates made parts for rockets. We walked around while she gave me what news she could of some mutual friends. Hanka had left Terezín for Auschwitz relatively late and knew of those who had preceded her, but she hadn't seen any of them again in the camp. In Auschwitz her mother had been separated from her during a medical check-up. Hanka explained how this was handled. The women had to undress and run naked towards an SS standing in the middle of the road who indicated with his thumb whether they were to pass to his right or left. Those who went to the side with Hanka were sent to work, those ending on the other side were never seen again—soon afterwards she found out about the gas chambers. Strangely, Hanka told me all this without any show of emotion.

'How come your mother was sent to the other side?' I couldn't help but ask. 'Before I knew you better I thought she was your sister.'

'I can't tell you. There were women in my group who looked much older. It was just a question of luck, maybe she wasn't running fast enough.'

'What happened to your father and brother?'

'I don't know. The men were separated from us well before the selection. My brother could be alive but I doubt my father is, he was a lot older than Mother. I never saw the men from our transport again.'

'And when were you sent to Dora?'

'About the end of autumn, before Christmas. The Russians were getting close to Auschwitz.'

'How were the conditions there?'

'Better. As you can see, I'm not in bad shape. At least they didn't shave our heads.' With that she took off her scarf to show me a stubble about two inches long and continued the story of her Odyssey.

'Then, when the Americans were approaching Dora, we thought at first we'd be transported to the south but the railway lines were bombed so we had to leave the train in southern Saxony and from there the guards brought us here.'

'How were the guards?' I asked, remembering ours.

'On the whole, fairly decent—some of them even shared food with us. Some girls escaped. I wanted to but then I thought I might as well stay with the transport as long as it was heading towards Prague.'

'Where did you sleep after you left the train?'

'In barns, or just in the fields, the weather was good. Anyway, it took us only a week to get here.'

We walked past a group of wizened-looking women sitting on the ground, but it was easy to see they weren't really old—their faces were like those of baby monkeys. Several of them were crying.

'Do you know who they are?' I asked Hanka.

'They're from Hungary but I don't know from what camp. They arrived a day after us, just before the SD left. When they got here they had to be de-loused and washed and some refused to go into the showers, they thought it was a gas chamber. The guards were burning all the files in the barracks where you are now so they may have thought the smoke came from a crematorium. But there was never a gas chamber here in Terezín.'

'What files, do you know?'

'It seems the SS kept the files from all the camps in Germany here. The fire was enormous with a lot of smoke, no wonder those women were afraid.'

We continued walking without purpose up and down the streets but always on the look-out for a familiar face. A prisoner from the Fortress met us. 'They're giving out food at the barracks, if you want some you'd better get there fast.'

'I suppose I'll be seeing you in Prague,' I said, turning to Hanka and hurried off. By now the barracks was seething with prisoners evacuated from the Small Fortress. The medical team running the dispensary didn't seem to be very strict about enforcing the quarantine, people were walking in and out without any control. I lined up for a piece of bread and some soup. When I went to return the empty bowl a man from the second yard stopped me.

'Somebody is looking for you. There, do you see that woman?' The woman was my mother, she had seen me too and was coming towards me. We embraced and her first words were, 'I heard you had been arrested and somebody told me that you were dead. It was only yesterday I found out you were alive.' Questions and answers were flowing on both sides. Mother told me Franta was no longer in Terezín—he had been shipped out in the autumn of the previous year—and we both speculated on whether or not he was still alive. Grandfather Joseph had been sent east in a transport much earlier than Franta so we knew there was no hope of ever seeing him again. Mother had remained in Terezín all the time. Her name was once on a list, she had even been given the wagon number when, just before boarding, somebody said to her 'But you don't have to go. Haven't you got a son from a marriage to a German Aryan?' Mother went right away to the ghetto council and from then on she was protected from further transports.

The news that I had been arrested and killed had been given to her by a woman from a mixed marriage who had been deported to the ghetto in the winter. She had learned that I was still alive only two days ago from Hana, a young woman she had made friends with in Terezín. Hana was a Gentile who had voluntarily followed her husband, Kamil, and they had a son who had been born there.

In the early autumn of 1944, Kamil had been shipped out, presumably to Auschwitz. Hana hoped he might be among the several hundred prisoners brought back by forced marches in February to be imprisoned in Richard, a small camp on the outskirts of Leitmeritz. This camp was actually an underground armaments factory located in an abandoned mine. Hana was determined to find her husband. Just before the guards left Terezín she slipped out to make her way to Dr Burian's home, the address my mother had given her. Utta was present when she arrived and offered to help in locating Kamil straight away. It was decided that my sister would lead Hana back to Terezín, which wasn't as simple as it might sound for they could have run into a police patrol. By various detours they made it safely and discovered that, in the meantime, the SS had left Terezín and the sentry posts were now manned by Jewish internees. Hana brought Utta to meet my mother for the first time, so she knew about my sister's visits to me in the Small Fortress and that I was in good health.

We went over all that had happened to us, there was so much she wanted to find out. I realized we hadn't talked like this for years; in the past, relations between us hadn't always been good. From the time I was seventeen or so we had never got along well and for almost a year we weren't on speaking terms at all. Now everything was forgotten. Once every bit of news that came to our minds had been exchanged, we discussed how best to plan our return to Prague. My mother wanted to stay put for a while until the situation became clearer. The *Wehrmacht* was still technically in control of the surroundings so she preferred to wait for a transport to be organized by the Red Cross. I was impatient to get home and told her I would make my way back at the first opportunity, but not before I had gone to Leitmeritz to see Utta. With that we separated.

When I reached the road from Dresden to Prague I found it full of troops and civilians fleeing southwards. This reminded me that the war wasn't exactly over yet so, instead of going to Leitmeritz, I decided to return to the Fortress. On my way there I was joined by another prisoner heading back for the same reason—we both agreed it would be best to await events. Strangely enough, after hoping for so long to get out of the camp, we now considered it a safe haven in the turmoil around us.

The gate was open and the yards looked deserted. All the dead had been taken away and the sick transferred to hospitals. I went back to my cell to find that many German inmates were still there—they had heard reports of Czechs lynching isolated Germans, making no distinction between Nazis and opponents of the regime. Unsure of how they would be treated they were afraid to leave the camp on their own, nor did they want to join the remnants of the fleeing army or the civilians on the road.

There was nobody in the laundry and the other cells in our yard were half empty. The only busy place was the printshop. On his own initiative the printer was still turning out certificates, not very official looking but, as he explained to me, he had been asked to do them for those who lived far away. A certificate would serve as a *laissez-passer*, since nobody had any identification papers. Staying on in the camp didn't make much sense to me: it was getting dark and there seemed no hope of finding anything to eat. I returned to the cell to say goodbye but my cellmates tried to persuade me to stay. There was more space now they argued, without the sick and those who had already left. Frigge wasn't there but then he didn't have to go far to get back to his parish: the prisoners left behind were mainly the Austrians and those who came from Dresden. I wasn't sure what to do but just then some inmates appeared with a slab of bacon, bread and a couple of bottles of schnaps discovered in the SD quarters where they had gone rummaging. That decided the issue, I was staying. When the loot was divided there wasn't much for each man but it was still better than what we used to get. The liquor made me a bit dizzy so I crawled back into my bunk to sleep.

Early in the morning an inmate from the neighbouring cell came to wake us up wanting to know if we could hear gun-fire. Together we climbed to the top of the fortifications and saw the road below packed with people on foot, horse carts piled with household goods and army trucks, all intermingled and heading towards Prague. This scene gave the impression that the road was the last open corridor leading from Saxony to Bohemia—the only escape hatch to the south.

Occasionally there was a lull but, most of the time, the road was so crowded that those on foot were left with only the shoulder to advance along. Motor-bikes and bicycles wound their way between the soldiers and civilians weary with the fatigue of sleepless nights, hunger and exposure to the elements. Loaded with bundles and wearing clothes unsuitable for the season, they looked what they really were, the image of a defeated nation, like the propaganda movies the Nazis had shown us after the collapse of France. There were whole families with children in prams, their eyes glued to the ground, nobody noticing us on top of the ramparts. It was a strange but, at the same time, fascinating spectacle. The Fortress walls were a good spot from which to observe the slowly moving human column emerging from Terezín, crossing the bridge and passing right below us. We figured the Russians had already taken Dresden and probably the railway junction where I had loaded coal, a place of unhappy memory.

Somebody climbed up to tell us soup was being distributed. It was noon, the time had gone by incredibly fast. I ran down, gulped the soup and quickly returned to my vantage point. The flow hadn't decreased but by now it was comprised, almost exclusively, of army personnel travelling in trucks, on motor-bikes and bicycles with, here and there, a horse-drawn cart. One truck had only three wheels and for the fourth a sort of makeshift ski which hit the pavement from time to time. Now the gun-fire was very close. A couple of *Wehrmacht* tanks went by, then more trucks and suddenly nothing—the road was completely deserted. Ten minutes, twenty minutes went by with still nothing in sight.

At last a bright-red German postal-bus came at high speed along the road leading from Terezín but, instead of taking the turn after the bridge, continued straight towards the Small Fortress. Who could it be? Why was it heading our way? We didn't have to wonder for long. Half-way between the bridge and the camp gate, the bus stopped suddenly. The driver realized it was a cul-de-sac and tried desperately to turn back, but the road was too narrow and the trees on both sides made manoeuvring difficult. The bus was inching slowly forwards and backwards until it was straight across the road. At that moment there were a couple of gun shots from very close by and the bus instantly burst into flames. We watched with fascination as the passengers tried in vain to get out through the windows.

A tank, followed by a second and third, emerged from Terezín. They didn't bother about the burning bus, or make the same mistake as its driver, and kept to the main road. More tanks appeared, with soldiers sitting on platforms to the rear of the turrets, while behind the tanks came trucks filled with more troops. The first of the tanks with a red star on the turret had now reached the road below us, its treads clattering on the pavement. The turret of the second tank was open, showing a soldier wearing an unusual leather helmet with ear phones. Tanks and trucks, now forming an uninterrupted stream of vehicles, were passing just below us. The soldiers wore grey-beige uniforms, quite different from the greyish-green of the *Wehrmacht*: none of them had steel helmets, just wedge-shaped caps on the backs of their heads and, instead of a jacket, a blouse worn outside their trousers and fastened with a leather belt. The men looked unconcerned and were talking and joking with one another as if they were out on an excursion. Some of them noticed us up on the ramparts and waved—by now we were quite a crowd. Between the rumbling of the engines and the clatter of the tank treads, we could distinctly hear the cheers coming from Terezín.

After a while the motorized column came to a halt. The soldiers began making signs to us to join them, and somehow, between the loose bricks and helping hands, I made my way down with others, crossed the moat and came up on to the road. Some inmates were already there. The Russians threw cigarettes to us—when I picked them up I noticed they were German. By the time it was getting dark, the convoy started to move and then halted again. A soldier sitting on the platform of the tank stopped in front of me asked, 'Ty voinoplenyi?' 'Are you a prisoner of war? Do you want to come with us?' On the spur of the moment I nodded. He stretched out his hand to help me climb up beside him. Somebody handed me a rifle and another a fistful of cigarettes, the whole procedure seemed rather informal. After crossing Germany they were visibly pleased with our friendly attitude. The column started to move in fits and starts. Once it was pitch dark progress was even slower—we advanced and stopped frequently—but, suddenly, in the middle of the night we were fired at from somewhere ahead. We jumped off the platforms and threw ourselves headlong into a ditch. The tank manoeuvred into position across the road and fired a rapid volley of shots. There were explosions all around us. From a soldier lying beside me I tried to find out from where the shots were coming, but couldn't make out his answer. Some thirty minutes later the shooting died down and everybody climbed out. There were some casualties up ahead. Among the dead, his uniform covered in blood, was an English POW who, like me, had been hitching a ride.

It was still dark when the column came to a halt in a village. The inhabitants lined the road offering the soldiers the traditional welcome of bread and salt; the Russians began handing out cigarettes, there was back-slapping, hand-shaking and embracing. I was giving away cigarettes as well, the supply inside the tank seemed inexhaustible. One of the men told me they had looted a tobacco factory in Dresden.

At dawn we moved out. The roadside was littered with burned-out Krupp personnel carriers, amphibious Volkswagens and trucks, some still smouldering. The tank on which I was riding got to the front of the column somehow. Two motor-bike riders were in front of us and the pace was brisk. The motor-cyclists motioned the first group of German soldiers we met to throw their weapons into the middle of the road where the tanks ran over them. As we advanced, more and more prisoners were taken until soon there was a solid file on both shoulders of the road walking in the opposite direction to us. The Russians paid no attention to them, no sign of hostility, it was as if they didn't exist.

Another stop. There was shooting to the right but this time nobody bothered to take cover and our tanks didn't fire back. It didn't last long and we resumed our advance. Groups of civilians were mixed up with the *Wehrmacht*. Here and there, on the far side of the ditches, families huddled in groups. The adults, ashen-faced, watched the advancing column in a non-committal way but the children waved to us. The civilians looked as if they had been on the move a long time—they wore shabby, crumpled clothes, anxiety showing on their faces. The road passed close to a railway line where a German hospital train was stopped in the middle of nowhere. Bandaged faces watched us from the windows while nurses in grey uniforms climbed down from one wagon and up into the next: they looked exhausted and here the picture of defeat couldn't have been more eloquent.

We passed through more villages with people lining the road, waving to us. The Czech flag and some red ones too were draped from windows and roofs. As the column approached the northern outskirts of Prague, a light plane in flames hit the ground a short distance away and erupted into a ball of fire. As we entered the suburbs, people massed along the streets greeted the Red Army and, in return, were given cigarettes. Finally, everything came to a halt not far from the spot where Heydrich's car had been ambushed. So much had happened since then that, to me, it felt like centuries ago. From the people around I heard that fighting was still going on in the city centre but it appeared that the Russians had no intention of entering yet. The soldiers had jumped off the tanks and out from the trucks to fraternize.

24

I couldn't bear to wait for the column to get moving. Giving the rifle to the nearest person, I made my way towards a bridge. Just in front of it was a barricade of torn-up paving stones piled waist high. I started to climb over but was stopped by a self-important busybody asking to see my identification.

'I don't have any,' I told him, then remembered the certificate given to me by the camp printer. While searching my pockets I pulled out endless cigarettes and still couldn't find it. At the sight of such riches the man's eyes bulged, so I gave him one, saying, 'If you want more, go up the road, the Russians are handing them out there.'

'You're from a concentration camp, aren't you?' pointing to my shaved head.

'Yes, I've just come in with the Russians. They've stopped around the bend beyond the hospital. I didn't know when they'd start moving again, so I decided to walk home.'

'You'd better be careful,' he warned, 'there is still fighting going on in the city. Sharp-shooters are hiding on the roofs.' I set off: once in a while I could hear shots in the distance. There were a few more barricades, most of them deserted, before I reached another bridge. In that part of town the river makes a loop and we lived some ten minutes from this second bridge. A sentinel stopped me as I was about to cross. 'You can't, nobody can go over.'

Hilda, my mother's friend, who had given me shelter in her country house before I left for the Beskyds, lived close by. I decided to wait with her until the bridge was open. Her flat was on the fifth floor, so I was relieved to see that the lift was working. I rang her bell, the door opened half-way and, behind it, I could see Hilda peering at me for an instant. She came out and threw her arms around

212

my neck. 'You know, if I'd run into you on the street I probably wouldn't have recognized you,' she exclaimed.

'Is it because of my hair?'

'No, you just don't look the way I remember you. It's not that you're thin either but you have a way of looking at me as if you were watching everything around you at the same time. Please tell me all, I've so much to ask you,' said Hilda.

'Is the phone working? I have to let them know that Mother is all right.'

Lida answered my call and I told her I had seen Mother and would be home as soon as I could. To Hilda I explained why I had come to her flat first, then started to recount events since we had last seen each other in the autumn. Later, while she was preparing something to eat, I had a bath. The bathroom door opened.

'Lunch is ready. I've brought you these. I can't imagine you'd want to put on what you came in, I suppose you know your pants are split.' She left the change of clothing on the chair.

After the meal I thought it might be a good time to try to cross the river again. Hilda came downstairs with me but when we reached the ground floor she stopped. 'Wait, I want to show you something,' she said and led the way towards the basement. A man was sitting on the steps leading down.

'This young man is a friend of mine,' Hilda addressed him. 'He has just returned from a concentration camp. I would like you to show him what you have in the cellar.' The man, the janitor of the building, took out a key and opened the door. Two dozen or so children and adults—mostly women—were squatting around the central-heating boiler.

'Here they all are. These are the Germans who were living in this house. They chased the Czech families out and took over the best flats.'

I looked at them. Everybody's clothes and faces were smudged with coal dust and their eyes betrayed fear. After we'd left the cellar I asked him, 'Why do you keep them there?'

'So they can't escape,' he answered.

'Where do you think they will escape to? At least you could have assembled them in one of the flats, not in the boiler room.'

'They are all Nazis and some were from the Gestapo,' he defended himself.

'The children too?' I asked.

'Isn't it horrible,' commented Hilda on the way out. 'I'm afraid to complain too much. After all, I'm from Vienna and he knows I'm German-speaking.'

I left the house in disgust. This time I was able to cross the bridge. Loiza and Lida awaited me: Hilda had phoned after I left to tell them I was on my way. I gave them what news I could about Mother but had no idea when to expect her. Our house hadn't changed, I noticed. Everything was in the same place as before—even the atmosphere was the same. Decidedly, we were not a family given to emotional outbursts.

After telling them all I could think of, I changed into my own clothes and left the house. I couldn't stay put for long. Heading towards the centre there were occasional shots but nobody seemed to be paying the slightest attention. The closer I got to the city centre, the denser the crowds. The Red Army was still nowhere to be seen, which was surprising. Why would the troops remain on the outskirts when there was no resistance anywhere?

From what I had learned since my arrival, street fighting had broken out five days earlier, which explained the barricades. At the time, most people thought the Americans, who by then had reached Pilsen, about fifty miles away, would keep on pushing forward. In expectation of this the population started an uprising, but the Americans stayed where they were. The *Wehrmacht*, having the upper hand in the city, nearly wiped out the poorly armed insurgents.

About the same time, contingents of the so-called Vlassov Russians were in the vicinity of Prague. These troops were made up of former Russian POWs who had chosen to fight the Soviets alongside the *Wehrmacht*. Some of these men could have been outright opponents of the Soviet regime but the majority were probably simple people who preferred to fight under German command rather than perish in a POW camp. In desperation, the leaders of the Prague uprising made contact with the Vlassov troops and, invoking Slavic brotherhood, implored them to switch sides to help them in their fight against the German troops. This they agreed to do, rather naïvely hoping that, in return, the Czechs would arrange for them to be given asylum by the Americans, expected to enter Prague at any moment.

Thanks to these units the uprising managed to hold on, sparing the city a blood bath and destruction. When the Vlassov troops found out that the Red Army had reached the northern outskirts of Prague, they withdrew to the south-west, crossed the Allied lines and surrendered.

But the Americans, refusing to recognize any deal made with the leaders of the uprising, extradited them to the Soviets as agreed in Yalta.

German civilians who hadn't escaped Prague were made prisoners by the mobs. Nearing the centre of the city I came across self-proclaimed guards supervising their captives in the demolition of barricades. Naked to the waist, with swastikas painted on their backs and foreheads, the Germans were being driven to replace the torn-up cobblestones. The jeering crowd gathered around was avidly watching, calling out to the guards if a prisoner slackened the tempo. History was repeating itself but it was now the Czechs who were showing a streak of cruelty: it made me realize that there is little difference between peoples when low instincts are permitted to surface. The spectacle was revolting, but a far worse sight awaited me.

In the square where I used to watch street-sellers hawking their wares, close to where Franta had lived, three bodies were hanging upside down suspended from lamp-posts, their feet attached by electric cables. The heads, with singed hair, hung about five feet from the ground, above a still-smouldering fire: the skin on the half-naked bodies had a yellowish tinge. All three men looked dead but the killing could only recently have taken place. The faces of the spectators were still gleaming with lust for revenge.

'What had they done?' I wanted to find out from a woman next to me.

'They're from the Gestapo. We caught them shooting at people on the barricades,' she told me.

'How do you know they were from the Gestapo?'

'Because somebody knew them. Anyway, they were hiding on the rooftops.'

'They must have been scared if they were hiding there. Don't you feel they should have been properly tried? This is no way to kill people,' I said.

Another bystander intervened and said threateningly, grabbing me by the arm, 'Are you defending the Germans? You're probably a collaborator yourself.'

The circle around the hanging bodies was now watching me, eager to pounce. The sight of the dead men suspended there wasn't enough, they wanted more. I wrenched my arm free.

'No, I wasn't a collaborator, I got back from a concentration camp only this morning. Look at my head. I've seen too much cruelty already and don't want any more of it.'

'Anybody could shave his head.'

'Wait, I can prove it to you,' I said, pulling out the certificate from the camp that I'd found when I changed at Hilda's. I showed it to the woman with whom the discussion started.

'Do you believe me now?' I asked her. Other bystanders were looking over her shoulder and the crowd around me began to disperse. Nobody said anything, as if they were ashamed, and I left too. A moment later I felt a hand touch my arm, it was the woman.

'I'm sorry, please forgive me, I didn't want to make trouble for you.'

Having no special plans, I decided to visit my friend Natasha who lived not far away. She was the eldest of three daughters of Russian *émigrés* from the First World War. The family was known to be very hospitable and we'd had great parties at their house. I imagined that my old crowd would meet at her home in the centre of Prague. Among those I found there were Lala and Olga. From the message which had been delivered by the camp electrician I knew they were married and I noticed I'd be a godfather, as promised, within a few months.

Mother, worried by my abrupt disappearance from the Terezín barracks, reached Prague two days after me. She had seen Utta again with her stepfather, Dr Burian, but this had only added to her confusion, as I hadn't gone to Leitmeritz. There had been an air-raid on the town and, at my mother's insistence, Utta had gone to the morgue to see if I was among the victims. She also told me that my sister went to look for Hana's husband, Kamil, in the Richard concentration camp. In a white doctor's coat and Red Cross armband, Utta bluffed her way in by brazenly declaring she was from the International Red Cross. The chaos there must have been complete and many things were possible that would have been unthinkable forty-eight hours earlier. Fortunately, she was able to locate him, but he was in bad shape, with typhus and a serious ear infection. She told the guard who was with her that the prisoner had to be evacuated immediately and taken to hospital. It sounds incredible but, without asking her to produce any written order, the guard consented. Not only that, at the gate as she was leaving, he even asked her if she would take him with her to Switzerland.

Less than a week after my return I ran into a former fellow-inmate.

216

While discussing recent events and recalling our last days in camp he casually asked what I was planning to do. When I told him that for the moment I was at a loose end he suggested I should see the secretary to the Minister of Information. This was a newly created organization that needed people with languages, he said.

'But I'm not a Communist.'

I wanted to be clear about it, knowing by that time that a large proportion of the employees in the Information Ministry were members of the Communist party: the Minister himself was one and had spent the war years in Moscow.

'Never mind about that, somebody like you doesn't have to be a Party member. Give the secretary my name and I'm pretty sure they'll find something for you,' he told me. Rather sceptical about my chances but not having had much luck finding anything suitable elsewhere, I took his advice and went to see the person he had recommended.

'Your name has been mentioned to me already,' the secretary, an efficient-looking woman in her early forties, informed me. We talked for a while before she gave me the name of the head of the French section, adding with an encouraging smile as I was leaving her office, 'Be sure to come back, whatever the outcome.'

The man was dour and elderly—he appeared to me to be suffering from stomach ulcers. During the interview it came out that he had been press attaché in Paris between the two wars and the conversation increased a few degrees in warmth when I told him how much I liked that city.

'As far as I am concerned you can have the job,' he assured me when we shook hands. However, as I later discovered, his opinion had little weight. He had been taken over from the Ministry of Foreign Affairs, mainly to pay lip-service to the policy that there would be representatives from all parties in every government department. In actual fact the hiring decisions were made by the secretary to the Minister, the woman I had been told to contact, a sort of Communist *éminence grise*. My interview with the former press attaché had been a mere formality. The acquaintance from the camp who had put me up for the job was also a Communist and, without my knowing it, already held an important post in the Party. He probably considered me a sympathizer or, at least, a so-called 'useful fool'—easily malleable material to be used as it suited them.

There were now four parties on the new political scene, the

Communists, Socialists and two centre parties, all participating in a National Union government formed in eastern Slovakia while Moravia and Bohemia were still under German occupation. There were no opposition parties; the pre-war right-wing groups were barred from taking part in public life, the rather unconvincing argument being that under German pressure they had passively accepted the dismemberment of the country.

Before holding elections, one of the first acts of the provisional government was to embark on a programme of far-reaching nationalization and agrarian reforms. Another was to undertake the expulsion of the Sudetens. The official reason given for their expulsion was that never again should there be a German-speaking minority within the borders since that had been the pretext for Hitler's occupation.

The day after my interview I started work at the Ministry. I was put to work translating leading articles from French papers to be incorporated into a bulletin for the use of government officials. On my second or third day at the office, my mother called to ask me to come home for lunch. As it was a fair distance to go, and we had a well-supplied canteen at the Ministry, I wanted to know why but she wouldn't tell me. When I reached home Mother told me to look in my room—I had no trouble in recognizing Franta in spite of his thin face, sunken cheeks and shorn head. He greeted me in a weak, plaintive voice. Pulling back the covers I stared at his stick-like legs covered in sores, his thin arms and protruding ribs. In the camp jargon he was already a '*muselmann*', somebody at the end of his physical strength.

Franta told me that from Terezín he had been sent to Auschwitz, then, with the Red Army approaching, he was included in a transport to Mauthausen. Whilst in Auschwitz, working in an armaments factory, he had stayed in fairly good shape: it was only after his transfer that he began to go downhill. It was clear to me that had the war lasted another two weeks he wouldn't have made it. The camp was liberated by the Americans who gave the inmates trucks to repatriate themselves.

With the beginning of summer the expulsion of the Sudeten Germans began. They had already been made to wear white armbands and their ration allowance was smaller than that for Czechs. No basic distinction was made between outright Nazis and the uninvolved. On paper, the so-called anti-Fascist Germans could stay on but, since the economic fabric of the community was being torn apart, this forced an overwhelming majority of Nazi opponents to leave as well. The carrying out of the expulsion order was entrusted to Revolutionary Guards, young individuals who had flocked to the border regions after the war with the idea of lining their pockets.

Dr Burian was among those deported in August. With his wife—Utta's mother—and their young son he was assigned to a small town in Saxony, near Dresden. Utta, who had proved her anti-Nazi convictions, was permitted to stay, didn't have to wear the white armband and received normal food rations. When her family left she came to live with us in Prague. My sister was understandably bitter about the unjust treatment meted out to the Burians and others.

About a fortnight after my liberation, when I saw Utta again, I delivered Schmidt's puzzling message. It was received with little comment—we wanted to talk of anything but those months. My own reaction was to try to forget everything to do with my imprisonment. Although at the time I still didn't know the full background of my shielded existence in the Small Fortress, I felt a certain amount of guilt at the preferential treatment I'd received. Utta too was attempting to block out certain memories and did not want to dwell on the undeserved difficulties her family was facing.

❧ 25 ❧

Fairly soon after his deportation, Dr Burian sent word that, in order to set up in practice again, he needed the medical instruments he hadn't been allowed to take with him and which Utta was looking after. It was decided that I should be the one to smuggle them out. Through my job at the Ministry I already had a passport—they weren't too easy to come by at that time. We arranged to meet at the flat of relatives of his in a Dresden suburb. When I arrived he wasn't there nor was there any message so, after hanging around until it was nearly time for my train home, I left the package with the relatives.

The trip gave me an opportunity to see at first hand the destruction caused by the raid which we had seen from our cell window. The centre of Dresden was completely destroyed. Since nobody lived there, trams were operating from one suburb to the opposite one with no stops in between. Dresden had been a beautiful city with tree-lined streets: all that was left of those trees were charred trunks with seemingly dead branches out of which, here and there, a few green shoots had sprouted. The houses were empty shells, fire-blackened and windowless. These ruins bore chalked inscriptions giving information on the whereabouts of the families who had once lived in them. Mainly middle-aged people and children were to be seen, apart from an occasional man in uniform with the insignias torn off. Side streets were still blocked with rubble. The only visible activity was being carried out by groups of women who were clearing the streets so that trams could run.

Well before the collapse of the Reich, anticipating the treatment the Czechs had in mind for the Sudetens, Dr Burian had entrusted my stepfather with a fair sum in cash as a hedge against unforeseeable events. A month or so after my trip to Dresden we received a request to send him the money. Loiza took me into his confidence as he had no idea how to get it to him. While smuggling instruments was hardly a serious offence, taking cash over the border would be another matter, the undertaking further complicated by the fact that neither mail nor telephone services had as yet been re-established between the two countries. The one person who I thought might be able to help was Frigge. He was back in his parish and we had kept in touch with one another. As the border ran only a few hundred feet from the presbytery he was known, at least by sight, to the guards there—it should be relatively easy for him to cross into Saxony. Frigge was dependable, trustworthy and, moreover, had a taste for risky undertakings, the ideal go-between, I thought. When I approached him he agreed to smuggle out the cash—all I had to do was deliver it.

It was my first visit to his village nestled in the mountains far from any railway line. There were still no buses running so it meant about an eight-mile walk. On my way I passed several groups of expelled Sudeten Germans slowly making their way up to the border. They looked tired and had probably been on the road for hours—their only possessions what they could carry. Young Czechs wearing red armbands on their civilian jackets were supervising the move. This ruthless and greedy gang was not above appropriating personal articles from the people they were accompanying. They had mistreated the Sudetens in countless ways, apart from chasing them out of their homes and taking them over for themselves. Valuable art works disappeared, sets of Meissen porcelain were broken in everyday use, entire libraries of rare books were sold to dealers and found their way to Switzerland.

The next day, on the way back, the same guards passed me but, this time, supervising the movement of workhorses from Saxony, I suppose to make their trip worthwhile. At the presbytery I met Frigge's sister and a Mrs Skopek who was living with them. We four spent a delightful evening together never imagining this would be the last time he and I would see each other. A few days later I learned he had been arrested, presumably with the money, because it never reached Dr Burian. All I know is that Frigge was eventually released and then deported but by the time he got out of jail all his parishioners had already been forced to leave. Much later I heard an unconfirmed rumour through Utta, or maybe her mother, that he had left the priesthood and married Mrs Skopek.

It was unfortunate that the smuggling attempt took place when it did, that is, in the autumn. In May of 1945 I could easily have made good Dr Burian's loss when strolling one day with friends in the park of a spa near Prague. In the centre of a gravel-covered oval we came upon an enormous pile of German banknotes of all denominations mixed up pell-mell; the soldier guarding this 'treasure' was busily raking back whatever the breeze blew away. To my question as to what the money was doing there, the Russian replied it was to be burnt. I'm sure it would have been possible to persuade him to let me have as many bills as I liked in exchange for a wristwatch, an ever-popular item with the occupation troops.

This was the closest I ever came to a fortune but, at the time, it never occurred to me, nor did it to my friends. The only explanation I have is that it happened very shortly after the war when the Reichmark was virtually worthless, at least to us. I had no idea that some of my acquaintances were already doing a brisk business smuggling the notes to West Germany and bringing back second-hand cars. I certainly missed a unique opportunity but I was completely out of step with the financial possibilities the period offered: I had no money-making aspirations and no responsibilities either. Getting my monthly pay cheque was enough for me.

In this I differed from my close friends. All three were married by then so had to look after finances more carefully than I did. Primus was managing the precision-tool factory but, unfortunately, not very efficiently, as his mental health was progressively deteriorating. Franta was called in to have a look at the books and discovered that, in spite of the control systems Primus was forever inventing, the accountant had been embezzling heavily for years. Franta had completely recovered his health and was running the business inherited from his father. Lala was on the verge of finishing his studies in architecture.

In October, Lala's wife gave birth to a boy in the Prague Clinic and, as promised, I was asked to be godfather. In those days, baptisms were frequently performed right away, so the ceremony took place in Olga's private room. When I arrived I found a priest, a nurse and both grandmothers waiting, with Lala nowhere around and Olga still a bit groggy. We waited a while but when it became evident that Lala had been delayed, and the priest began to get impatient, it was decided to proceed. The nurse explained what I should do, handed me the baby and took over as altar boy. The baptism proceeded without a hitch until we arrived at the moment when I was expected to give the priest

222

the name of the baby. Since I had no idea what name had been chosen, I turned to the others. Olga didn't answer and the grandmothers started to quarrel over the matter. Names flew back and forth to be immediately countermanded. The priest looked expectantly at me, it seemed it was up to me to decide. The situation was becoming more and more embarrassing and in desperation, so as not to offend anybody, I repeated half a dozen of the names I had heard called out behind me. As a result, nobody was pleased, not even the father when he got to the clinic after the whole thing was over and the priest had left.

A month after the baptism, the Soviet and American troops left the country and my war-time story could have ended there. Rather naïvely, I suppose, we hoped that, with the departure of the occupation armies and the coming general elections to clear up the ambiguous political situation, life would return to something comparable to what we had known before the war. Unfortunately, this was just wishful thinking. In a few months a better-organized Communist party consolidated its hold on the institutions. In the elections that followed over a third of the population voted for them, more than doubling the number of votes they had received in the last pre-war elections. A lot of support came from the adventurers who had taken over properties vacated by the expelled Sudeten Germans: it was somehow believed the government would now legalize these acquisitions.

Another factor in the increased support was that many people were convinced that a repetition of the evils of the Nazi system would be most effectively averted by giving their votes to the party claiming to be the champion of righteousness. With clever propaganda the Communists pointed out that, thanks to the sacrifices of the Soviet Union, the Nazi Reich had been destroyed and the Czechs were again a free nation. They warned, however, that Nazi ideology was not yet dead, and portrayed the Soviet Union as the sole guarantor that Nazism would never reappear.

My own doubts about the merits of the Communist system had been strengthened in, of all places, the Small Fortress. In our cell there was an ethnic German from one of the Baltic countries who had had the questionable privilege of knowing, from personal experience, not only the professed ideals of both sides but also how these regimes worked in practice, since his experience included stays in both Soviet and German concentration camps. While the treatment of prisoners may have varied in detail, in his view, the contempt with which both regimes held the individual was identical. I still remember his comment when we heard through the prison grapevine that, in order to placate the Western Allies, the Comintern had been dissolved. 'They'll invent something else. Their aims will remain the same and so will the way they treat people.'

While Czechoslovakia was still host to occupation troops, I had a chance to speak privately to a number of Russians, soldiers and officers. A surprisingly high proportion of them expressed opinions critical of the regime, especially about the chasm existing between the professed ideals and the aspects of everyday life. A friend of Lala's, a Yugoslav studying in Prague, lent me a book by Victor Kravchenko, *I Chose Freedom*, which made a deep impression on me. Some passages in this book were hard to believe, and I asked my Russian contacts to confirm them.

Gradually I reached the conclusion that the Soviet regime could stay in power only by force and terror and that, for me, this definitely wouldn't be one I would choose to live under. And the worst thing was that I began to suspect it was only a question of time before Communist rule would be installed in Czechoslovakia. Disappointment with the way the situation in the country was turning out was not only mine—it was becoming general—but, as yet, very few were concerned about an eventual take-over. My growing disenchantment coincided with an offer from the Ministry, to a few colleagues and myself, of a transfer to one of the two government news agencies. The attraction of the new job was that it offered the possibility of a later assignment abroad. I eagerly accepted the chance.

My stepfather was disillusioned with the way the government was interfering in matters of law. He had to defend a former member of the Czech parliament, a Sudeten being tried for high treason. Alleging that he never practised criminal law, Loiza tried to refuse: when he wanted to familiarize himself with the case he discovered that the file would be inaccessible until a couple of days before the trial. I well remember our discussion at table, one of the rare ones we had about his profession. In my stepfather's opinion the accused was being denied a fair chance of defence and the verdict had been decided upon beforehand. Loiza quite agreed that the defendant was a scoundrel but simultaneously maintained that under such conditions the law structure of the country would eventually collapse. The trial took place as he had foreseen and he returned home that evening visibly depressed.

From day to day I had been putting off the inevitable inquiry about Ondrej. It has always been a bad habit of mine to postpone anything disagreeable and, in this case, I was expecting the worst. Conscious that the blame was mine, I spent restless nights gathering my courage to take the first step in finding out what had happened. When I couldn't put it off any longer, I sent letters of more or less the same content to the first farmer, the smuggler and Ondrej's niece. To each I explained who I was—since I had given them all a false name—and recounted what had befallen me after leaving with Kupka. I received immediate answers, not only to my three letters, but one from Ondrej too.

He told me that he had been arrested a few weeks after me. Until the time of his arrest he had no idea I was in the hands of the Gestapo. Kupka visited him several times during the interval and assured him I had a good hideout and was in safe hands. Ondrej's arrest happened in a similar way to mine, away from his farm. One day he received a summons from the office that regulated the compulsory farm produce deliveries. At first he thought the charges against him were for selling something on the black market: it was only during the interrogation that he realized why he was being held. Like me, he was never tried. As he was of such a powerful build, the Gestapo in Vsetin used him as a hangman. Only after he was liberated did he find out that Kupka was an informer; all the time he was in prison he believed I was the one who had denounced him.

It was clear that the Gestapo had done everything to protect Kupka which confirmed my suspicions as to why I had been kept in isolation at the Vsetin Gestapo headquarters. Soon after Ondrej's arrest, however, Kupka got involved in another affair that blew his cover. People in the region started talking and my disappearance and Ondrej's arrest were linked to him. The underground kept close tabs on his comings and goings, which is how he got caught in a railway station close to the Austrian border soon after the German retreat. It seemed that during his first interrogation he admitted right away that he had turned me in.

A post-war law stipulated that anyone responsible for an arrest or deportation could face a life sentence: if the person denounced failed to return it was assumed he or she had perished and then the mandatory sentence was death. The investigations about my whereabouts had been complicated by the fact that nobody in the Beskyds and, surprisingly, not even Kupka, knew me by my real name. As I had given no immediate sign of life I was presumed dead. Kupka's chances had looked bleak even though, besides Ondrej, the other victims of his denunciations had returned. All this was described in their replies and they urged me to immediately contact the prosecutor's office in the district town where Kupka was being held.

In due course—early 1946—I received a convocation to appear as a witness. Before the proceedings I met Ondrej and, along with the smuggler and my farmer host, we decided to have a reunion afterwards. While waiting in the corridor I was approached by an elderly woman in black who introduced herself as Kupka's mother. Tearfully she told me the Gestapo had blackmailed her son for something foolish he had done and begged me to take pity on him and not aggravate his situation. Trying to console her, I pointed out that by the very fact I was able to attend the hearing, her son's prospects no longer looked as desperate.

My appearance as witness was short. Kupka, looking distraught and ill-kempt as anyone might in a similar situation, was sitting on the bench of the accused between two prison guards. I tried to catch his eye but he kept staring at the floor. At the end of my testimony his lawyer asked only why I hadn't come forward immediately after my release. Two other prosecution witnesses followed me, there was nobody for the defence. This type of trial was held with three judges but without a jury so the whole proceedings seemed more like a business deal. There were thousands of similar cases to be dispatched with assembly-line speed.

Within thirty minutes all those connected with the case were called back into the courtroom to hear the verdict. Kupka was condemned to life imprisonment without appeal. I had somehow expected his lawyer to ask the court to take into consideration the fact of blackmail but nothing of the sort was brought up. I watched Kupka as he disappeared through a side door between his jailors and that was the last I ever saw or heard of him. The courtroom quickly emptied: in the hallway was a group of people waiting for another trial to be held that morning. As Ondrej and I came down the steps of the courthouse I saw Kupka's mother ahead of us, walking alone. I have often wondered if he is still alive: is he living out his years in prison or has he perhaps been pardoned?

After the elections of May 1946, the Communists, with over one third of the vote, became the dominant party: the previous Prime Minister was replaced by the leader of the party and the cabinet reshuffled. As tension grew between the Western Allies and the Soviet Union—the Cold War—the internal political problems in Czechoslovakia seemed to increase in proportion. One country after another in Eastern Europe was falling under direct Communist control. In neighbouring Hungary and Poland the last vestiges of a democratic and pluralistic system were fast disappearing. Many Czechs were finally beginning to show concern at the turn of events although there was still a current of optimism. People argued that our situation was quite different since neither Poland nor Hungary had had a truly democratic regime between the two wars and were lacking the experience of governing with majority support in a freely elected parliament. Moreover, Soviet occupation troops were still stationed in both these countries whereas they had left us in November 1945.

I continued to think that a Communist take-over was on the cards but not imminent. I was still playing for time. Had I been really apprehensive I could have remained outside the country when I visited the West in the summer of that year but unless I was prepared to cut all ties with home and put myself outside the law, I first had to do six months' compulsory military service. The normal time was, I believe, eighteen months but as I was already twenty-seven my service, scheduled for the spring of 1947, would be shorter. Once that was behind me I hoped to be able to leave the country legally. About a year before it was due to begin, I met a very attractive woman at a party given by Helena. On first sight I was really taken with her—she had an unusually engaging personality—and our relationship began in a somewhat unconventional way. Another man there seemed as interested in Lily as I was but she did nothing to make her preference obvious. To get a clear field of action I suggested we leave the party for a night-club; the other fellow, just as persistent, tagged along. When it was time to end the evening it turned out my competitor lived roughly in the same direction as she did. I wondered how to make a date with her and there was no way of getting rid of him. When we were introduced I had missed Lily's surname and didn't want to ask Helena so I consoled myself that at least I would know where she lived.

As the three of us were approaching the entrance of her apartment building she pointed out a half-open window with a milk bottle on the ledge saying that was her flat. It wasn't clear to me if this clue was meant for my benefit but it decided my plan of action. We said goodnight and I continued walking with my rival for another couple of blocks, took leave of him and raced back to Lily's to be sure to be there first in case he had the same idea. Without hesitating, I scaled the necessary eight or nine feet and climbed into the room. In the darkness I could make out a cot with a small child in it and panicked, thinking I had entered the wrong apartment. A door opened and somebody came in—it was Lily all right, she had heard the noise and come to investigate. 'How could you know my husband wasn't here?' she whispered.

'I didn't even know you were married. I supposed that by showing me your window you'd made your wishes clear. The only thing I didn't know was if it was an invitation for me or for the other fellow, so I took a chance.'

'It was meant for you. I'd have preferred a more conventional approach but since you're already here you might as well stay.'

This was the start of an affair that turned out to have a direct bearing on my plans for the future. Lily had met Helena through her husband, a Sudeten, the son of a Communist member of the pre-war Czech parliament. Her father-in-law had escaped to Sweden when the Sudetenland was occupied in 1938 but his son stayed on, served in the *Wehrmacht* and married Lily at some point during the war. For reasons I never discovered, the Gestapo were interested in him: he deserted before the final collapse and, through connections, managed to join his father. In the meantime, a daughter had been born and mother and child were waiting for their Swedish immigration visa.

When I knew Lily better I asked her why her husband chose not to return now that his father had influential friends in the government. 'I really don't know why,' she replied. 'Personally, I'm not interested in politics, and I think his father has broken with the Party. He was in Moscow several times and always returned disappointed. My husband says his father is an idealist and the practical side of the regime didn't impress him.'

This revelation interested me very much and I wanted to find out the concrete reasons for his break. In my office I was working with people who had lived in the Soviet Union during the war and never heard any of them voice the slightest criticism. Our boss, with whom I was on good terms, had been the pre-war editor of the official Party organ, *Rude Pravo*—meaning The Red Right, or Law. He never missed an opportunity to praise life there, even though, as I later found out, his war had been spent in New York. I often tried to steer Lily towards the topic but each time she refused to be drawn. During one of our discussions she became irritated, reproaching me that I was obsessed with the subject. 'You always come back to the same thing. I've already told you several times I'm not interested in politics, and even if I were, please don't ask me questions like that any more. Try to understand my situation, I don't want to spoil my chances of going to Sweden.'

It slowly dawned on me that Lily didn't fully trust me: here I was sleeping with her and yet she was afraid of me. I began to understand how close friends and even members of the same family could mistrust each other. This was something I hadn't come across before and it disturbed me: I always spoke out quite openly with my friends. The fact that she had met me through Helena, whose convictions she knew, might have had something to do with it, or else she had been forewarned by her father-in-law not to go into the matter. So much greater was my surprise when, late that winter as she was boarding the bus for her trip to Sweden via West Germany, Lily told me, 'I was hoping you would ask me to marry you.'

'But you're already married,' I answered.

'Yes, but I would have stayed with you just the same.'

Shortly after her departure I received a letter from Stockholm with a passage that has stuck in my mind '. . . You'll surely remember the reason why I once got mad with you. I've spoken about this with my father-in-law. He believes your apprehensions are justified. The present situation is probably a temporary one and could change at any moment. Forgive me if I always tried to avoid the subject. Now it's up to you to draw your own conclusions and good luck . . .'

My military service was to start the following month, that is, at the beginning of spring 1947, so I faced a decision similar to the one I had had to make before my trek to Switzerland—what would be my best plan of action? If there were a Communist take-over during my service, I would be confined to barracks and, besides, fleeing in uniform wouldn't be easy. In the end I decided to wait, but resolved to keep some civilian clothes handy. On the appointed day I boarded the train for a small town in eastern Bohemia and underwent the usual medical. After spending a few days in barracks I was judged to be officer material and sent to a school in Brno.

There my ascent was relatively fast but my descent even faster. My social life was a very busy one as I soon made friends among the locals and often returned to the barracks later than my pass permitted—one particular night I was caught in the act of climbing the camp fence. The patrol took the business seriously and my efforts to persuade them to forget about it had no effect. As a result I spent a few nights in the military jail and, on top of that, had to undergo the ceremony of being down-graded from sergeant to private. While I considered it all a great joke, it upset the commander of the school, who liked me. He took me aside and told me that unfortunately, he couldn't do much about it. However, to keep me out of trouble he made me his personal chauffeur, which left me much more freedom. Between chauffeuring my commanding officer and driving trucks, my service was far from being a hardship. The news agency was holding my job and paying my full salary, so I was well off.

Towards the end of my service something happened to cause me serious concern. The United States launched the Marshall Plan. Czechoslovakia, whose economy was in very poor shape, responded at first with enthusiasm. Immediately after the government made public its acceptance of the aid, the Prime Minister, Klement Gottwald, and the Minister of Foreign Affairs, Jan Masaryk, were called to Moscow. On their return the newspapers published a report that the government had decided to refuse the American offer. This abrupt reversal totally shattered any illusion that our country was independent and, for me, it was an additional prod. As soon as I received my discharge and was back at work I was determined to be sent as a correspondent to Belgium, even if only for a limited time. Of course, I would have preferred an assignment in Paris but I was in a hurry and accepted what was open. My scheming was successful and, within two months, I was *en route* to Brussels.

⊰ 26 ⊱

Compared to Prague, Brussels, in December 1947, was dazzling, the Belgian post-war recovery impressive. I had made a few friends while visiting there for a short spell eighteen months before, and, through them, I got in with an entertaining crowd, going from party to party and enjoying the good food still unavailable at home. In short, it was a way of life I hadn't known since before the war. Through the people I met I hoped to find a job but I have to admit I wasn't going about it too methodically. The main obstacle to my being permitted to stay was that I had entered Belgium on a press visa so was limited in my field of action and, as long as Czechoslovakia was considered to have a democratic regime, there was no chance of applying for refugee status.

My social schedule and efforts to find a job left me with little time for the purpose for which I had been sent there in the first place. As time passed I started getting inquiries from the news agency as to what I was up to and why they weren't hearing from me. At first these inquiries were courteous but later they became downright threatening. Finally, a policeman visited me one day to inform me that I had two weeks in which to leave the country: they had received word through the Czech consulate that I was no longer employed as a correspondent.

Then I really began to look for a job, to be met everywhere with only promises. There was a slight chance of my being taken on by the Brussels office of a foreign news agency in which case my visa could have been revalidated but the job required me to be a photographer as well. When I went to the police in a last-ditch effort to prolong my stay, I was told my visa had lost its validity and there was no hope of getting a work permit.

After this categorical refusal there was no point in persisting so I

231

turned my attention to France and Switzerland. Both consulates gave me to understand that immigration visas took time and I knew I hadn't enough of that. While making the rounds of the consulates and seeing my prospects of settling this business fading with each visit, I hit upon a new stratagem—to return to Prague for a few days. I still had a valid passport which was already a great asset as they were getting more and more difficult to obtain. With a passport, and through the press attachés that I knew there personally, I was virtually certain I could manage an entry visa into at least one country. While I was rushing about Brussels during my period of grace, alarming news about the situation in Czechoslovakia began to appear in the Belgian press. According to these reports, certain of the popular, non-Communist members of the government had received parcels containing time-bombs. I considered this to be only a marked escalation of the tension between the Communists and the other parties making up the government but not so serious as to cause the final breakdown. I couldn't imagine it would create immediate obstacles to my plan although I knew I had to hurry to get a proper entry visa into a Western country before the situation became desperate.

With the intention of making my trip back as pleasant as possible, I boarded the train for Prague loaded with newspapers and magazines. There were very few passengers and when the train pulled into Nuremberg I was alone in the compartment with Belgian papers strewn around me. Immersed in an interesting article, I merely nodded and went on reading when two girls opened the compartment door asking in German if the places were free. They were conversing in Czech but I paid scant attention to them. At the same time, scraps of their conversation drifted across: they had been visiting American soldiers and were confiding in each other, listing the presents they had been given. The subject seemed interesting enough for me to concentrate on eavesdropping but if I wanted to hear more I had to go on pretending to read.

Their conversation gradually shifted from the rewards for their services to the services themselves, right down to technical details. It now became essential not to give myself away. Whenever they smiled at me I smiled back but otherwise pretended they could have been speaking Mandarin as far as I was concerned. Time was flying fast in such company but eventually we got to the border, which I regretted as I would have to show my passport.

There was a knock on the compartment door and two passport

officers came in. The girls presented theirs first then the officers turned to me. Intending to have my fun right up to the last moment I looked directly at the women as I pulled mine out. Their faces dropped and one even managed to blush.

'Anything to declare?' one of the officials asked.

'No, nothing to declare,' I answered in Czech.

'What will you think of us?' was their reaction as soon as the men had left. I assured them I thought only the best and would have liked to have added—at least as far as their professional skills were concerned. They said I had played a dirty trick on them but they certainly didn't hold it against me and we chatted and joked for the rest of the trip.

My parents were quite surprised by my sudden reappearance but I explained that I intended to leave again shortly.

'Your departure might get a bit more complicated,' remarked my stepfather caustically. I didn't inquire why, just thought it was his way of telling me I had once again done something stupid. At breakfast next morning, when my mother wordlessly handed me the newspaper, I realized what he had meant. 'Non-Communist Ministers Resign' announced the headline and below, in smaller print, 'All Workers Unite Against Provocations'. As soon as I had finished breakfast, I rushed to see the French press attaché. There were crowds around the Embassy building, but I made my way in through a back door and had to wait a while to see him.

'I need a visa. Could you help me to get it right away?' He looked at my passport and put it in his pocket.

'Let me take it to the consular section. I'll see what I can do for you. You might as well wait for me here.'

For about ten minutes I paced nervously up and down his office. When he returned he had the passport.

'Here you are and good luck,' he said with a knowing smile. I opened it and saw the visa stamp, which I quickly read, and then expressed my gratitude. It was a normal visitor's visa, valid for three months and extendable. Now what I still needed was a transit visa through West Germany. This was issued by the Allied Military Mission in another part of town but, with my French visa, it would be a mere formality. I dashed over to make it before lunchtime, got there before noon and tried the door—it was locked. Then I remembered it was Saturday and the Mission didn't work at weekends. I could still go by plane and in that case wouldn't need the transit visa. The airline office was close by but when I went in the ticket agent told me all flights were booked solidly for the next six days. Well, there was nothing further I could do, I would have to wait until Monday.

The weekend was full of foreboding. I decided to leave on Tuesday morning by the only direct train to Paris. On Sunday afternoon, I arranged to see Jean, my colleague from the news agency, as I wanted to find out how things stood there as far as I was concerned. Jean's father was Czech and his mother was from Dresden. Although a Czech national, Jean had been brought up in France. He spoke Czech with a strong French accent and had learned it mainly while serving with the Free Czech Forces in the West. I had been working in the Ministry for only a short while when Jean was hired, still in uniform, I remember, as he had no other clothes. Some months after he became established in Prague he married a French girl and I had been invited to the wedding. We always hit it off well and had both opted for the news agency when the opportunity came up. Later, his sister followed him and took a job with us as a French typist. Jean knew I had been fired but hardly expected me to show up in Prague.

'Everybody calls you a turncoat and bastard but I have the feeling this is mainly for public consumption. Most of the colleagues still like you, but don't dare to say it openly. Some probably even envy you. If they only knew you were here,' said Jean with a laugh.

'Listen Jean, I'm going to Paris. What do you want me to tell your parents?'

'Let them know that I'd like to go back. My wife isn't happy here and my sister isn't either. You know,' Jean continued, 'my father never wanted me to stay in Prague and he was terribly angry after I wrote that there was a position open for my sister as well. I don't know how he'll react to my message, we're hardly on speaking terms. But tell him that I'll need his help, at least for a few months.' I promised Jean I would see his father as soon as possible and then let him know his reaction.

On Monday I didn't bother to read the morning paper. I was in a hurry and left home early to be at the Allied Military Mission when the office opened. I gave my passport to the officer.

'I only need a transit visa, I'm going to Paris. Here is the French one,' I said opening the passport to the page with the new visa stamp.

'When do you want to travel?' asked the officer.

'Tomorrow.'

'I can give you a transit visa entitling you to travel within a month. But you probably won't be able to go tomorrow because we have just been advised, this morning actually, that all Czech nationals need an exit visa. Strictly speaking, I should give you the transit visa only when the exit visa is stamped in, but since you are here I'll give you an ante-dated one. That will save you coming back. Now you'll have to go to your Interior Ministry. Best of luck.'

He was an amiable, well-disposed person I thought, not the usual bureaucratic type one so often comes across: he could well have insisted I go first to the Ministry. However, the information he had given me hit me like a bombshell. What a fool I was to have come back just at the worst possible moment. Everything was so carefully planned and now I had messed it up. I felt like kicking myself for being such an idiot. Of course there was no question of my going to the Ministry for an exit permit. I had no valid reason for asking for one and in all likelihood they would confiscate my passport with the precious visa stamp. No, this new problem had to be tackled differently. I would cross the border into Bavaria clandestinely: once over the frontier everything would be fine, with my papers in order. Nevertheless, I went home feeling quite down-hearted.

Without saying anything to anybody I collected my skis from the basement, checked the bindings, oiled my boots and thought how to dress. It had to be something that would pass for ski clothes but could be used in town as well: even then, three years after the war, people were still strangely dressed, especially in Germany. It wasn't easy to sort out all I needed or to fit it into a rucksack. To save space I replaced my ski pants with grey flannels and decided to wear an anorak over my tweed jacket.

When I had everything nearly ready, I remembered I still had to get hold of some foreign currency. Anything I had in foreign money was with a friend in Brussels because I would have had to change it back into Crowns on the border: possession of foreign currency wasn't allowed. Once more in a rush, I left for a shop where I knew I could buy US dollars on the black market. Bad luck again, the shop was closed. That meant I would have to leave without any foreign cash because, if I postponed the crossing, it would become increasingly difficult with each passing day. There was a carton of Lucky Strike from Belgium in my luggage that would get me through Germany and, as for France, I would worry about that when I got there.

Evidently, Mother had guessed my intentions—which she didn't approve of—because I returned home to finish my packing and found that the skis and ski jacket had disappeared. I replaced the latter with one purloined from Lida and called Lala to ask if I could see him.

'Come over, Franta and Gaby are here for supper,' he said.

'You came back at absolutely the best moment,' he greeted me sarcastically when I showed up. 'You're an idiot, you couldn't have timed it better.'

Both Lala and Franta knew I was back, we had been in touch by phone, but I hadn't seen them yet. That evening our only subject of conversation was, of course, the latest developments. By then everybody knew that, in order to leave the country, an exit visa was necessary. All four were making fun of me and the way I had bungled my plan to get out in comfort and without problems.

'You know,' Franta remarked, 'your plans are usually good. The only trouble with you is you somehow always manage to mess them up.' I was walking up and down Lala's living-room like a caged animal. 'Lala, I need skis, could you let me have a pair of yours?' I blurted out.

'Sure, you can take my old ones. One was broken but I fixed it with a metal plate.'

'They'll be too long for you,' commented Franta. Indeed, Lala was well over six feet tall. 'You won't be able to ski on them. Anyway, what do you need them for?'

'I'm going to cross the border on skis tomorrow,' I announced, letting them in on my intentions.

'You're crazy,' everyone exclaimed together. 'Now is the worst time to do it. Wait until the situation clears up a bit.'

'No, I have to do it now. Every day I wait it will be more difficult, in a few days they'll have time to get organized.'

They all tried to discourage me and, as the evening wore on, our conversation became more incoherent. We were drinking heavily and the party broke up in the early hours of the morning.

'Let us know which jail you end up in, we can at least send you food parcels,' said Lala. 'And I still maintain you're an idiot. Have you stopped to think that in the next war I'll be a prisoner of the Americans but you'll end up in a Russian camp?'

'Good luck!' I heard them calling after me as I staggered down the stairs with the skis Lala had given me—they could hardly be called a loan. I was drunk but not enough not to realize I had only four hours of sleep ahead of me, my train to the mountains was leaving at seven in the morning. The skis didn't add to my sense of balance and I had to walk all the way home as the trams had stopped running a couple of hours earlier. Before falling asleep I set the alarm for six. Everything was packed and ready; I could leave before anybody in the house was up, it would be better that way.

I was awake before the alarm clock went off and left the house with ample time to catch the train. Luckily, nobody had heard me moving about. It was still pitch dark when the tram deposited me at the station, a place of momentous incidents in my life but, at that moment, I wasn't thinking so much about them. Some passengers on the train were busily discussing the latest events. The gist of the comments I heard went rather like this: 'Isn't it amazing that all those government members who resigned were actually traitors in the pay of the Western reactionaries, a good thing they were uncovered in time.'

These were the opinions voiced aloud and not necessarily those of the majority as most travellers kept quiet. History seemed to be repeating itself, it was unwise to speak out in front of strangers. Around noon I got off at a ski resort close to the Bavarian border, not far from the spot where, nearly four years earlier, I had crossed over on my unsuccessful attempt to reach Switzerland.

The hotel where I registered was only half full with skiers and a few Czech border guards. I thought it important to have some time in the vicinity to reconnoitre the terrain, so I studied the maps in the hall, put on my skis and spent a while on the slopes, until I could identify the lay of the land from the maps I'd looked at. When it was dusk I went back and, for dinner, ordered a dish I knew wouldn't be served either in Paris or in jail—roast pork with dumplings and sauerkraut, the same meal so often discussed in detail with my cellmates in the St Pancras jail.

During breakfast next morning in the hotel dining-room the radio was on full volume. The announcer was calling all workers and true democrats to a meeting in the centre of Prague where the Comrade Prime Minister was to deliver a speech. The broadcast went on to say that Fascist and anti-democratic elements were trying to sabotage the achievements of the working classes. The speaker was exhorting everyone to vigilance, reminding them they should listen to what the

Prime Minister had to say. That might make my crossing easier, especially if all the border guards were glued to the radio.

I left the hotel as soon as possible and, taking a slope away from the border, disappeared into the woods. Once under cover of the trees I made my way in the right direction. It was a sunny and crisp February morning, ideal for cross-country skiing, and there was nobody to be seen. The slope I was climbing began to even out and I came upon a kind of indentation, wide and shallow, somewhat like a ditch. This should be the frontier but I had no way of checking it since any markers were under snow. The trees in front of me began to thin out a little.

Close to the edge of the woods I stopped in my tracks when I caught sight of two men in *Feldgrau* sitting on a snow-cleared log, with their backs turned to me: one was enjoying a pipe, the smoke curling up into the clear air. I had never expected to be so elated at the sight of that particular shade of uniform, one I had so studiously avoided throughout the occupation, on my trek to Switzerland, in the Beskyds and the Small Fortress. So that was it, I was out of Czechoslovakia and over the border. In spite of being happy to see the German frontier guards I felt it better, remembering Poland, to avoid questions and complications.

Giving them a wide berth I continued on until I came to a road from where I could see the roofs of a village. As the skis had now become unnecessary, I stuck them into a snowbank with the poles alongside and walked leisurely down the road until I reached the first houses. It was close to noon with the most difficult lap of my journey behind me. With luck, in twenty-four hours I would be in Paris. I still had to be careful, however, as my transit visa from the Military Mission only entitled me to travel by train from Prague to Paris. I had to board the train as fast as possible.

Lost in thought about what I should do next, I found myself standing in front of the village church, one typical of Bavaria with onion dome and white stuccoed walls. This gave me an idea. I would see the parish priest—shades of Father Frigge again. I knocked on the door of the house by the church. An elderly man in a cassock answered.

'I would like to talk to you, Father. May I come in?' As soon as I was inside I said right away, 'I've just crossed the border and need marks. Would you be able to give me enough to get me to Nuremberg? I'll give you American cigarettes in exchange.'

He considered me thoughtfully, then answered, 'I cannot get involved in black-market deals but I could lend you some money if you promise to return it.'

'In that case, I'll make you a different proposition. You lend me the money and, as a guarantee, I'll leave you two packets of cigarettes.'

'That would be quite all right with me,' said the priest.

'Do you know the time-tables from here?' That was my next concern.

'There is a train in the afternoon but you would have to change, we have no direct connection to Nuremberg.'

'Does this train also stop at the next village, I don't want to board it here.'

'Why don't you want to get on here?' he asked in surprise.

I explained that the railway station was too close to the border—as a matter of fact I think the border went right through the building—and with only a transit visa I didn't want to be stopped by a control.

'There are no controls at the station but if you prefer you can go to the next village, it's an hour's walk. On this line trains stop at every station.' I asked him whether by any chance he knew when I would get to Nuremberg.

'No, I have no idea, I never go there. But if you get a connection right away, you should be there tonight. In any case, you have plenty of time so I suggest you stay and have lunch with me.'

I gladly accepted his invitation. During the meal the priest asked me about events in Czechoslovakia or, as he referred to it, 'over on the other side'. I told him what I knew but from his comments I could see he was well informed. 'It's a sad thing, one country after another falling into Communist hands. I wonder when it will reach us.'

'I don't think it will, Father. You have American troops here.'

'Let's hope you are right but half my relatives are living in the Russian zone and I am worried about them. It is as if we lived in two different countries.'

What he said was true and I couldn't console him. Germany was already divided and the situation in Eastern Germany was far worse than in the Western zones.

'I'll send you the money as soon as I can,' I said when leaving but we both knew the two packets of cigarettes I had left were worth more in barter than the cash I had been lent. The walk through the village and down the road took less than an hour. I caught the train with time to spare and reached Nuremberg in the evening.

I knew the city from before the war but wasn't prepared for the changes it had undergone: whole tracts of the old part were completely destroyed. To kill time I walked through the town but found it depressing. Passing a shop I stopped to choose a postcard and asked for a stamp for Czechoslovakia. The shopkeeper told me the price. 'I forgot my wallet, would you accept cigarettes?' I asked.

'That will do,' he told me when I pulled out one cigarette.

'Could you lend me a pen please?' 'With my best wishes!' I wrote and addressed it to Franta. On our last evening together I had promised to let them know as soon as I got to Germany. My family received word more or less at the same time. Until then, Mother apparently hadn't been able to decide whether I was off with a woman or in jail.

Wandering around with no purpose was getting boring and the train for Paris didn't leave until midnight. Besides, it was cold and I wasn't dressed for it. In front of a cinema the stills displayed caught my eye. They were showing *The Lost Weekend* with Ray Milland, a film I'd heard a lot about. At least it should be warm in there.

'Will you let me in for a cigarette?' I asked the cashier. She nodded, indicating with a movement of her hand that I could go in. The film had already started and, to my disappointment, the place was unheated, but in spite of the cold theatre I remained to the end, it was such a good film. I wondered what to do next: without ration coupons there was no hope of getting a meal. Finally I went back to the station even though I still had two more hours to kill.

The waiting-room was warm and crowded as well. Most of the people seemed to be foreigners, displaced persons with no desire to return to their homeland: some slept on benches, others on the dirty floor and quite a few were drunk. Looking at this dishevelled bunch reminded me that I was now one of the homeless myself. At last it was time for my train. As I passed through the ticket control I handed the man at the gate a cigarette which he pocketed without comment. The Prague–Paris express drew in alongside the platform. It was empty I saw as I settled myself in a compartment: what a difference from other times, this train always used to be packed. Now I could stretch out lengthwise and, better still, my situation had become legal—I was on the right train with a valid passport and French and transit visas. A minor problem was that I was without a ticket. Soon after the train pulled out of the station the conductor knocked on the compartment door. Silently I held out two cigarettes. He appeared to be satisfied, touching his cap as he closed the door. The car was well heated and I fell asleep almost immediately. Suddenly, or so it seemed, I felt somebody touching my shoulder. '*Monsieur, votre passeport, s'il vous plaît.*'

I jumped to my feet. The train had stopped for French passport control in Kehl—so I had slept through half of Germany. I reached into my pocket and handed him my passport.

'You are the first Czech national to pass through here since the events in your country,' the official commented.

'Yes, now we need a special permit to leave the country,' I remarked, still half asleep.

'Where is it?' he asked immediately.

Now I was fully awake and had to think fast. To tell him I had left illegally could cause complications and even result in a refusal of entry into France. It wasn't a question of being sent back but I wanted to avoid ending up in a DP camp in Germany.

'It's just a form and I handed it in to the Czech passport control at the border.'

He studied the visa, then handed the passport back.

'*Merci, Monsieur,*' he said and left the compartment. In a few moments the train was slowly clattering over the Rhine bridge and stopped again. We were in Strasbourg and I had, at last, accomplished what I set out to do nearly nine years earlier.

❧ Utta's Story ❧

It took many years for the full story to come out but my sister Utta finally agreed to contribute her version of the events as she recalls them for inclusion in this narrative. One mystery, however, will always remain—my perhaps life-saving transfer back to Prague from the coal-loading detail.

It may have been late August 1944 when I found an envelope bearing a Munich postmark in our post box. The address was written in an unusual and clumsy way. Inside were many closely-written pages composed in the form of a diary. There was no beginning and no signature but the handwriting was definitely my brother's. He described his aborted flight to Switzerland, his arrest and his fear of what the future might hold for him. After the war I found out that he had written these pages while in the Feldkirch jail and was lucky enough to be able to pass them on to a Ukrainian woman in the Munich prison.

I immediately applied for a permit to travel to Prague. At that time it was not possible to go from Leitmeritz to Prague without a special travel permit. To obtain one my stepfather gave me a fake prescription for the ear, nose and throat hospital there. On arrival I went straight to my brother's family and found them in a state of agitation—they had just been questioned by the Gestapo because he had succeeded in escaping from a transport some days earlier, but that was all they knew. I then got in touch with Lala as he was the most likely person to have any information about him. Lala told me that my brother had gone underground in

Prague and was looking for a contact with the partisans. As a person wanted by the Gestapo he couldn't stay in Prague for long. It was a strange feeling knowing my brother was hiding somewhere in the city and that I had no chance of seeing him. I am not sure of the date when all this happened, except that on the last day before my return, Marseilles was taken by the Allies and I was present at a celebration Lala and his friends organized for the occasion.

I must have returned to Prague again in September. By then Lala had my brother's cover address in the Beskyds and asked me to take some shirts and underwear from his home which he wanted to send on. I remember that my brother's assumed name was Matejka, an unimportant detail which has somehow stuck in my mind all these years.

Much later we received a card from my brother which had been sent from the Small Fortress, Terezín, asking for heavy boots and warm clothing. The news of this second arrest depressed me very much and made me feel helpless but I wanted to try by all possible means to do something for him.

It was an unbelievably lucky coincidence that the camp commander, Jöckel, was a patient of my stepfather's. He suffered from recurring ulcers of the throat and, when younger, had fallen into the hands of mediocre doctors. He therefore much appreciated my father's care. My stepfather called him right away. Jöckel was somewhat abrupt on the phone but, surprisingly, came to our house in a horse-drawn carriage that same day—even they were beginning to feel the petrol shortage. Our meeting really brought me more fear than hope. Jöckel was a hulk of a man and uncouth, his small eyes in a coarse face reminded me of a malicious animal, even though he tried to show a jovial side. His assurances that he would allow me a visiting privilege sounded very vague and, besides, according to him, my brother was in Prague for further interrogation so it wasn't absolutely certain he would be returned to the Small Fortress. To close the subject he advised us—my mother was present—that it might be better if I talked directly to Herr Bauer, the senior Criminal Secretary of the Prague Gestapo. I wondered about his attitude at the time and believe, even today, that he didn't want it known he was willing to put himself out on behalf of a prisoner, even if it was to such an insignificant degree.

244

My mother now made small talk in the old, genteel Austrian manner and I felt relieved to have her with me. She spoke about nothing in particular and gradually the atmosphere improved, until Jöckel touched upon the German war effort declaring, or rather shouting, that they had everything under control and how easy it was for him to recognize the enemies of national socialism.

'But how do you?' inquired my mother rather naïvely.

'For instance, when they have no picture of the Führer in their home.' There followed an awkward silence: naturally there wasn't a single picture of Hitler in our house. At that moment a grotesque idea came to me.

'Oh, I have something to show you,' I said and went to fetch a rather large portrait of my father which hung in my room. 'This is our Father,' I told him, holding up the painting for him to admire. He seemed impressed for my father was handsome, Germanic and exactly what those ugly Nazis would have wished to look like. Jöckel's reaction to the painting gave me the idea of taking a photograph along when I went to visit Bauer in Prague. I spoke only to his assistant and showed it to him. It might not have been to my brother's liking to advertise his German blood in this way but in any case it did no harm since the Nazis were putting so much emphasis on the 'Germanic' appearance.

First, my mother went to visit Bauer, but he told her to come back at a later date. When I saw his assistant, a visiting permit was again denied and, furthermore, I myself was interrogated for quite a while. However, my trip did have one positive result—I was told that my brother would be sent back to Terezín. On my return to Leitmeritz I phoned the Fortress several times but couldn't find out anything concrete and hoped that, through a call in person, I might at least get a clear answer.

And so, on a grey, autumn day I found myself walking towards the Fortress, reflecting on living in such vile times. I was twenty then and my brother twenty-five. What a way to spend our youth—and we hadn't spent that much of it together. I still pictured him as I had first seen him through the grille of our front door when he came to Leitmeritz to visit our paternal grandmother eight years before. To my eyes, this glamorous older brother who had travelled abroad resembled my father and we hit it off right away. Strange as it may sound I hadn't even been told of his existence before this meeting, though we lived only some forty miles from each other. From then on we met occasionally, always on my home ground. I hadn't met his Prague family.

When I reached the Small Fortress I found out that, contrary to the information given me on the phone the day before, Jöckel was still away, but his assistant Schmidt was available. He was in the canteen and a guard escorted me there. The canteen, a smoky, wood-panelled room with low-hanging, wrought-iron chandeliers had a strange, unreal atmosphere. All those men who spread dread and terror around them now sat in various stages of drunkenness, as though hoping to drown their own fear. I was taken to a table where six men lounged around looking as though they had been drinking for some time and the guard indicated to one of them that I wanted to talk to him. I was greeted with great enthusiasm and invited to join the group. Schmidt pulled out a chair for me beside him after introducing me to the others. The man sitting opposite was Czech and, to my right, was another civilian, a German, a particularly disagreeable character. I tried to speak to Schmidt but he was so drunk I didn't know if I could take what he was saying seriously. He assured me that my brother would indeed return to the Fortress and that I could count on permission to visit him. The civilian on my right laughed sarcastically while Schmidt was talking to me, interrupting with remarks like, 'You shouldn't be so foolish as to believe you'll ever see your brother alive again.'

The Czech tried to appease me, 'Look Miss, the gentlemen are a bit drunk, you mustn't take them seriously.' I thought this referred to Schmidt as well.

As he talked to me in his thick way of speaking, I scrutinized Schmidt's face. He was fair-haired with pinkish cheeks, not bad looking, but his blue eyes were half covered with drooping eyelids and this gave him a sort of hang-dog expression. I don't know how long I remained sitting with them all and I realized that I wouldn't achieve anything with this drunken lot. At the same time I couldn't find a decent opportunity to leave. Schmidt seemed to be interested in me and, to my astonishment, he haltingly declared, 'If you wish to have a personal relationship with me, you have to be discreet.' He repeated this sentence several times until our conversation was suddenly interrupted by the arrival of a woman with a child in her arms, appearing as if from nowhere. 'Oh, I see, we're drinking again,' she exclaimed.

Under any other circumstances I would have considered the commotion that followed extremely comical. All the men—not only Schmidt, whose wife she was—disappeared in a hurry. I looked closely at Frau Schmidt. She had straight, ash-blonde hair, sharp features and, naturally, like all Nazi women, not a suspicion of make-up. Following this scene a guard on duty accompanied me to the gate. I was very unhappy walking back home. No, I had no reason to expect anything good either from Jöckel or from this drunken Schmidt.

Against all my expectations, however, a few days later I received a phone call. My brother would be sent back and I could visit him on such and such a day and hour. So, I took the same walk back to the Small Fortress. It was a very different Schmidt who received me—he was sober and talked for a while about my work at the hospital before leading me to the barracks opposite the canteen. Inside stood a terribly thin, white-faced person with a shaven head. It took me several seconds to realize that this wreck was my brother. I put my arms around him but, to start with, he couldn't utter a word. His face had a nervous twitch. It was horrible.

Schmidt left us alone, which was unusual and actually not permitted, at least I knew that. I don't remember what we talked about or the questions we asked each other. We were probably too upset to carry on a normal conversation. The fact that Schmidt left us alone—this small humane gesture—gave me further hope. As he was escorting me to the gate after the visit I told Schmidt—by now I was crying—how worried I was about my brother's miserable appearance and that there were many cases of tuberculosis in our family. He replied, rather vaguely, that he would get him assigned to some better work. Encouraged by his remark, I asked, 'And could I visit him again soon?'

He didn't answer directly, he only said, 'I'll call you.'

My compulsory war work was in the radiotherapy and electro-massage departments of Leitmeritz Hospital. There we treated both in-patients and out-patients. About a week after my visit to the Fortress Schmidt turned up at the hospital for treatment for rheumatic pains in his shoulder. This 'coincidence' surprised me enormously. As he was leaving, he asked me when I would be off-duty. When I left the hospital that evening, Schmidt was waiting for me at the corner. He told me that since there was no other way to see me, he had asked for the treatment—he might have been accused of favouring prisoners if he was in touch with their relatives. However, he let me know he had arranged some other work for my brother and that he had something in mind regarding my next visit to the Fortress.

My first reaction was amazement that he of all people had to take certain things into consideration. There were pitfalls which even the absolute masters over life and death had to avoid. But I didn't give too much thought as to why he was willing to take the risks and felt only boundless relief over the miracle: I had established contact with the second most powerful man in the Small Fortress and he had promised to help. Strangely enough, I didn't doubt for a moment that he would not do so—not at all the same feeling I had when I left Jöckel.

We agreed that if I needed anything I would call him using the name Annemarie Schultz and he would arrange a meeting with my brother once a month, that is, when Jöckel was away in Prague on his periodic trips. From then on Schmidt came twice a week for his therapy treatments and waited for me at the end of the day to take me home. Most of the time we went for a short walk along the banks of the Elbe, while I recounted to him amusing happenings in the hospital. He would listen to my stories with little comment—he was a quiet person and I got used to his presence and began to feel at ease with him.

On my next visit to the Small Fortress I tried to convey to my brother that I was on good terms with Schmidt by letting slip a couple of times the familiar 'thou' instead of the usual 'you' when I addressed Schmidt in his presence. After the war my brother told me that my familiarity with an SS officer worried him greatly at the time. I couldn't tell him then how timid and reserved Schmidt was. He may have been a very strait-laced person because I remember the contempt he had for Jöckel's daughter, who was said to be a nymphomaniac. Perhaps he ascribed my reserve not only to his timorous attempts to be closer to me but also to inexperience on my part, or maybe he just wanted it that way.

In all, I saw my brother five times, three times in Schmidt's company and twice with other SS guards. These visits with

Schmidt present were almost relaxed. We talked about innocent things. I was able to give my brother a few pieces of warmer clothing and noticed with great satisfaction at each successive visit that his state of health was improving and he even seemed to be gaining weight.

How exceptional was this state of affairs became obvious when another guard was present. I had brought my brother some meat patties prepared by his friend Natasha, something she knew he liked very much. We behaved exactly as we would have done with Schmidt. Naturally, he offered me a patty and, for the sake of courtesy, one to the guard, but the man became livid with rage and I was stiff with fright. 'You dirty dog,' he shouted. 'Are you trying to bribe me?'

I cut the visit short, yet I felt so secure in my relationship with Schmidt that I complained about this and begged him not to assign the same man on any of my future visits.

It was well into the New Year when Schmidt first told me to advise my brother to declare himself German, or rather persuade him to do so. 'I was able to remove him from a transport list once, but . . .' he said without continuing. This I knew my brother would refuse to do and since it seemed the end of the war was approaching, I didn't worry about it too much.

As I've already said, I got used to Schmidt's company. There was so little—nothing to compromise me—that I had to do. Since we couldn't be seen together we arrived at our place of meeting separately. By the time I left the hospital it would be dusk and the blackout was a help. Sometimes we just stood on the bank of the Elbe, he would put an arm around me and silently watch the river. He spoke little about himself and was always careful not to show any weakness. He had children, two I believe, he was from Frankfurt and a Hessian by origin. When I questioned him about his profession he told me he was a shopkeeper and since I knew a drugstore employee in Dresden whom Schmidt closely resembled, I imagined that under normal circumstances he could have been a druggist too, selling soap and detergents, so fair, so rosy and clean while his shrew of a wife would have been looking after the cash register. Although I didn't give myself any illusions as to what prisoners could expect from him, he nevertheless lost, in my eyes, all appearance of menace: this man who kissed me timidly on my forehead, only rarely on my lips, who called me his

Princess and his Little Saint, this man with whom I played mock snowball battles or wandered in silence along the banks of the Elbe. Sometimes I spoke to him about my negative attitude to the Nazi ideology but he only smiled tolerantly, as one would to a child, and shook his head. He never tried to influence me; on the contrary, he avoided the subject.

Only once in our many meetings were we with anybody else and that was in the home of a woman who seemed to me to be a black-marketeer. Our hostess was on the familiar 'thou' terms with him. At one point in the conversation she said in her harsh, Leitmeritz accent, 'You must see about getting away from here soon, or are you going to wait until the Russians arrive?'

Hearing her speak so openly I was flabbergasted since I was present and could testify to it. Schmidt only smiled and answered, 'Now, now, we haven't reached that point yet.'

One morning, it may have been in February, I received a notice from the Labour Office. I was to leave my job in the civilian hospital and ordered to report to the SS Military Hospital in Leitmeritz. I tried every way I could to get out of this assignment; my stepfather intervened, also the head of our hospital, but without success. My stepfather had the worst fears as to what the end of the war would bring us and I was worried to death thinking I would be in an SS hospital at that moment. Finally, in desperation I called Schmidt. He came to meet me immediately. I broke down in front of him and told him it would be impossible for me to work with the SS while my brother was a prisoner, that I was sure I wouldn't be able to keep my mouth shut and would in all likelihood end up in jail myself. He quietly asked who had signed the letter and went straight to the Labour Office while I waited for him outside. How he accomplished it or how he, who officially didn't even know me, could have intervened on my behalf, I have no idea. When he came out he said only, 'It's settled.' A few days later the letter arrived confirming that I was to continue with my work in the civilian hospital.

When I first met Schmidt I was preoccupied with my own feelings; at the time I was getting over an unhappy love affair in Prague, a hopeless and one-sided relationship. And towards the end of the winter I fell very much in love with a Dutchman, a forced labourer, who lived with a family and was allowed to dress in civilian clothes. As a matter of fact, he wasn't permitted

250

to date me either but he was also getting radiotherapy treatments . . . all I had to watch for was that the two didn't meet.

It may have been towards the end of March when I had second thoughts about Schmidt's feelings. It was early spring weather and we went for our stroll by the river. Suddenly he stopped, turned me to face him and said, 'I'll get a divorce after the war. Do you think I could speak to your parents on our behalf?' I stared at him uncomprehendingly without being able to answer. But as he so often did, he interpreted my silence wrongly.

'You don't have to answer today,' he said.

That night I could hardly sleep. I realized that he dreamed of a life after the war, a completely unrealistic dream in which I, the innocent girl he believed me to be, would play an important role. But fortunately, he didn't bring it up again in the last weeks of the war. I don't know how often we met in April, but I do recall that once he broke off a forsythia branch in flower and gave it to me. Then, towards the end of April, Schmidt called me in great agitation and we decided to meet right away. He asked me repeatedly and with insistence to persuade my brother to declare himself German.

'I could release him immediately,' he said with emphasis, 'and as things stand now that would be of the greatest importance to him.' We discussed all possibilities. Jöckel was in the Small Fortress and not due to leave on his usual trip. Finally we arranged that I would call him the following week. In the meantime he hoped to come up with a solution.

I was in a panic for although the end of the war was in sight it seemed my brother was in extreme danger. 5 May was our agreed date and I tried to reach him the whole day without success. Only towards evening did the operator say with an ironic undertone I could sense, 'There's nobody there to answer, they've all gone.' That was the day Jöckel turned over the entire camp to the International Red Cross. About a fortnight later I learned from my brother that at noon on the 5th, as he was returning to his cell from his new job as Mende's orderly, Schmidt stopped him. He asked him to say hello to me and to tell me he was sorry he couldn't keep our last appointment, a message my brother was unable to understand. He hadn't yet realized the SS were in the act of pulling out. Moreover, he was ignorant of the fact that I was seeing Schmidt regularly and that our relationship was far closer than he might have imagined in his wildest dreams. What did strike him was their strange reversal of roles—it was now Schmidt's turn to face an uncertain future. It was only after the war that I learned of the crimes in which Schmidt took part but logically speaking I should have known at the time that one doesn't accede in innocence to a position like his. Thinking back on it, I simply couldn't see him, who was so reserved and timid in my presence, being guilty of so many atrocities. Nevertheless, when he was condemned to death I gave a lot of thought to the fact that without his help my brother most probably wouldn't have survived.

I have said he loved me, maybe that isn't the exact term for it. He imagined some kind of dream-life in which I played a certain role, one in which he was a good person and always helpful . . . maybe many criminals live such a dual existence. It was also strange that he saw me as an innocent, untouched girl. For a long time now I have wondered what quirk in his nature made him what he was. Was it that he was a staunch Nazi, an opportunist or simply an unscrupulous careerist?

I met many during those restless years with whom I so easily fell in and out of love. I can no longer recall some of their faces but Schmidt, this timid man who was a murderer, is unforgettable. I can still see him clearly, silent, looking at me in his baleful way.

When Hana came to visit Kamil in the section for infectious diseases, she told me that my brother was missing. He hadn't shown up at our house as he had told his mother he planned to do, so I called all the hospitals in town and went to the morgue as well. There was still some shooting going on and Leitmeritz had suffered a small air-raid—apparently the pilots mistook it for a target closer to Prague. I had to wait nearly a fortnight before I saw him again and when he arrived he was still worried by the treatment he had seen handed out to Germans in the city. But nothing like that happened in Leitmeritz, unlike Aussig where our former maid, a Czech, told us how Germans were being thrown off the bridge and shot in the water. Aussig was the railway junction where my brother had been loading coal.

He was visiting us when my stepfather's eighty-two-year-old aunt committed suicide the day she learned she was to be included in the first group to be expelled from Leitmeritz. At the end of the war, Father—and this would sound incredible to anyone who knew him well in normal times—distributed poison pills among the family, as he said, in case . . . I threw mine away and took them away from his mother as she was getting ready to take hers. This happened after my family had been expelled in August and when Grandmother was told to leave the house she had occupied for forty years. I was already living with my brother's family in Prague, so she had to go to a home for elderly Germans, a really depressing place. Even today, I wonder if I did the right thing. Grandmother didn't live long—she died in the Leitmeritz Hospital. The last time I visited her I was able to tell her that Father was establishing a practice again near Dresden and would soon be able to send for her, so maybe she died in peace. Neither she nor her sister who took poison were Nazis, unlike those distant cousins in Dresden where my parents and young brother went to stay.

My family wasn't meant to be in Dresden at all. They were there without ration cards but at least they had a roof over their heads. My father had the first of his attacks of depression at that time and took my little brother for a walk in the woods near the city, intending to poison him and then hang himself. He had some idea my mother would be able to manage better without them. By chance, they were stopped and searched by a Russian soldier who found the bottle marked with a skull and crossbones in Father's pocket. He jumped to the conclusion that Father had it in for the Occupation Army. At least, that is what he indicated in broken German, bringing them at gun point to the local Army Headquarters where my father was questioned by an officer who spoke good German and by a German Communist who had spent the war years in the Soviet Union. During the inquiry he was able to prove his anti-Nazi attitude by producing declarations from his Jewish friends. The Commanding Officer provided ration cards and a short while later my Father took over the practice of an ear specialist who hadn't returned from the war. When private practices were abolished and he had to take a job in the local hospital, father had another attack of depression,

253

but with time he came to realize he was better off without the responsibilities of a practice of his own. Moreover, in this way he was eligible for the good retirement benefits in East Germany.

❧ Epilogue ❧

Although the events described happened long ago, I don't believe I could have recorded them earlier as I found myself getting emotionally involved. When recounting a distressing incident I became depressed, and elated when I could write about success.

It might be of interest to relate what happened later to the people I have mentioned in my story.

Primus is still in Prague and has spent time in and out of mental institutions. He and I saw each other quite by chance in London in 1968 during the so-called Prague Spring. We were able to spend two full evenings together reminiscing and Lala joined us for one of them.

Franta and Gaby left Prague legally about three months after me and I met them on their arrival in Paris. They lived for a while in England and in 1949 moved again to settle in Canada. With their help, less than a year later, I joined them—France at the time seemed a dead-end for me. Franta divorced and married a girl of Baltic origin and they have two daughters. I am the godfather to his first and he is godfather to my youngest—both girls were born within weeks of each other.

Lala's older brother, Evzen, finished his law studies after the war and was sent abroad with the Foreign Service in 1946. He was later recalled but refused to go back: he and his wife settled in the States. Evzen has since died.

Lala, Olga, and their two boys lived in Prague until 1968. In the earlier years he had been discriminated against because of his brother's defection. He finished his studies in architecture and we were able to meet a few times in Europe when the government sent him out in the middle sixties to look over sport stadiums—his

255

speciality. Lala was working in London at the time of the Soviet invasion. Olga and their younger son got out of Czechoslovakia, arrived in Vienna and, from there, made their way to England. My godson escaped later. Today the whole family lives in Canada.

About eighteen months after I left, Loiza died in his sleep. Mother sold the house and moved to a much smaller one with a garden in a more residential part of town. Once she was of pensionable age she enjoyed several long visits outside the country. The house was shared with Lida's family until Mother's death at the age of nearly ninety—a mentally alert great-grandmother. Lida has two children. Her son, following family tradition, escaped, and lives in Canada.

Utta left Prague in the late summer of 1946, settled in Munich and married a Bavarian, now a well-known actor. Dr Burian died in East Germany about fifteen years ago; Utta's mother has also died. Her brother is a doctor and lives close to East Berlin.

Helena remained in Prague and I heard she went back to acting. I have lost all contact with her since my escape.

Elly, as far as I know, was reunited with her husband and they live in the States.

Ondrej remained on the land until the agrarian reform when farms were joined together into a collective. After that I lost track of him and all the others in the Beskyds. The region where I was hiding was made into a National Park some years ago and probably looks quite different from the way it was.

Eric and Feli returned to Austria and finally married. Both are now dead. In her will Feli left the castle to a youngish mason whose favours she enjoyed when well into her sixties. When relatives reproached her for this liaison she is said to have justified herself by explaining how good he was in bed.

I was told that Tonda, my fellow worker in the laundry, recovered from typhus but remained a partial invalid. He was granted a tobacco licence and opened a shop. I never saw him again, nor Lustyk, the kapo, and I don't know if the colonel survived. Once I left Czechoslovakia I lost all contact with the inmates of the Small Fortress, although there is someone living in Montreal who remembers me from when I used to come to the women's courtyard with Lustyk.

Natasha, my White Russian friend, married a Czech and lives in London. Lily eventually divorced, left Stockholm, and the last I heard she was in France. She remarried and has two daughters by her second husband, a Frenchman.

256

Jean, my colleague from the press agency, made it to Paris some months after I did. His father got hold of French passports for his children, Jean's wife always had her own. I arranged for a change of pictures and descriptions and had them sent by diplomatic pouch to the French Embassy in Prague. Jean is now a genuine Frenchman and has remained in the news business.

By a strange coincidence, in the early sixties, on another continent I came across the helpful officer from the Military Mission. He was no longer a Captain but the sales manager of a company I did business with in Caracas. I can't pretend that Ray Quesada and I recognized each other at first but, in general conversation, it came out that he had been stationed in Prague at the time of the putsch in 1948. As I had been the first person to apply for a transit visa on the day the borders were closed to Czech citizens, it was easily established that this wasn't our first encounter.

Leitmeritz is now Litomerice and completely Czech. The house where I was born is still a bookshop but I have no idea who lives above it. In the years since my escape I have never, for one single instant, regretted my decision nor have I ever felt the need to go back for a sentimental visit, knowing only too well that the country I remember no longer exists.

My Canadian wife and my children have visited Czechoslovakia separately and more than once. Much as they admire Prague as a city, they were far from impressed by conditions there. On his first visit my son wrote on a postcard: 'Dad, I'm glad you made the decision you did.' This one sentence summarizes exactly how I feel.

❧ Author's note ❧

I have tried to limit myself to recounting those events in which I was personally involved or as told to me by people close to me or by a reliable witness. To complete the story and fill in some gaps I consulted newspapers, books and US Army records, all of which information is condensed here.

The Small Fortress, under the jurisdiction of the Prague Gestapo, was in actual fact a prison and not a concentration camp although it quickly assumed all the trappings of one. Jöckel was appointed commander when the existing prison was reactivated in June 1940. As a police officer he had participated in the annexation of Austria in March 1938: six months later he took part in the occupation of the Sudetenland and, for a short time, was warden of a town jail there. After the take-over of the rest of Bohemia and Moravia he worked for the Gestapo in Prague.

The first inmates of the Small Fortress were, exclusively, political prisoners who were later joined by the so-called saboteurs, that is, people who had infringed the labour code. By 1942, when Jews were being interned in the nearby town of Terezín, any breach of the ghetto rules resulted in the offender ending up in the Fortress. In this same year the first batches of prisoners were sent in brigades to work outside. The prison administration received payment for this supply of manpower—by the end of the war as much as 20,000 Reichsmarks monthly—making it a profitable enterprise indeed.

The first women prisoners began arriving at around the time of the Heydrich affair when the third courtyard was set aside for them. The jail, originally planned for 500 held, by January 1945, some 6,000 prisoners. It is estimated that in its nearly five years of existence about

259

35,000 men and women passed through for varying lengths of time before being sent on to different concentration camps.

For those who died or were killed there, a civilian doctor from Leitmeritz furnished death certificates that invariably listed the cause as heart failure or pneumonia. This Dr Krönert was also the man who had declared me fit for transport after an inspection from a distance of ten feet. Until February 1945 all bodies were sent to the ghetto crematorium and the accumulated ashes thrown into the river flowing between Terezín and the prison. From that time, cremation was discontinued. The bodies—naked, with a name tag attached to a toe—were buried in mass graves close to the execution ground. When it was obvious that the end of the war was near, discussions began between Dr Geschke, head of the Prague Gestapo, and the German Secretary of State K. H. Frank on how to dispose of the prisoners: both men were well aware of Hitler's opposition to letting camps fall intact into enemy hands. The first plan was to gas all inmates of the Fortress, the ghetto and Camp Richard in Leitmeritz. Without proper technical facilities this idea had to be abandoned in favour of destruction by explosives. In the closing days of March or early April a group of officials from the Gestapo, with Jöckel and Schmidt, chose the most appropriate places for laying the charges. The prisoners were to be locked in their cells and any survivors disposed of with bazookas or flame throwers. I wonder if Schmidt's veiled hints to Utta were not a reference to this plan and, of course, I have no idea why it was never carried out: perhaps Hitler's death had something to do with it.

Dr Geschke may well have been the man to whose office I was brought before my first interrogation in Prague; such a luxurious office rather testified to his importance and Bauer, who was in charge of my case, referred to him as his boss. Another indication was that the man's face bore duelling scars, a fashionable mark of a university background and popular among German students before and immediately after the First World War—Geschke was a doctor of law. There can't have been many Gestapo officials in Prague with a similar background. As I had escaped in his precinct, so to speak, he may have been curious to have a look at me but I'll never know for sure if I had the honour of being punched in the face by such an important Nazi personality.

Negotiations to free the inmates were started immediately after Hitler's death. Dr Krönert proposed to Jöckel that, in view of the magnitude of the epidemic, all healthy prisoners be released at once, especially the women, as typhus had not yet reached their courtyard. This Jöckel categorically refused to do but, surprisingly enough, agreed to free about 200 inmates suffering from advanced tuberculosis. Perhaps this unusual concession was prompted by the fact that his elder daughter also had tuberculosis and he may have had some sympathy for those with the same illness. This was when Tonda was taken out although he was a victim of typhus. Was he freed by mistake or did he have influence? I know he was imprisoned for hiding a deserter, maybe a relative of his German wife. In addition to this humane gesture Jöckel agreed to impose a quarantine on the fourth yard which meant that no more work-brigades left the camp. There was of course a certain preoccupation that the typhus might spread among the civilian population.

Dr Krönert considered this one precautionary measure more than insufficient and went to Prague to confer with Dr Geschke. An SS doctor was sent to the Fortress for a tour of inspection: the sole result was that two additional latrine pits were ordered to be dug for the fourth yard. In the meantime, however, the released prisoners had alerted the Prague health authorities and a medical team with anti-typhus serum was sent out on 2 May, the day Jöckel left for Chemnitz in Saxony to take his personal effects to safety. In his absence Schmidt gave permission for the team to visit the first yard and the infirmary. Blood samples later confirmed not only typhus but cases of typhoid fever as well. The team was refused entry to the fourth yard, either because Schmidt did not want the true conditions to be made known or else because the XYZ prisoners were already assembled there prior to being taken to the execution ground. Incidentally, some twenty men of this group escaped the firing squad by not stepping forward when their names were called, which shows the state of confusion in those cells among the sick and dying.

In view of the alarming reports, and Schmidt's blunt refusal to allow an inspection of the fourth yard, the medical team sought out Monsieur Dunant, the representative of the International Red Cross, who quite by chance was then visiting the Terezín ghetto. He in turn intervened with Frank who, after some negotiations, finally agreed that the inmates be inoculated but not released. Because of Frank's promise, the team returned to the Fortress during the morning of 5 May but Jöckel refused them permission to enter. Leaving the doctors and nurses camped outside the gate, he called the Prague Gestapo for instructions and was told to await the arrival of an official. By noon nobody had shown up and the confusion grew even worse when the telephone and teletype lines with Prague went dead. Cut off from headquarters, Jöckel stayed holed-up in his office listening to the broadcasts from Prague with a Gestapo man translating, but neither could make head or tail of the conflicting reports, street fighting having broken out in the city the previous day. Schmidt, meanwhile, had begun negotiations with the medical team awaiting admission. He proposed to turn the camp over to them in return for the furnishing of vehicles with Red Cross markings. It is likely that the deal went through because later that day the SS and SD left the Small Fortress in an orderly fashion. Those of Sudeten-German origin probably headed for their homes nearby while Jöckel, Schmidt, Rojko and Wachholz with their families, and Mende drove towards Carlsbad, which was by then in the hands of the Americans. Although they travelled in civilian clothes with partially forged papers furnished by the Prague Gestapo, the group became nervous at a road-block and decided to split up. From Carlsbad Rojko, his wife and Mende went southwards, towards Austria. Jöckel's wife, with his two daughters, headed north to Chemnitz—now Karl Marx Stadt—where three days earlier he had brought their personal and household effects. It is not known if Frau Schmidt and her children and Wachholz' family went with the Jöckel women or stayed with the three men, that is Jöckel, Schmidt and Wachholz.

After the Fortress was declared a national monument, a memorial cemetery was laid out between the main gate and the road to Prague.

The following is condensed from an interrogation by the German police of an innkeeper friend of Jöckel's in Offenbach in October 1945.

My acquaintance with Jöckel dates from when we occupied the Sudetenland in 1938. Our friendship became closer when he was commander of the Small Fortress and it was discovered that my wife and his first wife were born on the same day. They invited us to visit them there while our son was in the Protectorate serving with the *Luftwaffe*. My wife and I stayed with the family for about eight days. For the funeral of Jöckel's first wife in December 1943 we sent them a small keg of sauerkraut through his sister. About nine months later he married Else (or Alice?) Benfer

262

whom I already knew. I used to see Jöckel when he was on leave visiting relatives and friends in Offenbach. He was generous because he invited everyone to my inn and always insisted on paying for his guests.

Late in June or early July 1945, Jöckel showed up at my house in a rather sorry state and stayed with me for four or five days. I gave him food and he never left his room day or night. I was able to have his shoes repaired by a cobbler I know. His sister, who lives in Offenbach, brought him a bicycle, provisions and clean laundry but I wasn't present at their discussions. From the talks we had I understood he eventually intended to go to Hamburg to try to find work as a shipyard worker. He knew he couldn't stay around Offenbach where too many people knew him and the police would continue their search. He said that there was no future for him here. When I asked him about finances he answered more or less that this was not his main worry and things were taken care of. Before leaving he confided to me that he would be going to Haiger to wait for his family.

Four weeks later, on a Sunday afternoon I remember, Frau Jöckel arrived in a heavily-loaded car with Red Cross markings. The two daughters, Hanne and Elfriede, and two men unknown to me were with her. The women were overjoyed to hear that Jöckel had stayed with me and should now be in Haiger. They unloaded the car with the help of the two men, stacked everything in the corridor and spent the night in my inn. The next morning the five reloaded the car and left. Frau Jöckel told me she had bought the car from the Red Cross for about three thousand marks and got permission from the Red Cross to keep the markings as they left Chemnitz with a transport of Dutchmen. She seemed full of confidence and believed the family would soon be able to start a new life. About four weeks after the first visit Frau Jöckel came to see me again, this time by train. When I asked how everybody was she told me that when Heinrich went to get his ration coupons and register his residence in order to do the right thing by the authorities, they arrested him because something wasn't in order with his papers and he ended up in the civilian annex of a POW camp.

Whether Frau Jöckel was ever reunited with her husband is an open question. Jöckel was arrested by the US Counter Intelligence Corps in Wetzlar on 1 July, very soon after he reached Haiger. His wife and daughters arrived in Offenbach only at the end of that month. For several weeks the Americans, not realizing the true identity of their prisoner, kept his family under observation in Haiger hoping to discover his whereabouts. According to Utta, an undercover agent started an affair with Hanne and found out that her father was already being held in a POW cage.

A questionnaire from the US Military Government, most probably filled out by the subject himself, provides the following information: Jöckel Heinrich, born 10 July, 1899 in Offenbach. Profession: house and sign painter, unemployed from 1930 to 1933; joined the Nazi party 30 December, 1931 (thirteen months before Hitler came to power). His membership of the SS dates from 30 April, 1933. From July of that year until the end of the war he admitted to having been an official in the police, stating the branch, however, as *Schutzpolizei* and not the SD and neglecting to answer the question regarding service outside the Reich proper. His yearly salary went from 2,640 marks in 1934 to 3,960 in 1944—actually not very much when I consider that to set up the diamond-buying business the brewer invested about triple that amount. However, Jöckel's income came not only from his salary; quarters were provided and his wife, who was running the SS canteen, must also have had a good income with no wages to pay. And then there was the confiscated jewellery and the gold teeth ... In principle all valuables had to be delivered to the authorities but it is more than probable that at least a part found its way into the pockets of the guards.

On 20 December, 1945, the assistant Chief of Staff, Counter Intelligence, signed a regulation form stating that the subject had been cleared through all interested sections of G-2 and the division had no further interest in him nor objection to his extradition. And so, Jöckel, his wife and daughter Hanne were handed over to the Czechs on 26 January, 1946.

My information about Wilhelm Johann Schmidt, SS *Oberscharführer* (Sergeant Major), born 1 December, 1911, in Frankfurt, married, one or two children, is very sketchy. His official title in the Small Fortress was *Hauptwachtmeister*—first adjutant. After getting away from the Fortress he established residence in Burbach, not far from Haiger. I have no date for when he was taken into custody but it was probably around the same time as Jöckel—all SS were automatically arrested. There is a cryptic note by an informer watching Jöckel's family that Schmidt was sent to jail in Darmstadt. The Czech government did not officially request his extradition until 22 March, 1946—nearly a full year after his departure from the Fortress—by which time he was interned in Zuffenhausen near Stuttgart. It makes one wonder why the Czechs waited so long before asking for his extradition and if this had some connection with Jöckel's interrogations.

In any case, the Americans wasted little time. On 10 April the same ominous form as the one for Jöckel was signed in the name of Lt. Col. Dale Garvey and by June of that year Schmidt was in Czech hands. As far as I could make out the only stipulation, when handing over the two men, was that the Military Government be informed of the date of their trials and verdicts. Incidentally, the same Garvey agreed that the war criminal Klaus Barbie would be a valuable asset to US Counter Intelligence in spite of his wanted status and eventually helped him to escape to South America.

Jöckel's trial began in Leitmeritz on 15 October. Among the witnesses were not only former inmates, as was the case when Rojko was judged, but also a couple of Gestapo agents; former guards from the firing squads; *kapos* under arrest; Dr Krönert, the signer of the death certificates; Schmidt, and Hochhaus, the SD in charge of the kitchen, who was actually free. To my astonishment I had met him in Leitmeritz the previous summer. He may have been just as surprised to see me but we didn't speak to each other although he must have known who I was. It was under his eyes that Lustyk and I had juggled soap and clean laundry for extra bread. It was only several months later that I heard the kitchen crew had given Hochhaus a favourable testimony, so he was left at liberty and turned evidence against Jöckel.

A fellow-inmate who assisted at the trial told me Jöckel's appearance had changed a great deal: he had lost weight, his hair was cropped and he was sporting a moustache which covered his whole upper lip—not the Hitler style we remembered. I imagine his frame of mind would have changed as well. Did he think back to the time two years before when, in Utta's presence, he defiantly reiterated his firm belief that Nazi Germany had everything under control? Did he regret his unshakeable faith in Hitler and German victory now that his wife was being held in the Small Fortress and his daughter Hanne had died in a Czech jail from untreated tuberculosis?

The trial lasted ten days. When he heard the verdict on the morning of 25 October he declared he was dying for Germany, asked the court for a stay of one hour to settle some family affairs and for permission to see his wife. He also asked that a change of name be arranged for her. Jöckel was publicly hanged in the courtyard of the Leitmeritz jail in the early afternoon of the same day.

Schmidt's turn to stand trial came two and a half weeks later: the proceedings took only two days. From the description of him during the trial he gave the impression of a bewildered man unable to fully realize why he was in the dock. His former colleague, Hochhaus testified that Schmidt was completely under the sway of his immediate superior and that the atmosphere in the Small Fortress improved to a slight degree whenever Jöckel was absent.

There were testimonies in Schmidt's favour from some of the inmates but several serious accusations were either proved, or admitted to by the accused. One concerned a woman inmate working in Jöckel's household whom the family took a liking to. When her execution was ordered by the Prague Gestapo, Jöckel arranged with Schmidt to have her believe she was being released. Her clothing was returned to her but, on her way to the main gate and freedom, Schmidt shot her in the back of the head. Another damning testimony came from a former *kapo* who stated that Schmidt had commanded the firing squad in the fourth yard when six men and a woman were publicly executed as a reprisal for an attempted escape. Schmidt was heard to threaten that at the next attempt every tenth inmate would be shot.

The most serious accusation, however, could not be proved: namely that he had been in charge at the execution of the XYZ prisoners on 2 May. Nor could it be established that he had had a hand in the decision to starve to death 387 inmates who came to the Fortress from Auschwitz in early February 1945. As a punishment for trying to escape during the transport their rations were as follows: Sunday, soup; Monday, nothing; Tuesday, 10 ozs of bread and coffee; Wednesday, soup; Thursday, nothing; Friday, 10 ozs of bread and coffee; Saturday, nothing. Although this order was cancelled after six weeks, the men were so weakened that only fifty-two survived to see the end of the war.

On 12 November, at 5 o'clock, Schmidt was condemned to death by hanging and the sentence was carried out three and a half hours later. On the 15th, as if by coincidence, the headquarters of the 970th

Counter Intelligence Detachment in Marburg, close to Schmidt's last residence, received a letter from his wife asking the whereabouts of her husband. Despite several requests by the US extradition board the Czech government never bothered to reply that Jöckel and Schmidt had been executed nor did they ever send death certificates as had been agreed when the two men were first handed over. The last inquiry, dated 21 March, 1951 came at a time when the Czechs had other things to fuss about; they were busy preparing a show trial for fourteen of their highest Communist Party functionaries and members of government of whom eleven would be hanged that same year. As for the other members of the Party which split up in Carlsbad, Wachholz was arrested in East Berlin in 1968 and condemned to death. I could find out nothing about Mende. I believe he was from South Tyrol and may still be alive.

Most of the guards of Sudeten–German origin were arrested and hanged. Horse Head, whose name was, I think, Soukup, committed suicide while awaiting trial. The memento I received from him has been the longest-lasting of all my souvenirs of the Small Fortress—a small lump on the forehead where he hit me with the gun butt that day of my return transport to St Pancras.